Stepping Up

Women's guide to
career development

Stepping Up

Women's guide to
career development

Nadine Kazerounian

The McGraw-Hill Companies

London   Burr Ridge, IL   New York   St Louis   San Francisco   Auckland   Bogotá
Caracas   Lisbon   Madrid   Mexico   Milan   Montreal   New Delhi   Panama
Paris   San Juan   São Paulo   Singapore   Sydney   Tokyo   Toronto

Published by
McGraw-Hill Professional
Shoppenhangers Road, Maidenhead, Berkshire, SL6 2QL
Telephone: +44 (0) 1628 502 500
Fax: +44 (0) 1628 770 224
Website: www.mcgraw-hill.co.uk

British Library Cataloguing in Publication Data
A catalogue record for this book is available from the British Library

Library of Congress Cataloguing in Publication Data
The Library of Congress data for this book is available from the Library of Congress

Sponsoring Editor: Elizabeth Robinson
Editorial Assistant: Sarah Wilks
Production Editorial Manager: Penny Grose
Desk Editor: Alastair Lindsay

Produced for McGraw-Hill by Steven Gardiner Ltd
Printed and bound in Great Britain by Bell and Bain Ltd, Glasgow
Cover design by Senate Design Ltd

McGraw-Hill

A Division of The **McGraw-Hill** Companies

McGraw-Hill books are available at special quantity discounts. Please contact the
Corporate Sales Executive at the above address.

ISBN 0 07 709802 1

Contents

Acknowledgements

There are many people to whom I am indebted for their help and encouragement with this book. First, I would like to thank Karen Harris for her generosity in helping with the interview programme and the desk research, for the ideas she contributed on structure and content, and for giving valuable feedback as each chapter was completed. Karen was too modest to share the front cover credit, but this book is dedicated to her for teaching me more about managing people and my relationships with them than I learned in a lifetime before we became friends. Much of the wisdom in this book is drawn from our many conversations over the years.

Most of the women we interviewed spoke warmly of the support they draw from their women friends, and I can identify with this very closely. At difficult moments what spurred me on was the thought that my friends were as keen to see this book in print as I was. For all their encouragement and enthusiasm I thank them from my heart.

A substantial part of this book is based on material from a programme of interviews with successful women. They gave generously of their time, experience and advice, and were very supportive of the concept for the book. Their names and occupations at the time of the interview (some of them have since moved onward and upward) are given below. I am greatly indebted to all of them and without their contribution the book would be considerably impoverished.

As a first time author I have been very much aware of 'standing on the shoulders of giants', since this book draws heavily on the research and writing of many other people. In addition to the footnote acknowledgements included in the text I should particularly like to thank Professor Susan Vinnicombe,

Dr Val Singh and the team at the Centre for Developing Women Business Leaders within Cranfield School of Management for allowing me access to their excellent research papers on impression management and related topics.

Several other authors and research organizations kindly agreed to substantial references to and quotations from their work, and they include: Susan Bird, Mary van der Boon, Jayne Buxton, Catalyst, Philippa Davies, The Domino Consultancy, The Equal Opportunities Commission, Professor Anne S. Huff, The Industrial Society, Elizabeth Mapstone, Mintel, Jane Sturges, Joanna Parfitt, Harriet Rubin, Avivah Wittenberg Cox and the Women Returners Network. My grateful thanks to them all.

Finally, my thanks to the team at McGraw-Hill for publishing this book and for gently (but firmly) guiding me through the writing and editing process.

Nadine Kazerounian

Contributors to the interview programme

Julia Barfield, Partner in Marks Barfield, architects of the London Eye.

Kate Barker, Chief Economist at the CBI.

Nikki Beckett, Chief executive, NSB Retail Systems Plc and Veuve Cliquot Businesswoman of the Year, 2000.

Lena Bjorck, Founder and managing director of catering firm Inn or Out.

Julie Bradley, Managing Partner at Devonshires, Solicitors.

Louise Campbell, Founder and managing director of recruitment company The Venture Partnership, specialists in dotcom recruitment.

Colette Graham, Head of Internal Communication, Centrica plc.

Professor Susan Greenfield, Director of the Royal Institution and Fullerian Professor of Physiology, Department of Pharmacology, Oxford University; broadcaster and author.

Carol Hambly, Financial Controller, Camelot.

Jeanette Hughes, Group Chief Auditor, Royal & SunAlliance.

Pat Jones, Partner, Ernst & Young.

Rt Hon Tessa Jowell MP, Minister for Employment, Welfare to Work and Equal Opportunities.

Joy Kingsley, Managing Partner, Pannone & Partners, Solicitors.

Martha Lane Fox, Joint Managing Director of lastminute.com.

Margaret McCabe, Barrister and founder of the Woman Lawyer Forum.

Judith Mayhew, Chairman of the Policy and Resources Committee, City of London, and Special Adviser to the Chairman at solicitors Clifford Chance.

Hilary Meredith, Managing Partner, Donns Solicitors.

Rabbi Julia Neuberger, Chief Executive, The King's Fund (health services charity); broadcaster and journalist.

Julia Penney, Vice President, Thames Valley Association, Chartered Institute of Accountants of England & Wales.

Fiona Price, Founder and Managing Director of Fiona Price & Partners, financial advisers specializing in women's finance.

Fiona Reynolds, Director of the Women's Unit, the Cabinet Office.

Sue Slipman, Director, External Relations & Compliance, Camelot.

Dianne Thompson, Chief Executive, Camelot.

Leigh Wood, Chief Executive, ntl, cable communication providers.

Preface

In September 2000 I had the great good fortune to take part in a women's conference – the Women's International Networking Conference, held annually in Milan. What was so special about this event was the opportunity it gave me to meet women from all over the world who had gathered in Milan to talk about the work and life issues closest to their hearts. The spirit of friendship they offered, the passion and conviction with which they spoke and their commitment and determination to change their own and all women's working lives was inspiring.

By that stage this book was already in progress, but what I took away from WIN 2000 has shaped its content and, I hope, helped bring it to life. For the remarkable thing was that women from so many disparate backgrounds and cultures should share broadly the same experience of what it was like to be a working woman today. The differences – where there were any – were differences of degree rather than of anything fundamental. The same issues and challenges confronted women from Russia to the Philippines: women were worrying about how to achieve work/life balance, how to get themselves taken seriously by male colleagues and how to tackle the structural and informal barriers to gender equality in the workplace, in politics and in public life. And, amazingly, women everywhere were confronting these issues with the same courage, humour, patience and resilience.

Certain sections of this book may lead some readers to conclude that the general picture is rather bleak. And it is true, women still have a long way to go to achieve equality at work – continuing pay inequalities prove this indisputably. But there was a spirit of optimism among the women at WIN 2000 from which we can all take heart. My enduring memory is of their conviction that women themselves have the power not only to transform workplace cultures but, more broadly, to bring about radical social and even global change through new styles of leadership and communication.

The millennium has seen the birth of a new spirit of feminism. Unlike what has gone before (and which alienated many women from the feminist cause) it does not hold men responsible for all the ills that beset women or incite us to the violent overthrow of our 'oppressors'. It is inclusive rather than separatist in its view of how men and women should interact. It urges us to teach men our language and to coach them in our skills. It believes fervently that women can win through by accepting responsibility for initiating change and *acting as if* their approach were the only sensible and realistic way of getting things done. More and more women have the self-belief to carry this off – witness those we interviewed, many of whom were outstanding for doing things their own way and for ploughing heedless through traditional male ways of working.

But, before we get carried away on a wave of euphoria, let us not forget the underlying power struggle that we face. Those who possess power are always reluctant to relinquish it and usually see any attempt to share it as a threat. We cannot expect the way to be easy. We will have to fight for what we want. But, in future, we must carefully choose our weapons. A new approach is needed – one that allows us to use our female strengths. In the past many women have tried to engage with men on their terms, only to find themselves disadvantaged and marginalized in a game whose rules they barely understood. Women must write their own rulebook now, using the tools of negotiation, persuasion and communication, rather than resorting to toughness, coercion and other traditional male power plays.

Through this book I wanted to support women's challenge not only to attain greater power but, more importantly, to redefine the way power is expressed and exercised within businesses and within society as a whole. The book aims to explode some of the myths and stereotypes that hold women back, to provide them with a toolkit of management skills and techniques, and to help them win credibility for the subtler methods that characterize many women's leadership style.

Introduction

The purpose of this book

The original concept for the book was that it should serve as a practical handbook for women managers or those aspiring to a management role. Rather than merely describe the challenges faced by women at work, I wanted to spell out in detail the strategies and tactics women could adopt when dealing with them. I looked to several sources for answers, and some of the most valuable and interesting material came from a programme of interviews conducted with successful women from a variety of business sectors and from public life. The book opens with an initial analysis of these interviews to see what traits high achieving women might share. The results were surprisingly consistent and are helpful, I think, in showing women that being female need be no disadvantage in a managerial career. Rather, it can actually be made to work in your favour. Additional material from the interview programme was used in Chapter Four to expand on some of the themes in Chapter One and to delve more deeply into how the women had achieved and managed their success, and what advice they could offer to other women looking to develop their careers.

How the content is presented

To set the context for women working in the 21st century I wanted to draw a picture of what this means, based on contemporary research. The first step was to examine the trends in work, society, technology and the economy that influence and prescribe women's options and choices. This forms the basis of

Chapter Two. As in all forms of strategic analysis, I thought it important for women to know where they were starting from as they plan their career paths.

Having described these issues the book moves in Chapter Three to an examination of gender stereotypes. The reason for this is that many younger women starting their careers now mistakenly believe they are entering a level playing field. They are seriously shocked when confronted with the reality, and I wanted to help prepare them for the gender issues they will have to deal with. This is done by examining the behaviours male colleagues are likely to adopt towards women at work and how various difficult scenarios can be successfully dealt with. Contemporary definitions of leadership are examined and the book considers the qualities women bring to management and how they can gain recognition and credibility for their management style.

As mentioned above, in Chapter Four leading women from business and public life share the secrets of their success and offer advice to women aspiring to a career in management.

Since training as an image consultant some years ago I have become a firm believer in the power of this process to build women's confidence both socially and at work. But in developing and delivering personal image workshops for the corporate market it became apparent to me that there were far wider challenges with which women needed help if they were to develop their careers successfully. The key issues seemed to be gaining recognition for one's achievements and raising one's visibility and credibility with those at the top of the organization. I gradually expanded the content of my workshops to encompass these issues and the distillation of the learning is contained in Chapter Five.

The development pattern of my own career has been far from straightforward. In the early years I set my heart on social work, but seeing the harsh realities of poverty, social deprivation and the shortage of resources to tackle these immense problems caused me to rethink. At university in the 1970s, the concept of a vocational first degree was almost unheard of, so I read the subjects I enjoyed best – philosophy and French literature. When I graduated I had the option of studying for a Masters in French, but decided that I needed to do something more practical (with a view to earning a crust) and so I enrolled for a postgraduate course in international marketing. I loved it, and subsequently embarked on a career in market research that took me around Europe and gave me an entrée into some of the largest corporations in the world, both conducting and selling research consultancy.

When I later married and was planning a baby I recognized that frequent international travel was hardly compatible with family life, and so I turned to university lecturing as a more viable option. I missed the adrenaline rush of consultancy, but enjoyed the teaching and course development work. And when I had my first child, like many women, I fell in love. I took three months' maternity leave (much of which fell over the Christmas holidays) and was fortunate enough to have a childminder close to my place of work so that I could see (and feed) my baby during my lunch break. But I hated leaving him and would dearly have loved to be a full-time mum. No such option was available to me though – mortgage interest rates were running at 17 per cent and we needed two salaries to meet the payments on our modest two-bedroom terrace.

Over the ensuing years, juggling an increasingly demanding career with home life proved difficult but not impossible. Being tired, irritable and often stressed became a way of life. Like most women I know, I got used to it and got on with it. However, it did make me question the advisability of having another child. I already felt I was short-changing the one I had. How would I manage him and a second baby? But I longed for another child to complete our family and remember my small son telling me how lonely it was to be an only child. Then something wonderful happened: we were given the opportunity of looking after a young relative of my husband's, a boy of twelve, who we subsequently adopted. During this time I studied full time for my MBA and moved out of teaching and into private sector training – more lucrative than university lecturing but also more stressful, since it required me to be away from home quite frequently. But my husband had started a business and so we had a degree of flexibility in terms of childcare cover when it was the au pair's evening off.

I often felt at this time like a serious underachiever – my MBA peers were streaking ahead into top jobs with telephone number salaries; my husband's business was growing fast, and I felt as though I were merely plodding along, not unchallenged by my work, but not really fulfilling my potential. Would it ever be my turn to shine?

About five years ago I had a potentially fatal car accident. Hit from behind (by a driver who didn't stop) my car spun out of control on a busy dual carriageway and ended up pointing the wrong way in the fast lane. I escaped with only minor injuries, but the incident marked a watershed in my life. I vowed in future to make every day count and to take charge of my life in a more positive way. I resigned from my job and started my own small consultancy business, advising small firms on business development and running personal image workshops. And then, just over a year ago the idea for this book came to me and I began to write. It has been one of the most fulfilling experiences of my life. I feel, at last, that I am doing what I truly enjoy.

All this is by way of introduction to Chapters Six, Seven and Eight. These have been written to support you through both the big issues – like achieving balance in your life – and in tackling the day-to-day issues at work that can help you operate more effectively and become a better manager. Many women lead very diverse lives: having fulfilling work is important, but they also want families, friends, outside interests and social lives. My message is that it is OK to want all these things simultaneously, if they are important to you, and to show you how other women have combined these elements without being superwomen. The key is to recognize that we all have choices, and that each of those choices entails consequences. Decide what it is you truly want and learn to live with what that entails. Don't waste your energy feeling guilty, or castigate yourself because you are not successful in other people's terms. Don't let others force you into choices you are uncomfortable with – it's your life and, as the saying goes, it's not a rehearsal.

To help you plan your future in a more focused way, Chapter Nine takes the form of a career/life planning framework. The women interviewed for this book were all great planners – their success didn't just happen, they planned and worked systematically to achieve it. You can do the same, if you wish.

Finally, Chapter Ten looks forward to the workscape of the future, to try to portray what shape our working lives will take and the skills and experience you need to acquire in order to take advantage of the many opportunities that will arise. I wish you well. Whatever stage of the journey you are at, fulfilling your potential through challenging work is a great voyage of discovery. I hope this book helps to chart the waters for my readers, for there are many rocks on which women's careers can founder. I have attempted to show where they are and to help guide you safely round them. Bon voyage.

I
What are women managers made of?

Introduction

Given the barriers to women's career development in the past, what is surprising is not that so few women reached the top, but that so many achieved it. What was it these women did differently that helped them succeed in the face of difficult odds? Did they have special influences in their background or early career? Were there lucky breaks or just lots of hard work?

We began this project by interviewing a group of successful women. They were drawn from a variety of business backgrounds, from the public, private and voluntary sectors, and from across a wide age range. What similarities and differences did we discover, and what can aspiring women today learn from their experience?

The early years

Family background

A common theme was the love and strength these women had drawn from supportive parents, and most often from an outstanding and unusual mother. These mothers were often professional women who pioneered the role of working woman in an era (1940s and 1950s) when social mores were very different from today. Judith Mayhew (barrister and Special Adviser to the Chairman at Clifford Chance), for example, was the daughter of a teacher who later became headmistress of a leading girls school in New Zealand. She had been widowed at the age of 34 with four children – three of them under five – and was forced by necessity to become the family breadwinner. Tessa Jowell (Women's Minister) is the daughter of a physiotherapist who always stressed the importance of educational qualifications as a means to independence. She herself was very proud of her qualification that had been hard won, in the face of considerable opposition.

Lena Bjorck (CEO of catering firm Inn or Out) was born in Sweden and recalled the strength her parents gave her because they wanted her to be happy. For them it didn't matter what she did in her career (at one time she wanted to be a policewoman). She was allowed to experiment and to fail, which gave her the courage to try things out even when there was a risk.

Many successful women now in their 40s and beyond share the experience of having been the first in their families to attend university. Sue Slipman, for example, came from a family of Eastern European immigrants who settled in the East End of London and was the first to get a university education.

Once at university some of the women met others whose parents had sent them there to find a husband. The women in our study would jokingly say their parents sent them so that they would not need a husband.

My father ran his own business and success and achievement was very important to us as a family.
Fiona Price, CEO Financial Services Company

Self-esteem

Most of the women we spoke to had, in their early lives, been imbued with a strong sense of self-worth and the idea that they could do whatever they were prepared to work for – certainly anything a man could do. Colette Graham (Head of Communications at Centrica plc) described herself as a shy person with a strong sense of justice. She thought her upbringing had been unusual and talked fondly of her parents as people who treated their children with respect and listened to what they had to say. In most cases the parents had imposed no specific expectations, only encouraged their children to get an education and some qualifications and to do what they found fulfilling.

Martha Lane Fox comes from an academic family background where the ability to debate and have a view was strongly encouraged. She travelled extensively as a child and was exposed to a variety of cultural influences that broadened her horizons. It is her family that keeps her grounded amid the mayhem of setting up and growing a high-profile dotcom. She has a close friend who worked in Chechnya during the worst of the hostilities. When things seemed to be difficult Martha's family would say: 'Just think of Millie in Chechnya' to help her put things in perspective.

Rabbi Julia Neuberger was an only child and her parents were passionate about education. It was assumed she would go to Oxford and then 'do something'. Her father was simply determined that she should be more successful than him and was a strong driving force in her career development.

Some of the older women in our study recalled mothers who had endured the hardships of the Second World War (1939–1945), left to cope without men, to earn a living and often to bring up their children alone. But with the return of the men from the war came the return of the women to the kitchen, and the consequent loss of both income and independence. Many of these women hated not having their own money and felt trapped by a society that expected married women to stay at home. (Up until the mid-1960s nurses, for example, were normally expected to resign as soon as they got married.) As a consequence they stressed to their daughters the importance of having the means to earn your own money.

Some women, particularly those born in the north of England, remembered being surrounded by very traditional attitudes to the role of women – it was commonly believed that women usually only worked until marriage and that if they worked thereafter it was only for pin money.

Several of the women we met had taken part in competitive sport. Fiona Price rowed at international level; Hilary Meredith was a champion trampolinist; Lena Bjorck swam competitively in her native Sweden. All have strong determination and a competitive spirit and have undoubtedly transferred their early training to the business context. Lena spoke of having a high degree of focus and self-belief, of setting goals and visioning achieving them. We discuss some of these techniques in Chapter Six.

Education

Many of the women we met had in common a strong academic streak. They had enjoyed studying for its own sake and were high achievers – some had attained first class honours, while others had subsequently taken a Masters degree. They had also gone on to sustain this level of achievement in the professional and business qualifications they had acquired, coming out with distinctions or finishing in the upper quartile of their group.

Several of the women had attended all-girls schools (usually grammar or direct grant) and felt strongly that this had been an advantage in shaping their attitudes. Dianne Thompson, bullied at a junior school from which she ran away, spoke of loving her grammar school where she suddenly blossomed. Equally, Julie Bradley felt single-sex education was best for girls, since it gave them opportunities to speak openly in an environment where they were not forced into gender stereotypes. She felt her teachers had been inspirational. Rabbi Neuberger too attributed her confidence in large measure to the fact that she attended an all-girls school and then a women's college at Oxford. Colette Graham attended a convent school where girls were expected to go on to university and study for one of the professions (medicine, dentistry or law). She did well, but went on to Queen's University to read international business and languages, before being recruited by Glaxo to their graduate entrant programme.

It is important to remember that women now in their forties and fifties, educated at all-girls schools, would mainly have been taught by women – many of whom would be unmarried (due in part to the post-war shortage of men, or because they had lost husbands or fiancés during the Second World War). These schools were usually led by a formidable headmistress, who with her staff would have created an environment of rigorous academic discipline where girls were expected to work hard and excel – at examinations, at sport, at drama and in music. Allowing yourself to be distracted from all this by the male sex was widely frowned upon – and considered rather 'common'. One of the worst epithets was to be called 'boy mad'.

Professor Susan Greenfield (Director of the Royal Institution) recalls being brought up with a strong work ethic – 'You get nothing for nothing and everything comes at a price'. And though she had ambition and drive, the prevailing ethos when she was young was that, for women, working in a bank was the pinnacle of achievement. She enjoyed learning and welcomed a challenge, and at Oxford, where she read philosophy and psychology, she felt accepted as a woman and free to be herself. This was very liberating because it made her feel all possibilities were open to her and that there were no limits to what she could do.

Similarly, Julia Barfield (partner in Marks Barfield, Architects of the London Eye) recalls that when she and her sister were younger their mother (a headmistress) assumed they would do whatever they wanted, that there were no barriers. This assumption gave Julia great confidence. She remembers too wondering what other mothers did all day if they didn't work outside the home. She has tried, however, to replicate the pattern set by her mother who always picked up her children from school in the afternoon.

Martha Lane Fox (27) provided an insight into the thinking of younger women. She and her contemporaries – graduates from Oxford – set their ambitions very high. She said of the Oxford experience:

It is an incredible platform to be able to believe you can do what you want. These women have achieved amazing things quite young. They are having phenomenal experiences and proving themselves better than their male counterparts.

This conviction, when they were young, that they could do anything – that there were no limits to their potential achievements – was a consistent theme among the women we talked to, and it still pervades their belief systems today.

Do believe you can do anything. Be feisty.
Rabbi Julia Neuberger, CEO, The King's Fund

Career influences

Mentors and role models

Apart from their mothers, few of the women in our sample had experienced role models – there were too few powerful women around – and many had begun their careers before mentoring became fashionable. Rabbi Julia Neuberger, however, believes strongly in the importance of female role models. Her own mother worked – employing a nanny and an au pair – and her grandmother (who would have loved to work) was hugely active in the resettlement of refugees. This established for Rabbi Neuberger a strong example of women having a role in society beyond the home.

CASE STUDY

Colette Graham described her experience of having an inspirational role model: 'The then head of corporate affairs at Glaxo was a woman who had achieved a high level of seniority at a time when there were no female role models to show the way. She became successful by being tougher and harder and by being overtly competitive with her male colleagues. She was a charismatic leader for her team and an inspiration to her colleagues. She inspired my vision of what a corporate communications function could be.'

We have so far stressed the importance of women mentors and role models – and we would generally hold that women are better able to support and advise other women than are men. (We discuss this further in Chapter Seven.) But there are examples of men who have taken genuine pleasure in helping develop the careers of younger women with whom they work.

CASE STUDY

Lena Bjorck shared with us the story of a restaurateur in Kent for whom she worked tending the bar. When she announced she was resigning to take a job in London, he refused to let her leave. 'You're not going – you're going to be an assistant manager in one of my restaurants', he announced. After three months the manager left and she was offered his job. 'He believed in me even when I didn't. He saw my potential, not my skills – and he acted on it', said Lena.

Vision and ideals

If you are driven by what you believe and it's rooted in real life, you will not be vulnerable to critics. Keep going and doing what you believe is right.

Tessa Jowell, Minister for Employment,
Welfare to Work and Equal Opportunities

One of the most impressive characteristics of the women we interviewed was their passion, conviction and vision for what they wanted to achieve. Several were motivated by social ideals and some indeed had been involved in left-wing politics early on. Julie Bradley in her youth wanted to 'set the world to rights' and flirted with communism. She tried criminal law but found she was not cut out for it:

I wasn't tough enough to face the daily tragedy of people caught in the poverty trap of debt and fines. Visiting Brixton prison was a real shock.

Julie Bradley, Managing Partner, Devonshires, Solicitors

Sue Slipman too was a communist at university and became the first ever woman president of the National Union of Students (NUS), an immensely powerful body in the pre-Thatcher years, when all students paid union subscriptions automatically and many were active in university politics and demonstrations. For her, work is 'incredibly important' and about 'being engaged in the world and making an impact'. Put simply, she wants to 'make the world a better place'.

Believe in your vision and don't listen to those who say you can't do it. It's better to try and fail than to do nothing.

Lena Bjorck, CEO Inn or Out

Tessa Jowell became a childcare officer in Brixton at the age of 22 and soon understood how myths and prejudices about the disadvantaged quickly become embedded into the regimes of care meted out to them. This fired in her a passionate belief that social welfare systems should ensure the dignity and self-worth of those they were set up to help. And from this have sprung many of the initiatives relating to health (anti-smoking), education

(New Deal) and childcare (Sure Start) that she and her teams have spearheaded in recent years under the present government.

I see the initiatives I have been involved in as a distillation of everything Labour is trying to do: to create the possibility for everyone to have a fair chance, to achieve personal dignity, and to have choice as a way to freedom. It is important to give people a sense of control and influence over their own lives.

Tessa Jowell

Skills portfolio

Developing a portfolio of versatile skills has been an advantage for many successful women. This is counter-intuitive to the normal female approach. Women generally believe that to get on one must develop ever more specialist skills and become expert in one field. Many women work hard to acquire additional qualifications in the belief that this will build their credibility. They end up in highly specialized functions in organizations – most commonly human resources (HR) and marketing – and wonder why the higher management jobs elude them. This is because board directors are most commonly recruited from the ranks of general managers, an area where few women gain experience. So generalists have an advantage in business, and several women in our study had benefited initially from a broad management induction programme as part of a graduate trainee scheme. Dianne Thompson (CEO at Camelot) recalled her first job with the Co-op where in 18 months she was sent on 15 external courses to develop her business skills. Meanwhile, the graduate programme at Glaxo was 'fantastic', according to Colette Graham, and was then consolidated by twelve months 'carrying the bag' as a sales rep to learn the ropes in the field.

However, if there is no appropriate training scheme in place, Jeanette Hughes (Group Chief Auditor, Royal & SunAlliance) has the answer – design your own. This is what she did when she joined Royal Insurance in the USA: formulated her own development plan that rotated her through different departments including assistant to the CEO. Unfortunately – or fortunately – this came to an abrupt end when, following restructuring,

Jeanette was promoted to Group Chief Auditor at the tender age of 30.

Unusual combinations of skills are increasingly attracting a premium and are more likely to prepare women for key projects and new opportunities. We discuss in Chapter Six the benefits of volunteering as a method of career development. Getting involved in work that develops new skills areas – finance, IT, project management, bidding and tendering, merger and acquisition activity – can be extremely advantageous when you are seeking promotion or a new appointment. Many of the women we interviewed had been astute in recognizing opportunities that could step change their careers.

CASE STUDY

During her time as a law lecturer, Judith Mayhew was involved in a ground-breaking project to develop an Anglo-French joint law degree – the first of its kind in the days before the Erasmus project promoted such activity. (The Erasmus project was sponsored during the 1980s by the EU, to promote integration of learning between centres of higher education across the EU.) The innovative nature of the project gained great visibility for those involved and confirmed for Judith the benefits of working at the cutting edge, both in terms of a sense of achievement and in terms of confidence gained. She sees herself as a practical lawyer and academic. She has since been appointed Special Adviser to the Chairman at Clifford Chance, in which capacity she is working on their community affairs strategy, building links with universities and developing client relations.

Sometimes the opportunity to acquire a new dimension of skills came about fortuitously, but successful women find ways in which to capitalize on this as their careers progress:

CASE STUDY

'I got a first in PPE¹ at Oxford and, after working in the City for a couple of years, I thought of returning to do a PhD. But my husband was transferred to Cambridge, so I looked for work in London (that's where most of the economist jobs are based). I was offered a post at the National Institute of Economic Research that had a very international focus and this set the direction of my career for the next 15 years. It was this experience that later got me a job as European Economist with Ford.'

Kate Barker, Chief Economist, CBI

Character traits

Drive and initiative

As one would expect, many of the women in the sample were very driven. Dianne Thompson, for example, always felt the need to prove her capabilities:

> *When I first moved to ICI in 1975 I was told I had to be 10 per cent better than the men. I said: 'That's OK. I'm at least 15 per cent better.*

Dianne Thompson, CEO, Camelot

Many women we spoke to had also developed the happy knack of being able to create opportunities out of a given set of circumstances where others might have seen only difficulties. Resilience and optimism, coupled with drive, are undoubtedly some of the key characteristics shared by the women in our sample.

CASE STUDY

Joy Kingsley (Managing Partner at solicitors Pannone) during her early career spent six months in a training placement in Wythenshawe. This culminated in her being asked to run the office, which she did for 10 years. During this time she became involved in management training via the local Chamber of Commerce. She discovered she had natural organizational skills and found management more enjoyable than purely legal work. However, at the same time she developed a nose for finding new work and built up the conveyancing side of the business (defaulting to repossession work during the recession). The business then underwent a series of mergers and demergers and when the shake up was over she found herself in the Managing Partner's chair – one of the first female Managing Partners in the country.

Most of the women we interviewed had spent their lives finding new ways of doing things and constantly seeking challenges. Many of them would say they had been lucky in their careers, but their good fortune was usually to work in environments where there was scope for their creativity, rather than to receive some unexpected windfall. Some had chosen to be part of a new venture that was breaking out of the old norms, having parted company with organizations where their talents were not recognized or the opportunities to express them were more limited.

I like to be in situations where I can make a difference and improve things.

Dianne Thompson

Martha Lane Fox, unhappy with the monolithic culture at Carlton TV and feeling trapped by politics and power wrangles was drawn to a new business paradigm with the creation of lastminute.com. She loved the original idea and was keen to see it become reality, not least because it's about doing things differently: relating to customer needs in a new way, through a new form of organizational culture, independent of traditional hierarchy and control systems.

After three years as Head of Communications at Glaxo Colette Graham began to get bored. It was an organization typical of the pharmaceutical industry where everything was clear, methodical and process-driven. She had had a great time and loved what she did, but her career seemed to be moving too slowly. Added to this, she had been in the same environment for too long (nine years) and needed to move on: 'I wanted to check if I really was good'. As a result she was recruited to Centrica – then established only three years – and has since enjoyed an 'amazingly exciting' time as the business embarked on a programme of restructuring, reorganization and growth through acquisitions. Colette's passion and enthusiasm for what she does is almost palpable. Steady state is of no interest to her: she derives her fulfilment from 'fixing things and making a difference':

I like to be able to make a personal difference by applying my skills and energy to business challenges. Putting yourself in

*difficult situations is high risk, but if you prove yourself
competent at crisis management then your credibility rises and
your visibility increases. You have to be passionate about what
you do and you must be able to feel there is a core of truth in
what you tell your customers.*

Colette Graham, Head of Internal Communication,
Centrica plc

Perhaps one of the most resilient women we talked to was Jo
Hansford, celebrity hairdresser who (with the help of her family)
manages a salon, a hairdressing academy and a haircare products
business. Having trained with Vidal Sassoon in the early years she
later went into business with Daniel Galvin, but the partnership
went sour and she was forced to leave:

*It was a terrible time and I thought of going back to work for
someone else until I realized I was talented – I just had to have
the confidence. Being let down by my business partner was
hard. But in the end it did me a favour, as I started out on my
own.*

Jo Hansford

But Jo was no stranger to finding opportunities, taking a risk and
working hard to make it succeed. She and her husband had been
doing it since they were married and first began investing in
properties, spending evenings and weekends renovating them
to rent out. The same entrepreneurial spirit had them running
market stalls at weekends too, to supplement the family
income:

*I am a great fatalist and take challenges and gambles – and all
challenges are positives to me.*

Jo Hansford

A very different character, but an equally resilient one, is
Margaret McCabe. When her marriage broke up it was at a time
when her father was terminally ill in Australia and she was
having a baby. She never expected to encounter discrimination,
but it hit her hard when her daughter was born (1988). She was
immediately relegated to the second division by the clerk at the

chambers where she was practising. Her income plummeted and she had no means of recourse, being self-employed. She experienced two or three years of major stress and was nearly bankrupt, but managed to find the courage to move on to other chambers (a 'voyage of discovery') before joining Pump Court. Here women constitute 50–60 per cent of the barristers in practice ('it's seen as a more radical set'). But her experience had touched a nerve and this led her to found the Woman Lawyer Conference as a forum to bring to light the issues holding women back in the legal profession:

I was astonished that it was me that took on the issues. I thought the law was a good profession and I had expected fairness. But I became a single parent and encountered discrimination, so I had no other choice but to fight. The foundation of equality is equal earnings and equal access to opportunity.

Margaret McCabe

Going the extra mile

Dedication to doing a good job – giving and getting the best for their clients, their teams and their organizations – was a recurring theme in the careers of successful women. One notable example was Hilary Meredith (Managing Partner at solicitors Donns). She has literally hiked several extra miles in her quest for evidence to pursue some of the cases she has undertaken to win compensation for those injured or killed while serving in the armed forces.

CASE STUDY

Hilary's talent lies in her persistence in digging for the story behind the cases she takes on. In one such instance she was instructed by the widow of a soldier killed near a reservoir. She literally put on her boots and hiked to the remote site. When she got there she questioned the manager of the nearby power station about the circumstances and was told that the reservoir was set to trip and overflow during heavy rainfall. The defence in the case had not revealed that their client was indemnified against such an occurrence. With this piece of information she was able to win compensation for her client.

It was Hilary's passion for justice and fairness and her persistence – a legacy from her days as an athlete – that spurred her to develop her specialism in compensation cases against the Ministry of Defence (MOD). She felt a great deal of empathy for the wives and children involved in some of the cases, and in the early days was often frustrated and angered by the intransigence of the MOD and its refusal to disclose information. But this just hardened her determination:

What keeps me going is the love of a fresh challenge. I never take no for an answer until I am satisfied I have achieved the best for my client.

Hilary Meredith

Some of the women in our sample had experienced difficulties in their personal lives, but here, too, they showed great courage and resilience in finding a coping mechanism and getting on with it. Dianne Thompson, for example, separated from her husband after a 21-year partnership. ('We weren't smart enough to realize the pressures we were subjecting ourselves to.') With a young daughter to care for she relinquished her high-flying job as MD of a large international company, because of the difficulty of managing the constant travel and long hours without support:

CASE STUDY

'I was devastated and only just holding myself together. My confidence was destroyed. I had no network to tap into but I did know a headhunter who was handling a marketing job for Woolworth. I hesitated because it wasn't in the same market as the other brands I had been involved with, but when they offered I took it. At the time it was a safe thing to do – I knew the ground (developing a new marketing and advertising strategy for the brand). We ended up winning the Advertiser of the Year Award for the campaign, which boosted my confidence. Soon after I was appointed director of marketing and instigated a culture and strategic change programme.'

Dianne Thompson

What's luck got to do with it?

▓ 'I've been as lucky as I've been smart.'
▓ 'How did I get where I am? Luck.'
▓ 'I stumbled into my career by chance.'
▓ 'It was all by accident.'

These responses were typical of the women in our sample when asked about their career path and how they got where they are today. We said earlier that the luck referred to usually had more to do with their ability to capitalize on a change in circumstances than with being given something they didn't really deserve. Margaret McCabe defines luck as 'the ability to recognize an opportunity'. This usually also entails a degree of hard work and applying oneself, so none of the women we spoke to had actually been given something for nothing. There were, however, examples of synchronicity – being in the right place at the right time and with the right set of credentials. There were many examples of how to turn circumstances to your own advantage. But in order to do that you have to feel empowered and entitled to do so.

CASE STUDY

'I joined Ford in 1985 as European Economist. Two months later my boss left and I had to take over his work. Once I had established my competence I was promoted to the job. But it was incredibly tough: it was very male-dominated then and people were suspicious of me – not only as a woman, but also as an outsider coming in. Surviving that was a real milestone that built my confidence.'

Kate Barker

What if you lack that feeling of empowerment? Jeanette Hughes talked about her feelings when she got her first big promotion:

CASE STUDY

'I had reservations about the new role as I'm not a confident person – which might surprise some people. Though the culture was changing at that time, the role of Chief Auditor had traditionally been a male one. It didn't hurt to be female then –

although there was no policy of affirmative action, the company was actively promoting suitably qualified women. Eighteen months later there was a reorganization and a new regional management structure was put in place. My predecessor was unhappy with the changes and left. It never occurred to me that I would replace him.'

Jeanette Hughes, Group Chief Auditor,
Royal & SunAlliance

We describe in Chapters Five and Seven how women can appear more confident by *acting as if* they have power and authority and how this, in turn, encourages a positive response from others.

The adaptability and flexibility of some of the women we spoke to was very striking. Put them down in situations where there's an unusual challenge and they flourish:

CASE STUDY

'I never had a career plan – I didn't have a clue. I thought at various times of being an actress, a prison governor or working in the media. It was never my ambition to be a CEO, I just wanted to work with bright, intelligent people. By chance I got a job at Spectrum by meeting one of the founder members, a really bright guy. It was serendipity that I ended up doing consulting work for media start-ups and developing my business planning skills. I came from an academic background and my three years at Spectrum changed my perspectives – it was a very different consultancy environment.'

Martha Lane Fox

Perhaps we should conclude this section with a telling quote from Joy Kingsley that puts the luck issue into perspective:

What I have achieved is down partly to ability but also to good luck – and the good luck could disappear. I never rest on my laurels and I'm always wondering – even after record results – what are this year's challenges?

Joy Kingsley

It seems the old adage holds true: 'Yes I've been lucky. And the harder I work the luckier I get.'

What fulfils successful women?

A consistent theme in the response to the question: 'What fulfils you about your work?' was the idea of making a difference, of getting one's contribution and value recognized. That is not to say that women do not enjoy power – they do, but usually as a means to an end. They see power as about having the resources and authority to get things done – and that's what makes these women tick. (Though in fact most of them fairly buzz and hum with energy and ideas.)

> *Titles mean nothing. I don't care who I speak to (to get things done). I'm not status conscious, I'm more interested in the purpose.*

Rabbi Julia Neuberger

Ambition and competitiveness feature significantly in the make-up of successful women, but these things are manifest in subtle ways. They are ambitious to get their agendas accepted and to push forward the issues in which they passionately believe. They experience competition not always in terms of winning, but rather in relation to winning people over to new ideas and better ways of doing things.

> *I'm ambitious for what I want to achieve – but being a minister is a means to an end, not an end in itself.*

Tessa Jowell

Both Kate Barker and Fiona Reynolds (former Director of the Women's Unit) spoke about the satisfaction of developing ideas, articulating them, persuading others to accept them and then seeing those ideas have an impact on the world.

> *I'm very driven by affecting the world and getting it right. I'm less bothered about hierarchical power. I'm a committee drone – I like to get things done. I'm quite enthusiastic about people getting things through and against sloppy thinking.*

Kate Barker

Judith Mayhew is also drawn to the idea of getting and seeing results (and talking about them) that she in fact holds down two full-time posts – Special Adviser to the Chairman at solicitors Clifford Chance and political leader of the City of London. Divorced in her 30s and with no children, she made a conscious choice to devote her life to public activity:

I have enjoyed unusual challenges all my life – I'm an optimist. I never thought about the difficulties, I just did what I wanted to do.

Judith Mayhew

A theme to which we will return in Chapter Four is the satisfaction successful women derive from 'doing it their way'. It is widely assumed that the desire for control in one's life through independent thought and action is a male characteristic. Not so. The successful women we spoke to often had a maverick streak that spurred them to adopt unconventional approaches, to take risks and to dare to do things according to their own lights.

I always felt you're put here to try to make things better.

Rabbi Julia Neuberger

A fascination for unusual work, especially where that work achieved an outcome for the greater good also featured in the responses.

The unusual nature of the work is compelling. Setting up the unique team of experts at Donns to support compensation claimants has been a major achievement.

Hilary Meredith, Managing Partner, Donns Solicitors

These women also derived immense satisfaction from their achievements. They communicated a real sense of being comfortable with who and where they were in their lives:

I love the work – it's intellectually and personally satisfying. I'm doing what being a lawyer is about – getting justice, fighting interesting causes and making a real difference to people's lives. After 18 years I feel I've got it right.

Margaret McCabe

The people dimension of their work was also immensely important. Dianne Thompson described the satisfaction of doing well for her team at Camelot and how touched she was when they cheered her on saying: 'Go on Di, do us proud', at the time she was presenting the rebid for the Lottery franchise. Sue Slipman talked of the satisfaction of bringing on her team, developing their skills and seeing them grow in confidence. This was reiterated by Fiona Reynolds:

Ninety per cent of the reward is the people you work with. Building alliances, winning people over, convincing them is a huge step forward. The greatest battle is won when the words come out of their mouths – then you know they believe in it and you've won their commitment.

Fiona Reynolds, Director of the Women's Unit,
Cabinet Office

Bringing others to new ideas was a recurring theme:

I liked studying and teaching was a natural progression. I liked the technical side – reading accountancy documents and then helping others to understand. You get immediate feedback with teaching – I'm not very patient and I like to see results. When I worked in insolvency everything took months and there wasn't always an outcome.

Julia Penney, VP, Thames Valley Association,
Chartered Institute of Accountants

Tangible results were important:

I always enjoyed a challenge and seeing material results – being able to say: 'I made this happen'.

Professor Susan Greenfield

Pitting yourself against difficult odds and succeeding also came through:

I always just ploughed through the middle of everything – and I just got away with it somehow

Hilary Meredith (speaking of the way she
dealt with bureaucracy and red tape during
her early days in the legal profession)

We'll let Julia Barfield have the final word in this chapter, since her contribution epitomizes what we – and many of the women in our study – hold true:

> *Success is about happiness and fulfilment – being a whole woman. Age brings a new perspective – family, friends, interests and work are no longer divided up and compartmentalized. You are a more balanced and rounded person.*
>
> Julia Barfield

Summary

Disparate though our group of successful women was in terms of age, background and career history, there were clearly discernible patterns in the life influences, character traits, attitudes and beliefs they shared with us:

- A supportive family that had engendered feelings of self-worth and stressed the importance of education.
- A strong work ethic and personal drive leading to high academic achievement.
- A desire to make a difference and the courage to do things their own way.
- The love of challenge and the willingness to stretch themselves and take risks.
- Resilience, tenacity and determination to resolve problems at work and in their personal lives.
- Making their own luck through sheer hard work.
- Setting challenging goals, planning and focusing on outcomes.
- Adopting a persuading and inclusive managerial style and being team players.
- Being dedicated to their work but not being defined by it.
- Staying true to themselves and not being seduced by success, status or propaganda.

We return to some of these themes in Chapter Four, where we consider how successful women deal with the challenges of being a woman manager.

The next chapter presents a picture of working life for women today. As we embark on our careers or seek to move up the corporate ladder in a new millennium, what is the broader context in which women are operating? How far have we come in our emancipation and what remains to be done before we can truly say we have achieved equality?

Note

1 Philosophy, Politics and Economics.

2
A snapshot of the year 2001

Introduction

In 1980 the United Nations reported that, though women constituted half of the world's population and performed nearly two-thirds of all work hours, they received only a tenth of the world's income and owned less than one hundredth of its wealth. It is beyond the scope of this book to consider the global condition of womankind, so we begin with a snapshot of what it means to be a working woman in Britain at the beginning of the 21st century.

Some of the questions that interested us were: How many of us are working and what kinds of jobs are we doing? What are we being paid for the work we do? How many of us are combining work with having a family and how are we coping? How many of us have reached the boardroom and who is running her own business? Are we having it all . . . or are we all about to drop from stress and exhaustion?

The news headlines

More women are working outside the home

According to government statistics the number of women working has risen by nearly one million over the past decade and we now account for 44 per cent of the labour force – representing 11.5 million women working.[1] Unsurprisingly, many women are opting for part-time work, with four out of five part-time workers being female, a far higher proportion than in other countries in Europe, Scandinavia, North America and Australia.

One of the most marked changes, however, has been the increase in mothers with young children returning to work – up from 24 per cent in 1979 to 67 per cent by 1996. There has also been a dramatic increase in the proportion of women who work through their pregnancies and return to work within a year of the birth. Half of all mothers with children under five now work, and of these 45 per cent do so full time.

The Future Foundation[2] has recently conducted a survey of 500 young women to assess their attitudes to work. The Foundation's Director, Melanie Howard, is quoted as saying: 'Women have now been raised with the same expectations as men', and that that includes the expectation that they will have paid employment.

I am a person, not just a baby-making machine, and I want the fast car and the nice house just like everyone else. I have the right to earn these things just like a man, and I don't expect to have the job of child-rearing dumped upon me.

Jo Persaud, participating in 'Talking Point'
online debate 12 June 2000

A key influencer is whether or not other women in the family have worked:[3]

All the women in my family have worked, right back to my great-great-grandmother. Work for me is about identity – I couldn't give it up.

Women are still opting for a relatively narrow spectrum of careers, though: half of all women with jobs work in clerical and sales roles or in personal services. (Not unexpectedly women outnumber men three to one in clerical/secretarial jobs.) That women occupy 64 per cent of all sales roles is probably attributable to several factors – for instance, the flexibility of telesales, where increasingly there is an option to work from home – as well as to the strength of women's communication and customer handling skills.

Women also predominate in public administration, education and health, where some degree of work flexibility is assured to accommodate the childcare and family responsibilities most women expect to take up at some point in their working lives. Indeed, there is strong evidence that the career choices of many young women are still constrained by the need for that career to accommodate a family at some future date. Teaching, catering, retailing, nursing and the other 'caring professions' all offer potential for part-time or flexible working to accommodate school hours and holidays. And women account for between 75 per cent and 90 per cent of all jobs across these sectors.

Sex role stereotyping is still prevalent

The most recent research findings by the Equal Opportunities Commission (EOC) indicate that male and female students in secondary, further and higher education still expect to enter different industries:[4]

KEY RESEARCH FINDING

Two out of five women intended to take up careers in education, health or related service industries, while men were most likely to opt for careers in research, IT or business.

Focus group feedback indicated that women's initial career choices – and consequently the salaries they can expect – are affected by the prospect of having a family in the future. As early as 1997 it was evident that girls were outstripping boys in the classroom, but they have yet to carry this through to higher education – and to subsequent employment. Even though girls outperform boys at GCSE level in science, maths and technology they are still opting for traditional female subjects at A level, degree level and in vocational training. Consequently males dominate in key subject areas such as computer studies, technology, physical sciences and economics.

The emerging new economy of Internet and high tech companies is characterized by rapid growth, burgeoning new opportunities and the relative youth of those involved in it. But while it might provide a more gender-neutral work environment than traditional sectors, women have less access to the jobs and money available because few of them have the necessary IT, engineering or even finance background.

Sex role stereotyping in education and training translates, of course, into job segregation, and consequently men and women tend to be employed in different kinds of managerial occupations. Production management in manufacturing is male dominated still, while most financial and office managers are female. Half of all personnel managers are women, while more than 40 per cent of managers in insurance and pensions are women. For it is in the dominant service sector in the UK that women are most successful. And within managerial occupations the overwhelming majority (about 90 per cent) of general managers, chief executives and other senior managers in large organizations are men. Data for 1999 from Remuneration Economics,[5] however, showed that the percentage of women directors had grown from 3.6 to 6.1 per cent, spurred perhaps by higher female representation in the new economy of dotcoms. But in many cases where women directors have been appointed, they tend to be non-executive rather than executive directors. Men and women also tend to be employed in different professions. Over 90 per cent of engineers and technologists are male, whereas over 60 per cent of those in the teaching professions are female. The inequality between the sexes is also evident in the further segregation of women into the lower status and lower paid echelons of their chosen professions. In teaching, for example, about 70 per cent of university lecturers are male while only 15 per cent of men work in primary and nursery education.

Table 2.1 Who does what – occupations of men and women

	Female % employees	Hourly pay (£)
General managers	34	20.21
Legal professionals	41	19.45
Health professionals	45	18.94
Specialist managers	32	18.88
Bus. and financial assoc. prof.	34	18.18
Other occupations (agricult. etc.)	22	5.15
Sales assts and check-out ops.	75	5.01
Catering occupations	63	4.94
Hairdressers, beauticians. etc.	89	4.84
Other sales and services	74	4.72

Source: *Women's Incomes over the Lifetime*, The Cabinet Office 2000.

In the legal profession more women than men are now admitted each year to the Roll of Solicitors in England and Wales, but men continue to dominate the upper levels of the profession. They are more likely to achieve partnership, whereas women are more likely to be assistant solicitors. While researching this book, however, we found changes afoot, with a surge of women solicitors – both in London and the provinces – being appointed managing partner. Legal firms are also attempting to accommodate both qualified and unqualified women through part-time and flexible working. There were even reports of women achieving partner status while on maternity leave.

Again, in the higher reaches of the legal profession the picture is less encouraging. Only a quarter of practising barristers are women and about 90 per cent of QCs are men. Women judges are still very few – accounting for less than 10 per cent of High Court judges – and woefully few are Lord Justices or Law Lords. There is little likelihood of rapid change in this very traditional and conservative sector and the recent experience of women barristers is described in Chapter Four.

Finally, within the medical profession the picture is not hugely encouraging either. Although women account for about a third of all medical hospital staff, only around 20 per cent of them are on career grades (primarily consultants).

Kamlesh Bahl, then Chair of the Equal Opportunities Commission, summed up the problem two years ago when she commented:

Most of our brightest students 'play safe', opting for familiar roles. This weakens the standard of candidates available to industry. It also means that women are limiting their earning potential. In 1998, on average, men still earn 20 per cent more than women.

Is the glass ceiling still intact?

A key indicator of progress towards equality of the sexes in the workplace must be the proportion of women in management and the professions. And though women have increased their share of employment in managerial roles and in the professions there remain considerable disparities.

KEY RESEARCH FINDINGS
ON FEMALE EMPLOYMENT

▓ Today, around one in five managers is a woman, compared with only 1 in 13 in 1989.[6]

▓ The gap closes somewhat among the professions where women account for about 40 per cent of jobs.

But despite the fact that more women are gaining business qualifications than men – whether through further or higher education, NVQs or modern apprenticeships – the disparity between the sexes persists. In marketing and sales, for example, where women vastly outnumber men in the lower ranks, only a quarter of the half a million managerial jobs are occupied by women.

The attitudes of some line managers are perpetuating job segregation as they demonstrate reluctance to promote women into traditionally male jobs for historical reasons.[7]

If part-time work is still very much the domain of women, then, as we have seen, the boardroom remains a man's world – less than 5 per cent of directors are female. Another EOC research paper – 'Management & the Professions'[8] – clearly demonstrates that women are still disadvantaged by the culture of long hours which largely excludes women with children, and the lack of family-friendly policies, particularly job sharing in senior positions. The authors of the report suggest:

Working long hours has come to be seen as an indicator of commitment and stamina and reflects a 'masculine' work culture. Whilst some individual men may not like working long hours, it is a requirement with which they are more easily able to comply.

Fundamental barriers to sex equality remain

Job segregation as a result of sex role stereotyping is one indicator that, contrary to popular opinion, women have not yet achieved true equality in the workplace. Further evidence, if any were needed, can be seen in the large numbers of people seeking advice from the Equal Opportunities Commission. Last year alone 16 000 people sought advice about sex discrimination and pay issues, indicating that the need for a sex equality body is just as vital now as it was 25 years ago when it was first set up.

The EOC research findings last year, unsurprisingly to many of us, revealed a worrying level of complacency about these issues among senior decision-makers (MPs, MEPs, life peers and political advisers).[9] For while nearly all were aware of the pay gap between women and men and recognized that promotion opportunities for women were much worse than for men, relatively few (just 43 per cent) thought that more needed to be done to tackle the problem.

While the issue of the pay gap is well documented and has received considerable recent publicity, the question of sexual harassment at work is less well publicized, except when newsworthy cases reach the headlines, such as that of Dr Kate Swinburne and her £1 million settlement from Deutsche Bank. Sexual harassment at work remains a serious problem, however, with 700 women contacting the EOC last year for advice. (Less than 5 per cent of harassment complaints are made by men.)

So, many of the old barriers to equality for women remain, with considerable effort required to ensure that it is recognized as both necessary, desirable and achievable in the workplace, as in our home and social lives.

The baby trap

While many women plan their initial careers in relation to the future families they will form, startling research from Mintel claims that the maternal instinct no longer exists for one woman in five.[10] Over the past two years the number of women choosing not to have children has risen from 15 to 18 per cent. It seems many women now are as unlikely to want children as men, a dramatic social change attributed by sociologists to women's reluctance to jeopardize their careers. And this trend will accelerate: within 10 years it is expected that around 25 per cent of women will be childless.

You know, if women cannot manage to work and get paid
handsomely and are stuck in the childbearing and caring roles,

*of course they will be undervalued. For this reason I choose not
to marry.*

Manisha, participating in 'Talking Point'
online debate 12 June 2000

Just as surprising is the evidence in the Mintel research that
women are now more career-minded: a quarter of women
surveyed saw their work as a career rather than a job, compared
with only one-fifth of men. This represents a complete reversal of
the position four years ago.

The financial and career disadvantages of having children
early are recognized by both sexes, particularly those under 35,
even when they are in long-term relationships. This is reflected in
the overall finding that one woman in ten was 'undecided' about
having children.

In her book *Farewell to the Family?* Patricia Morgan provides
evidence that the women deciding to have children late or not at
all are predominantly graduates. She reaches the bleak conclusion
that there must be adverse effects on the population if highly
qualified and experienced women are increasingly deciding not
to have children or to have fewer of them.[11]

This is supported by evidence from the Family Policy Studies
Centre that some women who are having babies are possibly
those least likely to be able to take care of them adequately –
single, teenage mothers (many underage) for whom a baby is a
source of status and an exit route from her parents' home via the
benefits system.

But in reality are marriage and motherhood bad career moves?
Research undertaken by the eminent sociologists Professors
Marilyn Davidson and Cary Cooper of UMIST found that
successful female managers were only 'a third to a half as likely
to be married as their male colleagues, and even fewer are likely
to have children'. Seventy per cent of the single women interviewed said that remaining single had been an advantage in their
careers.

If single and childless women are seen to have an advantage,
how do first time working mothers feel about their career
prospects? First, they tend to work harder during their pregnancies because they worry they may be seen to be slacking and
many fear they will in future be passed over for promotion and

pay rises. As a consequence some women delay having children because of misgivings about the effect this might have on their career.[12]

So what do employers think of women with children?

It seems that family formation does have a dramatic impact on women's prospects for promotion and equal pay. It is a seriously 'career limiting' move. An EOC survey of employers' attitudes provides some important insights:[13]

▪ Male line managers were reluctant to promote younger women in case they became pregnant (seen as costly, especially in small firms).
▪ Women were seen as less committed and less reliable once they had a family (because they might be called away for family emergencies).
▪ They were not trusted, so working from home was not an option.

Men are seen as more committed because they don't have the child to go back to, so they are rewarded for being able to stay away from the home.
                                    Female line manager, Glasgow

So, these typically male-held views are also endorsed by female managers. Even those women who themselves had taken periods of maternity leave and then returned to work quickly and without disruption, agreed with male colleagues that taking a break to have a child is detrimental to women's promotion prospects.

Moreover, in the wake of recent legislation on maternity rights and parental leave, Ruth Lee, Head of Policy at the Institute of Directors, revealed that 45 per cent of the Institute's members would think twice about employing women of childbearing age. The picture emerging is that further legislation to enable women with families to work is likely to impact adversely on the careers of all younger women.

That marriage and family should militate against a woman's career seems all the more unjust when we consider how these apparent encumbrances are viewed when attached to a man. He traditionally acquires a domestic support system that leaves him free to focus single-mindedly on the job and a set of responsibilities that tie him securely to the corporate bandwagon.

The presumption within many companies is that, once married, a woman's focus inevitably shifts to family life. This is compounded when she becomes pregnant and is subsequently relegated by her colleagues to the second division – 'the mommy track' as the Americans call it. Excluded from decision making and often stripped of authority, she soon finds herself isolated and out of touch. The myth of the working mother's lack of ambition becomes a self-fulfilling prophecy.

It's as though I don't count any more ... I'm relegated to less important activity and no longer taken as seriously. People are just waiting for me to have another baby.

Francesca, account manager in
a large public company

I returned to work full time a few months ago. I found I was not coping and asked to work part-time. My employer agreed but has taken away all my managerial responsibility and I am to do 'project work'.

Contributor to e-mum.com discussion
on problems returning to work, May 2000

Meanwhile the work paradigm of many companies (as designed by men and for men) – long hours and the requirement to be mobile – rules out for many women the possibility of continuing on the fast track unless they can find a radical solution. Few men volunteer to become househusbands – even when the woman is a significantly higher earner. In a random sample of over 2000 adults, only two men described themselves as looking after the home (compared with 12 per cent of women).[14] Meanwhile, as few as 3 per cent of fathers opt to work part time and, among those who choose to take care of the children, many still leave a large measure of the domestic work and responsibility to their working female partners. In short, househusbands don't provide the degree of support to their partners that housewives routinely do.

If my husband is asked to pick up the children at a certain time he'll be there. But as for remembering who has a music lesson or who needs swimming kit ...

Senior Lawyer

Reluctantly, many women succumb to the, often intolerable, pressures of trying to juggle work and home.

KEY FINDINGS FROM RESEARCH AMONG 560 WOMEN RETURNERS

Within two years 17 had gone part time; 19 had given up work altogether.

These results were largely attributed to the long hours required at work and the failure by employers to provide any flexibility. Even small concessions – for example, adjustments of 15 minutes to arrival or departure times – could not be allowed in some cases, while home working and job sharing were ruled out completely by some employers.

But many women do struggle against very difficult odds to maintain the financial independence that derives from having a job. Many women fear the consequences of relinquishing that independence and how it will affect the power balance in their relationship with their partner. And they are right to do so, if anecdotal evidence is any indicator.

CASE STUDY

Who would not have been incensed by the stories of some of the women who appeared on the 'Love and Money' TV series?[15] In one programme a husband made it abundantly clear that, since his wife had taken a career break to have their child, she had forfeited the right to any say in decisions affecting their lives. He added that: 'She would be in a stronger negotiating position if she was out there and bringing in the money'. The woman was given a house-keeping allowance and denied access to the joint bank account on the grounds that 'She would only spend it on fripperies'. She even admitted to having offered sex if, in return, he would pay the phone bill. The chilling conclusion was that when women relinquish their economic power some men would take advantage of that fact to bully and coerce them. Who pays the piper calls the tune.

Women lag behind on pay

In a study commissioned by Women's Minister, Baroness Jay, an attempt has been made to quantify the impact of motherhood on female earnings.[16] Women choosing to have a family can expect to earn almost £200 000 less over their working lifetime than their male counterparts doing the same job. Worse yet is the finding that many women are being paid less simply because of their sex, despite the Equal Pay Act introduced in 1970 to address precisely this inequality.

KEY FINDINGS ON EQUAL PAY

The research even revealed that women who put their career first earned much less than men. This puts the UK in the lower rankings across Europe – a poor 10th out of 15 countries surveyed on equal pay.

The reasons for this are several, including women's less aggressive attitude when demanding and negotiating pay rises. Also, if they take a career break, this is most frequently during their late 20s and early 30s, usually a period of high earnings.[17] But anecdotal evidence shows that blatant – and illegal – discrimination on pay has yet to be eradicated:

> *At my last annual review, I was confident I would receive a substantial pay increase on the grounds of my hard work and exemplary performance. I had exceeded all my targets and achieved all my objectives. Quite unashamedly, my manager proposed that I be given a smaller pay rise than my male colleagues – who had done less well than me – on the grounds that my partner is wealthy and I therefore didn't need the money as much as the others who had families to support.*
>
> Sharon, account director

This attitude is prevalent among female as well as male line managers:[18] they regard men as the main breadwinners whose key role is to provide for the family. Women are seen as secondary earners.

KEY RESEARCH FINDINGS
ON PAY (1999)[19]

■ For the first time women managers get bigger pay increases (on average 25 per cent higher) than male colleagues.

■ Executive pay gap narrows to an average 6 per cent.

■ The average female manager is 37 and earning £31 622 (by comparison her average male colleague is aged 43 and earns £37 235).

■ But in boardrooms there is staggering inequality: the average female director (41) is paid £66 711, compared with the £94 742 earned by her average fellow male director.

The Institute of Management, commenting on these figures, concluded that, taking into account that pay is influenced by age, experience and length of service, and that the average female manager is seven years younger and has served six years less with her current employer, the 1999 findings show that the gender pay disparity among managers is no longer 'significant'. But before complacency sets in, let us, for a moment, remind ourselves of the principle here: it holds that men and women should receive equal pay for work of equal value – regardless of differences in age or length of service.

The discrepancy in directors' pay can, in part, be attributed to the fact that few women occupy the highest paying board positions: those of CEO and finance director, another example of early career choices militating against women's later prospects.

... and are still tied to the kitchen sink

My second favourite household chore is ironing. My first being hitting my head on the top bunk bed until I faint.

Erma Bombeck

In addition to getting paid less, women are still responsible for the majority of housework (so no surprises there then). The EOC recently revealed that women spend twice as much time cooking as men, five times as long cleaning the house and eight times as long doing the laundry.[20] So the male attitude of 'helping', rather than accepting equal responsibility for domestic chores, still prevails. However, a least a quarter of couples surveyed said the man usually unblocked the sink (well, at least that's something to be thankful for).

The report's editor, Carol Summerfield, summed up the situation:

The traditional distinction between the woman's role of homemaker and the man's role as breadwinner has, to a certain extent, been eroded over the last generation or so. But despite the advance of women in the workplace the woman's role in the home has not changed so dramatically from that of her mother – it is still the woman in the partnership who usually has the major responsibility for household chores and childcare.

New men, where are you?

Undoubtedly, there are higher earning women who may be able to negotiate a more equal partnership or to pay for domestic help, but women earning at least a tenth more than their male partners account for only 16 per cent of all working women. Even when both partners are working, 80 per cent of women say they do most of the housework and childcare.

In the beginning, I thought it was going to be an equal partnership, but it's really not true. Women end up with all the burden of day-to-day living.

Lisa, married, two children.
Quoted on BBC 'Having It All' web page, 6 July 2000

Not unexpectedly the vast majority of women (93 per cent according to research findings by *Top Sante*),[21] find it difficult to juggle career and family life. This leads to stress among working women and frequently to disillusionment with their jobs. Many of the 5000 women surveyed felt they were overworked, under-paid and at breaking point from stress.

KEY RESEARCH FINDINGS

- 75 per cent of working women experience health problems as a result of stress
- Three out of five worry about the impact on their children's emotional well-being of their short temper and impatience.
- Over half said they had shouted at their children because they felt stressed.

I feel as if I do everything and don't have a life of my own. I feel very isolated and sometimes have a weep or a shout.

Julie, married, two children.
Quoted on BBC 'Having It All' web page,
6 July 2000

A prime cause of these problems was lack of support from both partners and managers. For, at work, women reported they felt they had to work harder than men to get promotion – despite being faster and more productive – and that having a baby was damaging to their career prospects. These factors plus the lack of crèche facilities (available to only 6 per cent of those surveyed) and the failure of most bosses to make any allowances for family responsibilities, leads many women to feel overworked and underpaid.

KEY RESEARCH FINDINGS

- It comes as no surprise that four out of five women would give up their jobs if they did not need the money.
- Most women work primarily for financial reasons: only 23 per cent of women said they would stick with their careers if money were not an issue.

I work for financial necessity. I'd give it up if I could.

Sarah

I've always been ambitious but the main reason I work now is for the money . . .

Linzie
Both quoted on BBC 'Having It All' web page,
6 July 2000

I have to go back to work after the birth of my baby in order for my family to survive – 'wanting it all' has nothing to do with it, I'd rather stay at home if I could.
Ingrid Solberg, contributor to BBC 'Talking Point'
e-mail debate 12 June 2000

Interestingly, the *Top Sante* sample was skewed towards women in the upper socio-economic groups, with over a third of respondents earning more than their partners. Relatively few of these women, however, enjoy being the main breadwinner. Some of them, working as many as 50 hours a week, are undoubtedly victims of the long-hours culture prevalent in many organizations. Half of them work full time, but most of those with pre-school children resent having to do so. They would prefer to work part time or to job share and many would like the opportunity to work from home.

The reality is that only about a quarter of women are employed on some form of flexible working – most commonly flexitime – and in 1998 fewer than 2 per cent of women were working from home, though this may have risen recently with the growing trend for teleworkers to operate from home.

Sharon Parson, editor of *Top Sante*, spoke for many of us when she said:

Women are invaluable to the workforce and they have fought hard for managerial, skilled and director level jobs. But they are also still expected to take the bulk of responsibility for the home and family as well as hold down a demanding full-time job and they're exhausted.

Sisters are doin' it for themselves

KEY RESEARCH FINDINGS
ON ENTREPRENEURSHIP

Figures released last year show women accounted for 30 per cent of new business start-ups in the UK (these totalled 232 000 in the first half of 1999).
Source: Nat West Bank Small Business Services[22]

The rather disappointing ratio of 70 : 30 men to women entrepreneurs has remained fairly constant over the past 15 years. But if women are less inclined to initiate new ventures than men, businesses launched by women have just as much chance of succeeding as those started by men. Indeed, some small-scale studies and anecdotal evidence suggest that, once established, businesses run by women are more likely to survive than those run by men.[23] This may be because businesses owned by women tend to grow at a slower rate than those run by men and so are less likely to become overextended. Nat West also found that women are more realistic in their business planning than their male counterparts, as judged from first-year sales projections.

Regarding the smaller number of business start-ups by women, there is growing evidence that we still find it difficult to gain access to venture capital – in the USA, for example, only 6 per cent of businesses started by women attract venture capital.

Sadly, women-owned businesses appear also to be ghettoized in the same way as women's employment. They gravitate towards certain service sectors including domestic services, retail, professional services, catering and leisure. As we saw earlier, these are the sectors that offer greater flexibility in working hours, an issue of prime importance for working women with families. These choices reflect too the pre-existing vocational qualifications and work experience of the women entrepreneurs.

We return to the issue of setting up a business in Chapter Seven when we consider the advantages and disadvantages of running your own enterprise.

Summary

While, undoubtedly, much has changed for women over the past century – with the pace of change accelerating dramatically in recent years – many areas remain to be tackled if women are to achieve true equality:

■ Pervasive gender stereotyping that restricts opportunities for women (and men) by designating certain careers as "men's work" or "women's work".

▨ A continuing pay gap of around twenty per cent that without concerted action will remain unchanged.

▨ Complacency among politicians and policy-makers towards enduring inequalities.

▨ The need for more women politicians to represent women's issues at senior government levels and to bring fresh perspectives to work-life issues.

▨ Long working hours that disadvantage those with families – especially women – and result in high levels of stress with serious economic consequences.

The next chapter considers in detail the myths and stereo-types that are still holding women back at work, and proposes strategies women might use in overcoming them.

Notes

1 Office of National Statistics, March 1999.
2 'The Sexual Renaissance': www.futurefoundation.net.
3 BBC Online 'Having it all', 6 July 2000 at www.bbc.co.uk/education.
4 Equal Opportunities Commission, *Attitudes to Equal Pay*, Spring 2000.
5 *National Management Salary Survey*, published annually with the Institute of Management.
6 *National Management Salary Survey*, Remuneration Economics and IM, 1998.
7 *Attitudes to Equal Pay*, EOC, ISBN 1 84206 029 5.
8 *Briefings on Men & Women in Britain*, EOC, ISBN 1 87 03 58 61 9.
9 Research conducted by IPSOS-RSL for the EOC, Summer 1999.
10 'Pre-Family Lifestyles Report', Mintel, December 1999.
11 Patricia Morgan, *Farewell to the Family?*, The Institute of Economic Affairs, second edition, 1999. Now available from www.civitas.org.uk.
12 Research by Johnson & Johnson, July 2000.
13 Equal Opportunities Commission, *Attitudes to Equal Pay*, ISBN 1 84206 029 5.
14 Johnson & Johnson, op. cit.
15 'Love and Money', Channel 4, March 2000.
16 Katherine Rake (ed.), *Women's Incomes over the Lifetime*, HMSO, 2000.
17 Juliet Mitchell, Senior Lecturer, Cambridge University, Faculty of Social and Political Sciences.
18 Equal Opportunities Commission, *Equal Pay – Omnibus Survey & Class of 2000*, ISBN 1 84206 029 5
19 *National Management Salary Survey*, op. cit.
20 Equal Opportunities Commission and Office for National Statistics, *Social Focus on Men & Women*, October 1998.
21 *Top Sante* survey, June 2000.
22 The NatWest Small Business Research Trust, Quarterly Survey of Small Business in Britain, October 1999.
23 Cited by the Equal Opportunities Commission in *The Labour Market*, ISBN 1 84206 017 1.

3

Women at work: exploding the myths

Introduction

Many of the barriers to women's progress – commonly known as the 'glass ceiling' – are the consequence of myths and stereotypes about women's employability and effectiveness. On Radio 2 some time ago, Ruth Lee of the Institute of Directors declared that, based on her experience in the City, women lacked ambition and didn't have the 'killer instinct'.[1] By contrast, the famous social anthropologist, Margaret Mead, was once asked by the US army to determine whether women should be allowed to participate in armed combat. She came back with a resounding 'No'. 'Give a woman a gun', she warned, 'and there's no telling what she'll do.' So, opinions vary markedly regarding women's capacity for aggression.

Other gender myths abound, and many are used as excuses not to recruit or promote women: they get pregnant and leave; they can't cope at the top; they are less committed than men; they score poorly on the 'harder' skills of negotiation, decision making and strategic planning; women are not effective leaders and they are difficult to work with.

This chapter draws together evidence from a variety of sources to explode these myths, for not only are they used against women, but so pervasive are they that women themselves (as we saw above) are in danger of believing and even of perpetuating them. What can women managers do to break down these preconceptions, and how can they ensure that their behaviour does nothing to reinforce them?

We look particularly at the issue of leadership. Perhaps the single most important determinant of business success: what is the ideal leadership style, and how can women managers develop it?

Some gender stereotypes at work

The concept of gender stereotyping at work has been documented since the early seventies,[2] but the ways in which women collude (whether consciously or otherwise) in this process was brought forcibly home to me while studying for my MBA. Of the 160 or so students, only about 20 were women and, in a situation where women were heavily outnumbered, it was interesting to observe the resulting behaviour. Six stereotypes were clearly observable:

■ Den mother: good listener; focused on the problems of others; took on waifs and strays; matronly appearance.

■ Big sister: slightly aloof; quiet and ironic manner.

■ Little sister: petite and cute; fun loving; off-beat.

■ Tart: flirtatious manner; dressed provocatively.

■ One-of-the-boys: played darts and pool, dressed in jeans and T-shirts; boyish appearance.

■ Victim: quiet and unassertive; mousy appearance and drab, shapeless clothing.

The common denominator was that none of these roles in any way threatened the men. Nor, unfortunately, did any of them really command professional respect. They were all modes of behaviour associated with particular forms of dress and demeanour that avoided the challenges of competing with men as equals. When one woman, during a debate about equal opportunities, proposed that some forms of positive action should be introduced to level the playing field, she was greeted with a barrage of objections. Subsequently, in a satirical paper circulated among MBA students, she featured prominently in the headlines as: 'Dog gets on its hind legs and barks.' Clearly, women were not to be taken seriously, and if they demanded change then they must be brought to heel through abusive language and ridicule.

The female gender roles outlined above are those with which most men are comfortable, and women commonly adopt them (both at work and socially) in order to avoid the kind of confrontation that provokes men to anger and resentment. They are 'safe' alternatives. While recognizing that choosing to be proactive is not an easy option when it comes to challenging these stereotypes and adopting more 'authentic' behaviour (that which is true to our own principles and values), I believe that the alternative (doing nothing and acquiescing) can be just as stressful.

Beverly Stone has written eloquently about the moral responsibility of the individual with regard to culture change in organizations.[3] She speaks of 'taking responsibility for our own behaviour' by understanding that it is dictated more by what goes on inside our heads – fear and uncertainty – than it is by external circumstances. Looking back on past mistakes, the author sees that she regrets more the things she did not do than the things she did. Why did I hold back from acting when I was treated unfairly, when my credibility was undermined and even when I was bullied? What would I have had to lose if I had followed my conscience and protested? In retrospect, very little. What I lost by staying silent, however, was my self-respect. As Stone puts it, I have at times been guilty of 'wasting life by playing safe', and those feelings of guilt and regret stay with you long after the event.

Now, it must be acknowledged that in reality it is far easier for some of us to stand up and be counted (very easy for me, with hindsight) than it is for others. Some of us choose to be active and some of us choose not to be, often because of circumstances that constrain our actions – our job options are limited; we need the money; some of the positives outweigh the negatives – so we struggle on. But it is important to remember that you may feel better having confronted the politics that are holding you back, even where the outcome is not entirely favourable. (These issues are pursued further in Chapter Seven.)

CASE STUDY

One of the women in our study, a partner in a professional services firm, described what it was like to achieve partnership in a traditional, male-dominated culture: 'I came into the profession with no expectation of partnership – it seemed beyond what I could achieve. The firm was run by men from the "old school" network, with a strong belief in their power and entitlement. At assessment boards I had feedback that the assessors doubted I had the edge as a manager when it counted. They expected it would take me another two and a half years to reach senior level. This made me angry and I thought: "I'll show you." I realized that I was too quiet. I was working to make life easier for those above me and they didn't see it. I had to manage upwards and confront the attitudes of the partners who were very directive and allowed me no initiative, no platform for decision making. So I stopped aiming to please the bosses and gave them feedback that they were passing me all the grunt work they didn't want to do. I got a secondment to an international project team and this gave me the chance to show what I could do. For the first time I felt I could be myself, an equal contributor with valid opinions. This really moved my career on and subsequently, at the assessment centre for partner, I not only passed, but finished in the top quartile. The assessors said: "You came out as a real tiger." It was gratifying to surprise people and upset their preconceptions about me.'

Let us now consider some of the gender myths that are widely perpetuated about working women.

Women get pregnant and leave

As time goes on, more women will rise to the very top jobs. But they should not have to struggle against the odds. Companies can benefit from allowing more flexible working hours and from holding jobs open for women to return to when they have had their family. After all, if they have spent thousands of pounds training female employees, they should want to reap the benefit of their investment.

Zena Jones, Opportunity Now[4]

It is a fact that two out of three highly qualified women will take a career break at some time, usually for family reasons (though occasionally for personal development).[5] For 60 per cent of women the duration of that break is less than a year (and nearly half return to work within six months). But very few – less than 20 per cent – take their career break as part of an employer's scheme, since these are not yet widespread. Most women work at least four years before taking a break and switch jobs infrequently thereafter (only 1.57 times on average). Yet research among human resource managers (60 per cent of whom are women) showed that they sometimes recruit a man in favour of an equally good woman because they believe the woman might leave or go part time when starting a family.[6] Given the predilection of males to job hop during their early careers, one has to question who in reality looks the better bet – the woman who works four years, has six months off and then shows a high degree of loyalty or the man who jumps ship every couple of years?

*I feel I'm much more employable now (at 41) that I am
divorced and past childbearing age. I think I was held back in
my career because companies don't want the hassle of
employing women who might get pregnant.*
                          Karin, Swedish HR Director of a
                          multinational company based in Italy

We have already highlighted the worsening skills shortages across the European Union. Therefore one might reasonably expect that employers and other organizations – specifically the professional associations to which many women belong – would be at pains to ensure that women who do take career breaks return to work afterwards. But all the evidence points to the fact that few employers have in place appropriate policies and provision for career breaks, and that professional associations are failing dismally to provide support for their female members. But, more of this in a moment.

*Inflexible and outdated employment practices are still the major
career barriers, and highly qualified women put flexible family
policies at the top of their lists for choosing a new employer.*[7]

In the Women Returners to Work (WRN) sample, some 43 per cent of women did indeed move on to a new job after their career break. And the most commonly cited reason for doing so? To take advantage of more flexible or family-friendly policies. Another reason given was to find better promotion prospects (17 per cent). Only 4 per cent in fact moved jobs to take up part-time work. Among the women who were temporarily unemployed (199 out of 1276), only 7 per cent wanted to return to their previous employer. And what were the reasons for this? The barriers to career progress experienced by over 70 per cent of the women are significant indicators of the cause:

MOST SIGNIFICANT CAREER BARRIERS

Inflexible working practices	44 per cent
Lack of childcare	38 per cent
Old boys' network	30 per cent

What is more, one in five women taking a career break returns to a lower grade job, further evidence that such breaks seriously damage women's prospects through loss of seniority.

KEY RESEARCH FINDING

50 per cent of women reported that they had no contact at all with their employer during their career break.

When I returned to work after my first child I was immediately made redundant. I had made clear my intention to return on a full-time basis – I couldn't afford not to. I had organized a nursery place and got the baby on to a bottle. I couldn't claim unfair dismissal, so I had to go freelance. It worked out very well though: once word got round, I was very quickly inundated with work.

Liz, training manager

Typically women on career breaks experience a high degree of isolation – both from their employer and from their professional association. Despite employers' fears about losing out on their investment when highly trained women leave, there is little evidence that the majority make any effort to retain women going on career breaks or to facilitate their subsequent re-entry to the workplace. This results in a drop both in confidence and in skills levels, particularly for women on extended breaks (of a year or more), factors which can cause women to leave the job market all together. As a consequence, this pool of talent is not simply lost to individual employers, but also to the particular profession as a whole. Where this happens, women often change careers, choosing forms of employment where the challenges of work and home are more easily accommodated: teaching, lecturing or self-employment. Fewer than 15 per cent of organizations are affiliated to bodies dedicated to improving women's situation at work (through childcare provision and equal opportunities). And there is little evidence of employers and professional associations working together to tackle issues related to women's employment.

CASE STUDY

A solicitor from Leeds, quoted in the WRN report, stated that three of her colleagues had taken career breaks. Two were now working on supermarket checkouts, thanks to the inflexibility of the law firms for which they had previously worked. They were effectively excluded from returning to the profession for which they had trained and qualified.

QUESTIONS TO CONSIDER

■ What processes and policies does your employer have for career breaks?

■ How could you become involved to help your company develop a creative response to the support needs of women returners?

■ Could better re-entry schemes be developed to include work shadowing, work placement, buddying and mentoring?

Some examples of good practice can, however, be found. Ernst & Young, for example, has an Office for Retention in the USA, responsible for the retention, development and advancement of women professionals. Its director is Deborah Holmes, who was recently recognized as a Global Leader for Tomorrow by the World Economic Forum.

Resistance to change or lack of political will at senior level led many professional associations to be unwilling to have their lack of initiatives for women made public or potentially challenged.[8]

If employers are doing little for women returners, few of their professional associations fare much better. Policies and practices on career breaks are rare, and where they exist the information is poorly disseminated. Relatively few associations focus on women members specifically in terms of equal opportunities policies. Many fail to monitor the progress of women members at all, or even to track pay differentials. In a world where retraining and up-skilling are a critical part of self-development, many professional associations are failing to support women returners through training, careers guidance and job search. This is probably attributable to the fact that women are poorly represented on the decision-making bodies of their professional associations. Much greater diversity is needed at the top of these associations if the interests of women are to be better served.

Part of me feels that a separate network for women is self-defeating – I want women to be part of the mainstream. Fortunately, more of the younger women members are now coming onto the Committee, but problems getting babysitters preclude many women from active involvement. Even single women have difficulties – one that I know has to work until 9 or 10 pm just because she has no family ties.
　　　Julia Penny, deputy president, Thames Valley branch,
　　　　　　　　　Institute of Chartered Accountants

(The Institute of Chartered Accountants does try to involve women members with children, both at national and at branch level, for example through career planning courses and evening workshops costing as little as £30.)

ACTION POINTS

- If you don't belong to a professional association, consider joining one.
- Set your sights high and aim to change things from the inside to make the association more women-friendly.
- Lobby for better training, career guidance and job search facilities.
- Ensure there is a policy to retain women members during career breaks (reduced membership fees; keeping women on an active list).
- Help the organization to promote networking to support women with information and other back up to facilitate re-entry after a break.

■ Think about setting up a job share register and database for part-time vacancies.

Women are tied to their husband's careers

Another widely held assumption is that married women are a liability in terms of flexible deployment: they are not free to relocate or take on additional responsibilities because their husband's career comes first. Therefore, women must be less committed than men because personal issues come before work. Research has shown that, when asked, women are prepared to relocate to further their careers.[9] But because they are *assumed* to be unwilling to do so, they are sometimes passed over when opportunities arise simply because they are expected to say no.

Women want long-term careers in their organizations but suffer from lack of prospects because their roles within the culture are poorly understood:

> *Thus women, for the time being, will still be viewed as poor bets for organizational commitment and long-term employees, and will remain a minority in the higher levels of management.*[10]

In fact, in order to reconcile the demands of work with children and family, many successful women and their partners choose unconventional relationships, with the man taking a career break to assume responsibility for the family – sometimes for several years – to allow the woman's career to move forward unhampered. This is now the case for many senior women in the USA and the UK.

CASE STUDY

Leigh Woods, CEO at NTL, did not foresee, when she first married, that her career would take off as it did. She took each step as it was offered, rather than having a long-term plan to reach the top. And when, after her first two babies, she found she was earning more than her husband (even when working part time), they took the decision that he should stay at home. During this time he took a Masters degree and now that the children are more independent he may think of returning to work.

A supportive partner is the cornerstone of a successful career for many women:

I could never have achieved what I have without my husband who has massive faith in me. Also, I am blessed with massive energy levels – it helps.

Jo Hansford, hairdresser
('The best colourist on the planet' – *Vogue*)

But here too organizational cultures lag behind today's changing social norms. Many dual career couples are now deciding that the woman's career – for a period at least – should take priority. And we can expect this trend to continue and even to accelerate. The very high levels of academic achievement attained by women, allied to their higher career expectations and supported by the growing number of 'new' men (who do not want or need to be defined primarily by their jobs) is creating a new climate of opportunity. And companies must adapt to these changes: decision-makers must shift their perceptions of what women want and eliminate bias from selection processes based on outmoded preconceptions of gender roles and behaviour.

Women can't hack it at the top

KEY RESEARCH FINDING

Some of Britain's most successful women leaders in public and professional life say women still find the world of work inhospitable to them.[11]

The implication of this myth is that women are simply not tough enough to cope with life at the top of an organization – they get their chances, but leave before they achieve their full potential. Indeed, so widespread is this myth that many women stick with careers in which they are unhappy, denying their inner voice simply because they feel they have to prove to others that they can 'cut it'.

Another two years of this will be enough – I want time for my friends and family. But does that mean I'm not ambitious?

Woman entrepreneur

KEY RESEARCH FINDING

Women leave jobs mid-career more because their professional life does not match their values than for reasons of bringing up a family.[12]

Other reasons why women employees don't stay beyond a certain level of seniority are to do with:[13]

- feeling isolated and unsupported in male-dominated organizations
- wanting to stop, take stock and restart their careers, often in their own companies.

Of course, the consequence of this wastage has been to diminish the pool of talented women for the top jobs, as well as reducing the number of role models and mentors available to younger, aspiring women. What is more, as the employment market is depleted of experienced people, this adversely impacts upon creativity and innovation. And the phenomenon is well documented, particularly in the USA: women are increasingly opting out because their work compromises their values and even their sense of self to an intolerable degree.

What do I get out of my work? Well, self-fulfilment and a good lifestyle – it's good not to have money worries. I enjoy what I do, but I don't love it.

Senior woman accountant

Many of the high achieving women we interviewed were quite clear: work is interesting and fulfilling (and they were highly committed to it) but it isn't real life. And several at the top of their profession were already planning their exit route, not in order to run away from what they were currently doing, but in order to embrace something more fulfilling and meaningful. Work for many women is what you do to earn enough money to move on to higher things in terms of self-actualisation. Women are highly motivated by the ability to change things, to make a difference, to do something useful – hence the recurring theme in our research of women 'wanting to give something back'. Yet the rewards at the top of an organization have little real meaning for most women – status, hierarchical power, deference from others and some better 'toys' (though 'the money is nice'). The price of this achievement is too often remoteness from what's happening, and many women find the 'hands-off' role unsatisfying. They like to work with a team and to see tangible results from their efforts. As Elizabeth McKenna has pointed out,[14] even the very word by which we describe this life-changing process – *downshifting* – has connotations of something less valuable, when in fact what these women want to do is enlarge their lives beyond the relatively narrow confines of corporate life. And here's the rub: for men to have quality of life goals is considered laudable, for women it is apparently an admission of defeat ('She's just not up to the job').

I won't be in the profession for more than another 10 years.
There are all sorts of other things to apply my skills to. I want
to find something I can do to put something back.

Senior woman lawyer

ACTION POINTS

▪ Avoid isolation by joining a women's network – either specific to your profession or drawn from a wider group of women in your area.

▪ Plan some long-term goals for your career and prepare for the day when your needs may diverge from what employment in a company can offer.

▪ Ensure that, through your personal development programme, you acquire the skills and experience that will ultimately enable you to move into an entrepreneurial or creative role if that is what you aspire to.

Women are not ambitious

Definitions of success are different for men and women. The
informally accepted definition of success in an organization
tends more closely to match the one held by men. This often
results in women being perceived as less ambitious.[15]

Subsumed within the myth that women cannot cope in senior positions is the idea that women lack ambition. It is this assumption, according to the Industrial Society, that lies behind pay inequality and the failure of companies to develop and promote women employees:

KEY RESEARCH FINDING

Although women say they work because they are ambitious, men think women work because they want independence and to escape the home. Consequently men assume women are not interested in promotion.[16]

This is, of course, compounded by the fact that, as we shall see in Chapter Five, male employees make active representation to their bosses for promotion, pay rises and involvement in interesting work that looks good on the CV. Many women, by contrast, are less direct and expect to be rewarded simply for working hard and doing a good job. We demonstrate in Chapter Six how ineffective these tactics are compared to those used by male employees to develop their careers.

Research from the Centre for Developing Women Leaders[17] has shown that many men in fact *define* career success in terms of position and pay, and while these criteria are relevant to women, they are not central to their view of success. Achievement, recognition and influence are more important to women: job content comes before job grade. But it is the male definition that is informally accepted in organizations, and because women fail to comply with it they are seen as unambitious.

And if women are not ambitious, where is the need to train or promote them – particularly as they are likely to leave (or worse still, stay and cause all sorts of problems) when they have children? These attitudes are deeply entrenched in many organizations, including the recruitment function where prejudice is rife:

> *There is huge discrimination at the point of recruitment where male managers have a preconceived idea of the perfect candidate which will often be a male stereotype.*
>
> Paul Burns, Industrial Society[18]

Even in job roles where the objective criteria indicate the need for skills widely acknowledged to be more closely aligned to a 'feminine' style of management, men are routinely appointed ahead of equally well-qualified women. For example, fewer than 15 per cent of international managers working for UK companies are women, and yet the inventory of skills required for the job includes the following: interested in people, consensual, participative, facilitator, team builder, culturally sensitive, collaborative, communicator, and so on. Research found that informal selection systems – those that allowed personal preference to prevail over objective criteria – were the predominant selection methods for international posts.[19] These were therefore heavily gender biased because, almost invariably, men were making the selection decisions.

While gurus may think that a paradigm shift of feminisation in management is crucial ... in Britain managers continue to confirm traditional practices and reinforce male behavioural responses ... women's preference for relational processes and organizational development is rarely valued or formally acknowledged within recruitment, appraisal and performance measurement.

Su Maddock[20]

So when we unpick what is really holding women back we find that it is not their lack of ambition, but an unholy alliance of discriminatory recruitment and selection processes, and the fact that both success and commitment in organizations are defined according to male paradigms.

ACTION POINTS

■ Through your networks and professional organizations help to lobby for reform in recruitment and selection procedures by raising awareness of the gender bias that frequently occurs.

■ Find out what your company's HR department is doing to help eradicate discrimination.

Women lack the harder skills

KEY RESEARCH FINDING

Women executives score higher than their male counterparts on a wide variety of measures – from producing high-quality work to goal setting and mentoring.[21]

Until recently it seemed firmly established that women managers scored high on the people dimensions of leadership (concern for and understanding of others), and poorly on the task-oriented issues (drive, decision making, competitiveness, risk taking).

Competing in a man's world is what I want to do. I'm very much in touch with my male side. I'm really competitive, and I find confrontation stimulating. But I keep those qualities in check. I use my feminine traits – empathy, collaboration.
                   Nina DiSesa, creative director, McCann Erikson[22]

Much has been written about women as 'transformational' leaders: those who enable their subordinates to develop their skills and then empower them to act. Typically, transformational leaders:

- Encourage participation
- Share power and information
- Build others' self-worth
- Enthuse and energize others about work.

When this was also linked to findings that women saw organizations differently, not as hierarchies, but as networks to facilitate the free flow of information, it seemed that the 'feminization' of managerial style must become the model for future managers. Indeed, most of the behaviours that are instinctive to many women managers are critical for the success of businesses now and in the future. These include the ability to create environments where intuition is prized, where uncertainty is managed, where new opportunities can quickly be seized and where the focus is long term.

Women get high ratings in exactly those skills needed to succeed in the global Information Age, where teamwork and partnering are so important.
                        Professor Rosabeth Moss Kanter[23]

Now, though, the softer skills will take on new importance as this century unfolds, the harder (traditionally masculine) skills will still have a significant role to play. This creates a dilemma for women, since they have often been assumed to possess the softer skills *to the exclusion of* the harder. An either/or gender stereotyping has taken hold: women are nurturers and carers and therefore they cannot concurrently be decision-makers and risk-takers. The two sets of skills have been assumed to be mutually exclusive. In fact, the more she exhibits her nurturing side, the less competent a woman is often assumed to be in terms of transactional skills.

From experience we know this to be nonsense, and to reconcile the two aspects of leadership – both of which are indispensable (different but equal) – the concept of androgyny was developed. This was based on the assumption that effective managers combine both male and female characteristics in their behaviour. Increasingly it has become accepted that a style drawn from the 'best of both worlds' is more effective than a style polarized either to the masculine or to the feminine.

Being a woman in this job is important. I'm dealing with big egos, big personalities. Fragile, high-maintenance people. If I didn't have a strong nurturing component I couldn't do it.

Nina DiSesa[24]

More recent research by Vinnicombe and Cames[25] has examined the attitudes of male and female managers of different nationalities in relation to a set of 24 attributes. These included both 'instrumental' (task-oriented) and 'expressive' (people-oriented) characteristics. Respondents were required to rate themselves, their superior and a successful manager. The results showed that more women saw themselves and their superiors as androgynous (65 per cent of managers rated as androgynous were female), while the males were more sex typed (57 per cent). Women showed higher levels of task orientation than in any previous study and saw themselves as less expressive, completely over-turning existing gender assumptions. Both the men and the women emphasized the need to combine task and people issues in their leadership approach, but the women ranked themselves higher on both dimensions than the men.

KEY RESEARCH FINDING
Women score higher on 'hard', task-related issues than on 'soft' skills, but feel they need to adopt even more 'masculine' characteristics to succeed.

Both saw the gap between themselves and a successful manager as the need for greater task orientation. However, while men saw successful managers as androgynous, women saw them as male. This indicates that middle management thinking about what defines managers is in transition. But while men seem to be accepting the need for greater people orientation to balance their task focus, women seem to be rejecting their expressive side. Though they meet the criteria for combining the best of both worlds in a gender-neutral managerial style, they appear to think they must become more masculinized in order to succeed.

Perhaps the explanation for this lies in the ambiguity of most organizational cultures and in the informal networking and promotion systems that perpetuate the *status quo*.[26] Male attitudes may have shifted from 'Think manager, think male',[27] but the reality for most women – reinforced by the informal culture – is that (male) senior managers recruit in their own image. Traditional notions of male and female roles support this view and ignore women's abilities, despite women scoring higher in competence tests. Even though senior managers say that women should be promoted (espousing the need for change and the importance of greater diversity), most organizations continue to exclude women from the higher levels of decision making, perpetuating the concept: 'Think *successful* manager, think male.'

Comprehensive studies carried out by consultants across the USA (where the evolution of the woman manager is rather more advanced than in Europe) provide compelling evidence that women managers are more than equal to their male counterparts across the spectrum of management skills. These included strategic planning and analysis. (Men occasionally scored higher on strategic ability and technical analysis, but these differences were not statistically significant.)

KEY RESEARCH FINDINGS

Women managers' strengths are greater than men's and their weaknesses are less pronounced.[28]

The research,[29] derived from complex performance appraisal techniques, shows that women managers are overall more effective than males. Again, this completely overturns the conventional wisdom, myths and stereotypes that have so long held back women's careers. Women have been shown to out-perform men in many intellectual areas including producing high-quality work, recognizing trends, generating new ideas and acting on them. All the data, of course, beg the question: if women perform so well, why are more of them not at the top? And even in the USA – where 45 per cent of all managerial posts are held by women – only six of the US top 1000 companies are run by women.

First, there is the pipeline issue: insufficient women are emerging from the ranks of middle management. In the USA, as here, this is due in part to the fact that women (as Professor Susan Greenfield highlighted) seek careers where they can 'work with people'. Thus they find themselves in specialist, female-dominated posts like HR and PR – jobs that rarely lead to the top. We talk in the next section about 'women's work', and there is no doubt that women's management strengths have long been undervalued because what they do is often invisible – it is vital but often goes unnoticed. Women are seen as workhorses: fit for the demands of tough middle management, but not for the plum jobs at the top. Confronted with this reality women, as we have seen, often leave the workplace to do their own thing – to the extent in the USA that over 9 million women now run their own business, double the number 12 years ago.

But, interestingly, the increasing recognition of women's management skills is prompting a new hiring bias in the USA: women are being picked in preference to men because it is believed they will do a better job. The head of global services at IBM was reported in *Business Week* to have said he chooses women because they think through decisions better, are more collaborative and are motivated by what they can do for the company, rather than by self-interest. By contrast, however, it is many women's experience that their skills and approach to management often baffle their bosses. By practising delegation and empowering their teams through coaching and facilitation they are seen to be looking after their people rather than looking out for themselves. This is counter-cultural in many organizations. It still remains for many companies to recognize that people skills are also business skills, since it is well established that people who are inspired and feel cared for by their bosses also perform better. Yet when women manage in this way their intentions are often misunderstood – what they do has the hallmarks of a kind gesture, of being 'nice'. The business value is often overlooked.

KEY RESEARCH FINDING

Corporate selection committees are still heavily biased towards recruiting leaders they see as 'heroes' (tough minded risk-takers), despite recognizing the need for leaders to show collaborative skills.

We refer in Chapter Five to the importance of impression management (the need to consciously influence others' perceptions of us at work), and here, as elsewhere, women's strengths can also prove their downfall. For while women are adept at getting buy-in to an idea by persuading others they thought of it, this means women often miss out on taking the credit. Getting their ideas accepted and acted on is more important. Meanwhile their male colleagues are often basking, not only in their own glory, but also in whatever is reflected off the work of others when they can.

We have established how the concept of leadership is changing, but the importance of interpersonal skills is still not fully recognized in practice. This is demonstrated in the double standards for selecting top managers. Males score highest when they are forceful and assertive and worse when they are cooperative and empathetic. The reverse is true for women: they are downgraded for assertiveness and score higher if cooperative. Yet, as we have established, the capacity for collaboration is not seen as the stuff of which top managers are made.

There can be no doubt that women have the talent to be effective and even outstanding leaders and managers, better than men if the researchers, academics and futurologists are to be believed. But while the 'comfort fit' of an individual (based on subjective judgement) continues to carry greater weight in recruitment and promotion decisions than the objective assessment criteria in formal evaluation systems, women will be held back.

Women's work

Sharing experience with other women has confirmed for me the notion that women's careers often stall because they are too useful in the administrative jobs they perform at the lower levels of management. And, vital though this work may be to the smooth running of many companies, it is largely invisible. Like housework, people want it done, but they don't want to know how, and the need for it is only recognized when it is neglected and everything falls apart. Lack of visibility for their contribution is often compounded for women by self-deprecation ('I was lucky') when they succeed, failure to claim recognition ('It was a team effort') and having little or no decision-making authority.

We create our own problems by saying 'I can't not do it'. Also as women we pick up a lot of jobs by default – no one else wants to do them.

Julia Penny

Also, the downside of being a 'transformational' leader is that motivating and supporting people is time consuming. We have only to compare ourselves with our male colleagues who use a more directive style – they are usually the ones on the golf course with the clients on Friday afternoon, while we are back at the office clearing the decks after another hectic week's activity. What is more, the nurturing style can, if we are not careful, create relationships of dependence, whereby our subordinates work less autonomously. And this, in turn, takes up our time in unnecessary supervision.

Women behaving in this manner have been described as 'wives of the organization':[30] they think about others, organize details, are deferential, negotiate, make peace between combatants, use persuasion and positive reinforcement to get things done – and their work goes largely unnoticed. The time required for all this activity also displaces opportunities for learning and promotion, and it reinforces gender stereotyping by feeding expectations that a woman's role should be to support other leaders rather than to be a leader herself.

'There's a sort of unconditional love that develops when you're a mother. You believe in people, and you accept their

*weaknesses, their frailties, their moments of irrationality. That's
what helps build very strong teams.'*

Shelly Lazarus,
CEO Ogilvy & Mather[31]

What makes us take on this role of organizational wife? Professor
Anne S. Huff[32] points to several factors including our sensitivity
to the feelings of others and the way we take responsibility for
things left undone. By contrast, most male managers (at work as
in their domestic situation) have the ability to switch off and
withhold involvement. This reinforces their status, ultimately
contributing to their success:

■ They detach themselves from 'trivia' (they are too important
  for such distractions).
■ They focus on the high-profile aspects of the work (it gets
  them greater visibility).
■ They haven't time for the mundane because their work is
  more important (they 'take a strategic view').

When women take care of the 'maintenance' work it also
reinforces the male patriarchal relationship with which many
men are comfortable: it allows them to see women primarily as
carers and does not require them to treat women at work as
equals.

Lack of alternative role models has also conspired to entrap
women into the 'wife' role at work. According to Professor Huff,
because we are unable to define ourselves in terms of ambition,
power seeking and ability (both because of our socialization and
because of prevailing gender stereotypes), some of us default to
what we know and to what is culturally acceptable in many male-
dominated organizations:

*In short, professional women in organizations often make
themselves and others more comfortable by filling the
social roles our culture has established – mother, sister,
wife, lover – and the most attractive of this set, especially
for the professional woman, appears to be the role of
wife.*

Professor Anne S. Huff[33]

How can women resist both the internal and the external pressures to take on this role? Huff identifies seven behavioural changes on which we should focus.

ACTION POINTS

- **Learn to say no** Resist invitations to take responsibility for secondary (low status) activities. Focus on work where your efforts make a difference – and get you noticed.
- **Let go of trivia** Channel your perfectionist tendencies and manage your time in the direction of key tasks that *must* be done right and away from things it might be *nice* to do.
- **Let others take their share** Men particularly need to learn to take on relational tasks as part of their remit – attention to detail and concern for others must be everyone's job.
- **Take the pressure off other women** If you want a job doing well do you rely too heavily on women colleagues? Involve males more and let them learn about the small stuff.
- **Learn to focus** The downside of the ability to multitask is that it distracts us from the main goal. Learning to be more single-minded is central to emancipating ourselves. We must stop feeling guilty when we say no. We must let go the unnecessary detail. We must practise being more like our male colleagues.
- **Forget misplaced loyalty** We must remember that if we are dissatisfied at work we have the option to voice our objections or to leave. Our sense of obligation often prevents us from exercising either option. If your talents are not appreciated, take them elsewhere. Do not live in hope that things will get better – you must act to make it happen.
- **Become more self-aware** Our preoccupation with the needs of others often distracts us from what we ourselves feel and need. This is important in developing our careers: we must decide where we are going and concentrate on those things that will achieve our goal. Serving others selflessly may make us feel good as women, but our time and energy would often be better directed into developing and deploying our professional skills and in making a visible and valued contribution to the organization.

*The increase in the numbers of women at work has also
changed the atmosphere of the workplace and helped to create a
more natural and sociable environment than the testosterone-
filled offices and factories of the past.*

Richard Reeves[34]

It is up to us to resist the lure of becoming wives of the organization. Otherwise we risk perpetuating the gender myth that
relational tasks and 'housekeeping' detail are primarily the
responsibility of women at work. It is tempting in predominantly
male organizations to want to 'humanize' or indeed 'feminize' the
workplace. But if we take on this issue it is a short step for
people to assume it is exclusively our responsibility. Organizational change on this scale must be led from the top: we can be
part of the process, but we cannot *as individuals* initiate it. (That
is not to say that *collectively* we cannot press for change.) We
need to save our pioneering spirit, our time and our energies for
climbing the organizational hierarchy.

Women are not creative or innovative

*Women may be visible in management and in senior positions,
but their creative energy is too often lost within the stresses and
strains of working and living within still dominant male cultures.*

Su Maddock[35]

The issue of creativity is problematic because it involves perception and judgement – it cannot be measured objectively and, like
beauty, it is in the eye of the beholder. I cannot say I *am* creative.
I must wait to be perceived or judged as creative by others. The
following framework[36] describes the three necessary conditions
for creativity. There must be:

1 A field of endeavour (music, science, business) which has a
  set of rules or norms.
2 Work (book, product, theory) that goes beyond the rules or
  norms of the field.
3 Judges who know the rules and norms of the field, see the
  work created and judge it innovative and valuable.

From this we can see that failing the criteria for creativity may be only tenuously related to ourselves or our work. In male-dominated organizations the rules and norms are highly inflexible (and known as 'the way we do things round here'). Women's creativity often operates outside that range, and as a consequence is often dismissed. For example, intuition is hugely important in the creative process and can be defined as our ability to know something without reference to analytical thinking. Organizational cultures are deeply entrenched in what can be measured and verified: the analytical method is the norm. By contrast women often intuitively 'know' things, but hold back from voicing their thoughts because they feel they have insufficient data to back them up. Alternatively, they propose their ideas with poor conviction and expose themselves to being ridiculed or ignored. (They often weaken their case with tag statements like: 'This may sound stupid, but . . .' or 'I'm probably completely wrong about this, but . . .').

And in many cases the ideas we are trying to articulate are difficult to describe in terms our male colleagues can understand and accept because they are often about new ways of working. So while we try to nail the proverbial jellyfish to the wall, our male colleagues switch off or look bemused. In this way our brand of creativity often runs counter to organizational norms and we may lack the confidence as well as the vocabulary to propose our ideas boldly. As a result, others respond negatively and our ideas carry little weight. It is the difficulty of trying to get our male colleagues to learn our language and enter a new kind of dialogue.

Intuition functions with little or no information and is especially adept at sensing future trends, assessing multiple factors, embracing positive changes and seeing the big picture . . . Since intuition can be trained and developed, it is high time that it receive serious attention and be incorporated into the decision-making and innovation process.

Nancy Rosanoff[37]

ACTION POINTS

■ Visibility of our creativity is crucial, particularly to the senior movers and shakes within the organization. As we will show in Chapter Five, women do not routinely manage the impressions they make, nor do they bring their achievements to the attention of their superiors. Other people sometimes claim credit for their ideas and output, and women (who dislike confrontation) sometimes stand quietly by while this happens.

- Getting your work accepted as innovative and valuable is also tricky. Again, it involves overcoming many of the gender stereotypes that pervade organizations. Men may be uncomfortable listening to a woman's ideas – too often we want to press for change and some men will prefer the *status quo*. Women's solutions often require the dismantling of hierarchies and abandoning the tried and tested ways of doing things to find a way through – and men resist this (the old ways may be bureaucratic but they're what we know). The 'not invented here' syndrome sometimes occurs, whereby men close ranks against a woman, blocking her proposals.

- Find a champion to support your ideas. Whether we win recognition for our creativity is dependent on who is judging our work and the context in which they are assessing it. In order to overcome resistance, one option is to enlist the help of those with influence. (This is why mentoring and networking are so important.) And since timing is so critical, we must be sure to prepare the ground before sowing our ideas (again by networking, using people we trust as a sounding board and taking informal feedback).

- Finally, persistence pays dividends. Successful people never give up on something they believe in and persevere through setbacks. Go create.

Women are bitches to work for

This is held to be especially true in their relationships with other women.

KEY RESEARCH FINDINGS[38]

- Women managers were judged more effective and satisfying to work for, and more likely to generate extra effort from their teams.

■ Women were more charismatic, inspirational and considerate than males.

Research in Canada was carried out by Professor Karen Korabik[39] to discover how women at work help and support each other. The findings showed strong solidarity in the women's behaviour, expressed through the formation of coalitions and alliances. This usually occurs in organizations when under-represented groups reach 30 to 35 per cent of the population and newcomers group together to change the organizational norms to make them more acceptable. The women surveyed were active in a range of initiatives to help other women including mentoring, working to modify organizational politics and supporting the rights of female employees. The survey overturns existing ideas about the Queen Bee syndrome, where all women who achieve power are assumed to ignore or even to subvert the careers of the women coming up behind them.

CASE STUDY

'I was recently transferred to a city branch of a large accounting firm. When I arrived I hoped the senior female manager would be supportive. But she wasn't. It's as if she has come up the hard way and is still struggling to be better than the men. The way she dresses is very plain Jane, no nonsense (black or navy and white). She's very bright but seems to find it hard to relate to others (bit of a schoolmarm). We organize activities for the women staff, but she never joins in. She doesn't cope well under pressure and can be very brusque. She always thinks she's right and when she's not it takes her a long time to admit it. It's never the right time to ask her for help. Though she has had feedback about her behaviour she seems unable to change.'

Viv, senior chartered accountant

The Queen Bee syndrome is most evident in firms where token women face pressure to assimilate to male behaviour. This entails either denying your femininity and becoming one of the boys, or accepting the humiliation of reduced status as a woman. This state of affairs creates taboos against women helping each other, for not only is this seen to betray the entrenched male values, it also exposes senior women to accusations of discrimination when they initiate women-friendly policies. Old boys networks go largely unchallenged (because they are established and inconspicuous), but old girls networks (because they are new and visible) are labelled 'favouritism'.

Women are tearing down barriers in organizational settings but they need to be encouraged to do it more openly.

Karen Korabik[40]

Women in the minority in organizations are routinely marginalized and excluded from informal groups where vital pieces of information are exchanged. Being 'in the know' is a critical aspect of organizational politics – and as outsiders women find it difficult to flourish. So the temptation to become one of the boys is almost irresistible – if you don't drink with them out of hours, sharing their jokes and chit chat, you won't be party to the inside track. Acceptance into the group means conforming to its norms and values, and those don't include helping other women. Those values do, however, often promote men's superiority and perpetuate female gender stereotypes. So women's acceptance into these male groups is at best tenuous, and any challenge to the prevailing attitudes (by refusing to participate in sexist banter for example) is met with accusations of incompetence and marginalization. Isolation is very difficult for most women to cope with, and it is fair to say that some token women in the past (they know who they are) have been less than sisterly to women co-workers and subordinates. But as more women are integrated into the workplace the Queen Bee syndrome is disappearing and women are learning to operate collectively to improve their working lives.

Women and leadership

A different approach

We have seen that women managers sometimes mimic male behaviour, specifically when their numbers are limited (tokenism), but that more usually they are a force for change, being motivated primarily by the desire to 'make things better' and the lure of challenging work. This focus on improving oneself and one's organization gives rise to a different approach to leadership:

KEY RESEARCH FINDINGS

Male managers are predominantly traditionalists, while women are more visionary and catalysts for change. Visionaries are natural strategists.

Professor Susan Vinnicombe[41]

We describe in Chapter Ten how the role of managers is changing and how British managers are largely failing to meet the challenges of the New Economy (3i research). Flexibility, responsiveness and the ability to harness the creativity of others are the characteristics of visionary leaders. They work to transform their organizations, enabling them to exploit new opportunities. Traditionalists, by contrast, default to conventional ways of managing by focusing on processes and systems. They fail to embrace change and are easily deterred by difficulties. And while the traditional command and control managerial style was effective in a steady state economy, today's business leaders must move beyond the hierarchical power base to establish new kinds of relationships, not only within their own teams and across their organizations, but through partnerships outside their companies. The key skills of the future are the ability to inspire, to stimulate ideas, to listen and to empower people. This is the toolkit of the 'transformational' manager.

CASE STUDY

Colette Graham of Centrica says that when it comes to getting things done, she doesn't like hierarchies and manages her team in a consultative way – everyone has a role in working together. Having become a senior manager at a relatively young age she finds it more disarming to others simply to be herself. She prefers to persuade rather than to resort to table thumping and has made a point of recruiting people who do not expect to be directed. She describes her management style as 'muck in' and sees herself as responsible for ensuring the highest quality output that the team can manage. Colette believes this is all common sense – being a leader you ultimately carry the can for what goes wrong. So make sure you manage things in such a way that nothing is likely to go wrong.

Transformational leadership

Over a decade ago it was established that women were more likely to adopt a transforming style than their male counterparts, because women want primarily to motivate others and to achieve shared objectives.

As a minister I am in a powerful position to achieve good. Women get their satisfaction from completing a task. The least rewarding aspect of public life is just being there and turning up.
Tessa Jowell, Minister for Employment

Women have long understood that people skills are important, not only as an adjunct to their formal status, but also because people perform better when their contribution is valued and when they feel good about themselves. As well as being able to inspire their teams to rise to challenges, women managers are skilled in being able to identify potential roadblocks to change, and in using their skills to persuade people so as to overcome resistance. They are also willing to listen and negotiate when managing change: being collaborative rather than competitive with colleagues, they are more concerned to achieve a workable outcome than to assert they know best and push their agendas through.

There is a new way of working that women are not frightened of. Women hear what is going on and really listen. Behaviours or issues that block change are often unspoken, but women can often understand what these might be. They are sensitive to personal agendas.
Sue Slipman, Director, Camelot

Personal empowerment

Our research among successful women confirmed previous findings about personal empowerment. Their ability as leaders springs principally from a high level of self-esteem – they themselves feel empowered and in control, and they are therefore able to empower others. This, allied to their passionate belief in their vision for change, makes them inspirational leaders.

Within this reside two key principles of leadership that women managers must adopt:

1 Feeling in control (internal locus of control)
2 Focusing one's efforts.

Locus of control

This concept holds that some individuals believe they are the passive objects or victims of external circumstances (external locus of control) and are therefore unable to influence what happens to them. Others see themselves as masters of their own destiny (internal locus of control), able to manage life's events to their own advantage. We could argue whether this feeling is innate or acquired, but the key issue is to try to take control and to engender positive feelings of self-esteem. (We describe in Chapter Five some methods for doing this.)

> *Women take on responsibility for things that are not always their fault. Losing a client has wide-ranging implications for a woman. Guilt is a female thing. Men would say 'Well, I didn't like that client anyway. He was a pain in the rear.'*
> Senior woman lawyer

We saw at the beginning of this chapter that there are several female stereotypes that trade on women's socialization into deference and humility. From this spring some stereotypical female behaviours, including helplessness. Not being in control and appearing helpless are, as we saw, ways of avoiding both responsibility and confrontation. Within paternalistic organizations this behaviour may be the norm for women (most of whom will be subordinate to men), and it is difficult for women managers to counter established patterns and expectations. While many women have successfully transcended these difficulties by using their charm and charisma to get what they want, others have, admittedly, resorted to bullying or nagging.

Some of the most successful women, however, are those who have had the courage to defy the rules and norms of behaviour – not necessarily by challenging them openly, but by charting their own course and doing things in their own way, often in the face of criticism and hostility.

I have never allowed myself to be a victim – it's a mentality that women are easily drawn into. There's nothing that you can't achieve – you just have to dare to dream it. The legal profession is slow to change and I didn't want my daughter to encounter the same problems, so I started a campaign to change things. Now I speak at conferences all over the world.

Margaret McCabe, barrister and founder
of the Woman Lawyer Conference

KEY RESEARCH FINDING
Getting results is one of the skills at which women score highest.[42]

Focus

The second issue, that of focus, is referred to later in Chapters Six and Seven. But it is worth making the point here that we must not allow our ability in multitasking to diffuse our efforts and distract us from our primary goals. Organizations require us to focus on fairly narrow targets: spreading our energies across too many projects makes us look ineffective. Taking on too much also leaves little time for networking and building alliances – activities vital to our career progress. Perfectionism and concentrating always on delivering results can also leave us without the time and energy to think about strategy and vision, and these are key qualities for managers at the top.

The most important thing is focus and being rooted and in touch. Otherwise you risk dissipating your energies across too many fronts. You have to be ruthless and remember that whatever you choose to do excludes the possibility of doing two or three other things that also require your time. Prioritize. Be clear. Judge where you are needed most.

Tessa Jowell

Don't be typecast

Two of the most insidious aspects of female behaviour are self-deprecation (playing down our achievements) and deference (allowing the opinions of others to override our own). Attributing our successes to luck rather than good management and undervaluing our own contributions (because they are non-conformist), makes us look (and feel) as though we are not in control. Because it is defined by male values, leadership in organizations is all about appearing in control and being goal oriented. Established gender stereotypes make it difficult for some of us to break out of old behaviour patterns – not only others, but we ourselves often expect women to be modest and deferential to authority. So women are caught between a rock and a hard place – damned for conforming to stereotype and damned if they don't – because they are assessed and judged in ways that are not objective.

A strategy suggested by one of the women in our study for overcoming the disadvantages of being a (relatively young) woman interacting with male authority figures is not always to acknowledge that others are more senior and experienced, and to express your views regardless. Admittedly this takes courage and a few successes under your belt to build your credibility. But if we are ever to change the *status quo* we must take some risks. We know that our transforming style works – every management guru in town says so. Perhaps then we need to learn to talk with more confidence about alternative ways of working. And though the gurus refer to the 'feminization of management' we don't need to use the same vocabulary. The business case for adopting a more people-focused approach, of empowering teams and encouraging their creativity is already well established and the process should therefore be seen as gender neutral rather than quintessentially 'feminine' (and by extrapolation, different from and inferior to a 'masculine' style). We need to get away from thinking about management and leadership in terms of ideologies – masculine versus feminine – and focus much more on demonstrating what *works* in practice.

It's still a challenge to find an effective style of leadership. Initially I was in really deep water, but I eventually found a balance between an authoritarian and a 'loose' management style. I try to be approachable and to let people get on with things, but within clearly stated goals and parameters. The key to leadership is to understand that within a diverse team people will have very different motivations, and so need to be managed differently.
Carol Hambly, Financial Controller, Camelot

Increasingly, younger successful women see their skills as gender neutral. Though they recognize that their inclusive and nurturing style can be seen as 'feminine', taking the right approach to getting things done has nothing to do with gender.

I'm driven and a perfectionist. I make things happen which usually gets me what I want. Many of my qualities are gender neutral and I like to think I take the best approach.
Jeanette Hughes, Group Chief Auditor,
Royal & SunAlliance

I have never been conscious either of advantages or disadvantages in being a woman. My strength is persuading skills and these are gender neutral. Women do find it harder to be dictatorial, but thankfully that sort of style is less and less effective.
Colette Graham, Head of Internal
Communications, Centrica plc

Winds of change

A recurring problem holding women back has been the assimilation of younger, more egalitarian males into the paternalistic values and behaviour of more senior managers as they move up the organizational hierarchy. But, as we saw in earlier chapters, men, too, are changing. They want greater balance in their lives;

they have wives with careers and daughters with aspirations. The changing social context of their lives must ultimately spill over into their work, modifying their attitudes and behaviour towards women colleagues.

Meanwhile, though there are strong forces perpetuating male-defined work paradigms, there are equally strong countervailing pressures accelerating change. Skills shortages, the compelling business case for new ways of working, the restructuring of gender roles in society and women's growing confidence in their leadership qualities are conspiring to erode traditional business cultures. Gender roles and stereotypes are not permanent constructs, and while it has been difficult for women to fight them individually and in isolation, a new era is dawning. The sheer numbers of women in the workplace – both now and in the future – allied to the unstoppable pace of economic, techno-logical and social change, *demand* a new response from businesses. Those that fail to meet the challenge and accept that their companies need to reflect the diversity of their marketplace by employing more women in senior roles will simply not survive.

Summary

Many myths and gender stereotypes are holding women back, but the research evidence is compelling: women have precisely the skills needed by business in the twenty-first century and they make excellent managers. To deal with gender bias:

■ Stay true to yourself and be courageous in confronting the issues.
■ Avoid isolation by joining professional women's groups and sharing experience.
■ At work, signal your career aspirations clearly and demonstrate that you are ready for promotion.
■ Don't get stuck with all the routine work – delegate.
■ Understand the informal culture in your company.
■ Find a mentor and get into the key networks.
■ Extend your managerial skills through training and development.

■ Develop your own approach and show how it benefits the business.

■ Be confident, take calculated risks and be proud of your achievements.

■ Choose women-friendly companies where your talents are recognized and rewarded.

■ Monitor your job satisfaction regularly: if dissatisfied, move on.

In the next chapter we look at some of the issues discussed here in relation to the research we undertook with successful women in business and public life. What challenges did they encounter and what can we learn from their coping strategies?

Notes

1 Jimmy Young programme.
2 V. E. Schein: 'The relationship between sex role stereotypes and requisite management characteristics', *Journal of Applied Psychology*, vol. 57, 1973.
3 Beverly Stone, *Confronting Company Politics*, Macmillan Business, 1997, ISBN 0 333 68154 1.
4 Quoted in *Telegraph*, 4 October 1999.
5 'The role of professional associations in facilitating the re-entry of highly qualified women into employment', Women Returners Network, March 2000. EU Project 0084.
6 Saxton Bampfylde Hever, October 1999.
7 Quoted in *Telegraph*, 4 October 1999.
8 Ibid.
9 G. Coates, 'Integration or separation: women and the appliance of organisational culture', *Women in Management Review*, vol. 13, no. 3, 1998, MCB University Press.
10 Ibid.
11 G. Coates, op. cit.
12 Research by The Change Partnership and The Tavistock Consultancy Service cited on BBC News online Friday, 3 December 1999.
13 J. Marshall, *Women Managers Moving On: Exploring Career and Life Choices*, International Thompson, 1995.
14 Elizabeth Perle McKenna, *When Work Doesn't Work Anymore*, Simon & Schuster, 1997.
15 Susan Vinnicombe and Hilary Harris cited in *People Management* feature on Women and Leadership: 'A gender hidden', 6 January 2000.
16 Industrial Society research into equal pay, cited in Crème, *The Times*, 25 October, 2000.
17 Vinnicombe and Harris, op. cit.
18 Ibid.

19 Savita Kumra and Hilary Harris of Cranfield School of Management, 'Sex role stereotypes in management: of square pegs and round holes'; presented at EGOS Colloquium, July 2000.

20 Su Maddock, *Challenging Women – Gender, Culture and Organisation*, Sage Publications, 1999.

21 Haberg Consulting Group, USA, quoted in *Business Week*, 20 November 2000.

22 'Powerful women: these women rule', *Fortune*, vol.140, no. 8, 25 October 1999.

23 Quoted in *Business Week*, 20 November 2000.

24 Ibid.

25 Susan Vinnicombe and Isabelle Cames, 'A study of the leadership styles of female and male managers in ten different banks, using the Personal Attributes Questionnaire', *International Review of Women in Leadership*, vol. 4, no. 2, 1998.

26 Susan Vinnicombe and Hilary Harris, op. cit.

27 V. E. Schein, 'Managerial sex typing: a persistent and pervasive barrier to women's opportunities', *Women in Management: Current Issues*, Davidson and Burke (eds.), Paul Chapman, 1994.

28 Reported in *Business Week*, 20 November 2000.

29 Ibid.

30 Professor Anne S. Huff, *Management Focus*, Cranfield School of Management, Autumn 1996.

31 G. Coates, op. cit.

32 Anne Huff, ibid.

33 Ibid.

34 The *Observer*, 23 July 2000.

35 Su Maddock, *Challenging Women – Gender, Culture and Organisation*, Sage Publications, 1999.

36 'Creativity' by Mihaly Csikszentmihalyi, cited by Joyce Wycoff of thinksmart.com.

37 'Can intuition be an active part of the innovation process? You bet!', Innovation Network: thinksmart.com.

38 Bass and Avolio (1993) cited by Su Maddock, op. cit.

39 Professor Karen Korabik, University of Guelph, March 1999.

40 Ibid.

41 Professor Susan Vinnicombe (1987) cited by Su Maddock, op. cit.

42 Schein, op. cit.

4

The secrets of our success: women at the top share their experience

Introduction

What is wrong today in the business world is that success is defined one-dimensionally. This notion that success is only measured by how much money you have made and how powerful you have become isn't, and shouldn't be, acceptable.

Avivah Wittenberg-Cox[1]

Success in business and public life is usually defined according to established male paradigms: having a position of power, managing extensive resources and receiving a high level of remuneration. While the women we interviewed fitted these traditional criteria, both they and the authors would add a codicil: women define success in much wider terms. It is also about personal fulfilment and a sense of doing something truly worth while, allied to a happy personal life and deep friendships. Our work and our personal lives must be in reasonable balance, for when they are not we feel we are underachieving in some important area and strive for redress. In Chapter One we looked at the early influences, character traits, attitudes and behaviour of high-flying women in order to find some common patterns and experiences. Now we probe more deeply to ask how they produced their often remarkable achievements; what challenges they experienced; how each developed her particular style of leadership; whether there are downsides to life at the top; and what advice they would hand on to those who aspire to follow them up the career ladder.

This advice ranged comprehensively over all aspects of building your career, so that in this chapter we are able to pass on their recommendations for 'How to': get yourself hired; set goals and milestones; get help through networking and mentoring; be an effective leader; meet career challenges and cope with the downsides. Our group of successful women also tell you how they see the world of work panning out for women in the future, across the various professions and in corporate life. Finally, from the outstanding women entrepreneurs we spoke to we pass on some vital tips for setting up and running your own business.

Getting started . . . getting on

Know yourself

At as early a stage as possible in your career it is crucially important to understand who you are, what your values are and in what type of work environment you are most likely to flourish. Nikki Beckett, for example, had first intended to become a barrister but soon realized that her 'noisy, outgoing personality' (she was always being told off for this in her teens) would be ill-suited to the conservative, understated world of the law. But in the dynamic and vibrant environment at IBM in the 1980s she fitted right in.

Another helpful piece of advice to those starting out on their management careers was to give yourself a chance to know yourself by not making major choices too soon. Women have traditionally allowed others to close doors of opportunity for them, but to succeed in a man's world you need determination. An important point was the need for women to draw their motivation from within themselves and to understand that if we look for it from outside we will often find negativity and patronizing attitudes towards us.

I really want women to have more confidence to grasp opportunities. One of our women employees worked her way up from secretary to lawyer, gaining distinctions along the way. You must believe you can do it.

Julie Bradley

Seeking self-knowledge by taking on challenges and testing yourself was an important theme. Not only does this process bring personal insights, it also builds self-esteem. A senior woman accountant had found leadership training invaluable in developing her thinking about how to change her life direction:

Many of us, given a role, will play it. But how do we define for ourselves the role we want and give ourselves permission to play it? ...You never know yourself until you've tested yourself.

And as you progress in your career it is vital to keep asking whether you are still challenged by what you do. Do the rewards match or exceed your expectations? You must also continue to gauge the organizational culture – are you still in tune with its values? If not you may need to move on. Nikki Beckett recalled how, after an exceptional career at IBM, she subsequently became disillusioned with the company in the early 1990s. As it lost market leadership, so management resorted to cost cutting and downsizing, when earlier decisive action could have avoided such consequences. No longer able to believe in the policies she was responsible for implementing, she made the decision to leave. This is, in part, what prompted her to set up NSB Retail Systems – a desire to recreate the spiritual purpose that had first attracted her to a career at IBM. Recognize that your perspectives too may change over time and be prepared to move on to something you might enjoy more in terms of personal fulfilment, was the message from many women we spoke to:

Understand what you are dealing with in corporate life and recognize that not everyone is suited to it. Be creative in your thinking about work and look for something where perhaps you could have some entrepreneurial involvement.

Some of the successful women in our sample told us that their careers had developed largely by accident, but by the time she reached 21 Nikki Beckett had already written a life plan, making an inventory of her skills and assessing her strengths and weaknesses. Throughout her life she has read widely in order to gain personal insights and to learn techniques that help her achieve her objectives. The exercises throughout this book and the chapter on career life planning are designed to support you in your quest for greater self-knowledge and faster progress in attaining your goals. Nikki, with her expanding multi-million pound business, is compelling proof that this process can work.

Getting hired

When you have a portfolio of marketable skills and good technical expertise you hold the cards. This gives you bargaining power when negotiating for terms and conditions.

Julia Penny

Knowledge and experience relevant to the job in question are, of course, taken as read – without them you will not get through the first sift. According to recruitment agency head Louise Campbell, the key criterion that decides who gets hired is cultural fit: will the individual get on with other people in the company? This is notoriously difficult to evaluate, but the good news for women, particularly in the New Economy, is that there is a growing need for teams drawn from a broad cross-section of society to reflect an increasingly diverse and international marketplace. Young male entrepreneurs, too, are very positive about employing women. Unlike many of their counterparts in large corporations they have not adopted gender-biased attitudes as a result of pressure from older managers to conform to established norms and values through a sort of rite of passage sexism.

When looking for a new job always ask: 'Is this organization a good vehicle for my career?'

Louise Campbell

The importance of checking out the employment practice – as opposed to the stated policy – within any organization you consider working for was emphasized by Kate Barker. She also had some advice about choosing a profession:

Ask questions: how many women are doing this or that? What's the culture regarding hours – is evening or weekend working standard practice? Will it change? Look at the norms of the profession or sector you have chosen and ask how flexible a career you will have. Will it always be a struggle or could there be periods when it could be done at a lower pitch? Economist jobs, for example, are nearly all London-based. I wish I'd done law – it's more portable.'

These views were confirmed by other women, one of whom suggested looking at the top of the organization: if the senior managers have conventional marriages with wives at home, they will not appreciate the problems encountered by working women and the crises that will arise.

Speaking about the underrepresentation of women in corporate life, Leigh Woods suggested that many businesses would be stronger if they were better able to deploy women's skills in teamworking and juggling multiple priorities. Though not in favour of positive discrimination if this means not recruiting the best candidate, she nevertheless believes that HR departments could and should try to access more women candidates by thinking differently about the way job specifications are defined. They should be actively seeking employees with the ability to multi-task and thinking laterally about ways to look for evidence of such skills. Employers also need to be redefining the skill sets of the future and learning to write job descriptions differently to attract the right people.

The most successful women I know have made very good choices in terms of employers, with whom they've stayed a long time, so they can prove themselves and so put a little bit of flexibility in their working lives thereafter. It's a lot easier for women if they choose companies that are not male strongholds.

Avivah Wittenberg-Cox[2]

Know your stuff

Be first rate in terms of your skills for the job.

Margaret McCabe

A recurring theme among the women we interviewed was the importance of absolute professionalism:

Sheer professionalism will prevail.
Nikki Beckett (talking about gender discrimination)

Speaking of the challenges of working in a city law firm, Judith Mayhew mentioned the need to be more competent than the men: 'Being average won't do'. She felt that women had many admirable qualities to bring to the workplace – their collegial style, intuition, courtesy and perfectionism. These qualities can, however, result in women being perceived as less ambitious, dynamic and competitive. In particular, women needed to try to be more focused and to resist the temptation to multitask too much, particularly when juggling work and domestic responsibilities.

In male-dominated corporate environments the issues are similar. Kate Barker felt during her time in the automotive industry that she too had to be better than the men:

People are waiting for you to fail and are unforgiving of mistakes. Also, when gender equality issues come into a promotion, you want to prove you weren't just recruited because you're a woman.

But while being professional may have become second nature to many of us, achieving recognition for our knowledge and contribution can pose significant challenges:

Though inwardly confident in their own abilities to achieve almost anything, many women do not outwardly appear confident. Men find it easier to tell a good story. Women are more reticent and people take all this at face value.
Senior accountant

In Chapter Five we stress the need to manage the impression you create in order to win opportunities and move up the promotion ladder. Women at the top have internalized this lesson and are skilled practitioners in gaining visibility and creating opportunities to shine:

Build value and understand your value. Then you can say: 'This is what I'd like you to do to keep me'. In order to get to

*the top you have to do your own PR. Know your own
importance and take the initiative. Don't feel you always have
to be invited. Men don't.*

Julie Bradley

Building your value in the eyes of senior management was an
issue many women focused on, since they felt it important to
lay the groundwork before asking for concessions like flexible
working or a four-day week. Kate Barker, for example, appreciated that significant exceptions were made for her after the birth
of her second child because she had established her worth, and
this had been hugely motivating:

> *The right time, for your career, to have a baby is when you
> have established your worth to the company.*

In Chapter One (and elsewhere) we refer to the critical importance of gaining a solid business grounding, the foundation upon
which your professionalism must be built. But while the trend for
many women is to specialize early, successful women tend to aim
wide in their career development. For Nikki Beckett her early
business training was the vital element in enabling her to start her
own highly successful business, NSB Retail Systems. She joined
IBM in 1979 (having chosen at 18 not to go to university), and
embarked on a 'fabulous' training programme that took her
through every major division in the company. Eventually she
chose the field of general management, which became the
springboard for her first major opportunity: to lead a team
developing business relationships with major corporations.

At this point it may be useful to consider the qualities required
for general management, since it is a proven route to the top
taken by many men, but too few women. There are two key
elements: the ability to manage resources (budgeting) and the
skills of leadership. The first requires some basic management
finance know-how (if you don't have any, then take steps to
acquire some). The second Nikki describes as the ability to
inspire people to give something extra, even to take on an
impossible task. But both of these skill sets come into play when
we look at what a general manager does: she needs to be
successful at selling ideas and concepts by persuading others that

they are well founded, that they will fly. (Later in this chapter we will look at some techniques recommended by successful women for getting your ideas adopted and bringing people on board with your plans.)

Lots of women say they don't like the financial side of business. But it's just not made attractive. Young women don't identify with your average finance director.

Rabbi Julia Neuberger

An added skill that women bring to the party is our ability to ensure attention to detail without losing sight of the goal, one of our greatest assets.

You don't need to lose the big picture to be a completer–finisher.

Nikki Beckett

Nikki's success running the business development unit subsequently led to her being seconded out to run an equity investment company in which IBM had taken a holding. This enabled her to gain the experience of building a business while she was still employed by IBM. How she went on to launch NSB and the secrets of her outstanding success we will reveal shortly when we look at the advice she and others offered about starting a business.

CASE STUDY

Gaining specialist skills in Internet recruitment and becoming one of the top three performers in the organization for which she then worked gave Louise Campbell the confidence to be herself and ultimately to leave and set up her own business. Of working in corporations, she says that it is vital to develop the knack of being a chameleon, reflecting the norms of the organization, while at the same time retaining your own integrity. Self-knowledge and a keen awareness of your environment enable you to respond subtly and sensitively to the challenges you encounter. She calls this 'being political in a non-manipulative way'. For Louise, being successful in her field stems from an understanding of different client environments and matching what you do to how they operate. Whether within our own or a client's organization, we need to observe the subtleties of internal politics (a potential minefield) and assess the broader picture – something at which women are very adept.

Establish your goals and milestones

Decide what you want your life to be. Pursue your goals and be prepared to live with the consequences.

Joy Kingsley

Setting realistic career goals and believing you can achieve them was something that many of the women endorsed:

I was not remotely surprised by my success – I worked and planned for it. You must plan and be certain of your objectives. Anticipate problems. Chunk them up in order to deal with them. You have to set measures and celebrate when you have achieved them.

Nikki Beckett

While taking the long view is important we must also learn to recognize opportunities and seize chances by creating them out of the circumstances around us, according to Judith Mayhew. Having a flexible mindset and maximizing the opportunities we have now, rather than hoping they will turn up at some point in the future, can help us make the most of every day. The process of seeking opportunities and gaining experience is vital in building your self-confidence. Start small to build some initial successes and eventually you will have the courage and confidence to take on the big tasks and challenges.

This issue of creating opportunities was a common theme among the successful women we talked to. We saw in Chapter One how Hilary Meredith, inspired by the plight of victims in damages cases, made this work her own. Similarly, Joy Kingsley described how she 'developed a nose' for new business – a skill she practises to this day – and built up the legal office she managed in the early days. Her organizational skills and tenacity also proved invaluable as the firm expanded and moved through a series of reorganizations, leading ultimately to her appointment as managing partner. Finding your niche will undoubtedly help you move your career forward. Look at your portfolio and determine what it is you do well, whether designing and setting up processes and systems, breaking down barriers to achieve results quicker, working collaboratively with others or business planning and innovation. Capitalize on your natural adaptability and keep developing new skills, layering these on your core discipline. Ask yourself what you feel passionately about and let this guide you in setting goals and planning your future.

Vive la différence

Interestingly, when Nikki Beckett was voted Veuve Cliquot Business Woman of the Year (2000), she was reported as saying that, far from being a disadvantage, being a woman had opened doors for her that might otherwise have remained closed. In her experience it had a certain novelty factor in some environments, and this had created opportunities for her rather than held her back.

Several other women we spoke to concurred: being a woman need not count against you if you know how to make it work in your favour. At a very basic level, client service companies will often include a woman in teams pitching for business. While many of you will cry 'Tokenism!', some women had found this a useful way of getting in the front line and grabbing an opportunity to show what they were made of, both to clients and to senior colleagues.

The deck is not, in my experience, stacked against women. Any one can do it. Women can have the advantage because they are unique and different, and they should use this difference as an asset.

Leigh Woods

Naturally, it is important not to be too overtly feminine. Judith Mayhew advises that we remain always businesslike in our dress and behaviour, but learn to avoid setting up male aggression by remaining neutral and focusing on getting things done. This was also the view of Julie Bradley with regard to attempts by male colleagues at bullying and intimidation:

> *Don't react. Reply completely deadpan. It would cost you a lot of angst, time and effort to reply in kind – and they wouldn't be able to cope with it if you did.*
>
> Julie Bradley

In a more positive context, both Kate Barker and Julie Bradley had found advantages in learning to play on being different. Julie advocated using your femininity to allow you to adopt different roles, for example in order to interact more effectively with male colleagues and clients who find strong assertive women threatening. Tempting though it may be to dismiss such men as 'wimps', the fact remains that we will encounter them and having a workable strategy for persuading them to accept our agendas is vital.

> *Women know how to open up a dialogue in a non-threatening way, creating the perception that it's easier to raise issues with women.*
>
> Julia Penny

Kate Barker had found it effective to seek out a champion or mentor who would provide support and allow her to do things differently. She also believed it was important not always to play by the company rules. For example, while working for a major car manufacturer with a strong consensus culture, she was not afraid to disagree with the received wisdom and to challenge the status quo. To affirm her value, however, she always set out to draw on her expert power as an economist and to deliver what the company needed from her, however difficult.

The successful women we interviewed had learned to capitalize on some of the traditional female qualities: being comfortable with change, thinking intuitively and using their insight into how other people think and feel about issues. Their ability to grab hearts and minds had enabled them to inspire others to share their vision and work to achieve it.

Wanting success in your own terms is important. In some professions women sublimate their softer side and become aggressive. There are lots of negative impacts from battling against problems, rather than using your intelligence and your own style to manage them.

Senior accountant

Don't carry a chip on your shoulder

Seemingly in contrast with advice about using your femininity was the view that women should almost try to forget they are different from men and focus on being professional. But, according to Louise Campbell, the key is to understand how you are different so that you can successfully make your own way through without raging about inequality.

Women are not disadvantaged. They have infinite capacities and need to use them intelligently to get what they want. Understand that men and women are different, and when things happen, don't respond emotionally. Develop awareness and insight and take time to stand back and assess the situation.

Louise Campbell

Julie Bradley reiterated this sentiment:

Some women become bitter and blame every setback on the fact that they are female. You need to understand that sometimes things don't work out and let it go. Look forward.

Julie Bradley

Avoid false modesty

Women are usually less confrontational, less ego-driven and less likely to seek the limelight than their male counterparts according to our findings. Women often prefer to let others be seen to shine rather than take the glory for themselves. But there is nothing feminine about false modesty:

If you act like a doormat you'll be treated like one.

Women need to take credit when it is due to them, so that they become more visible and their potential for promotion is made apparent to the decision-makers.

Assume there's not a problem – that you're taken for what you are.

Julia Barfield

Speak up

Both Julie Bradley and Kate Barker underlined the importance of trying always to have something to say at meetings. 'Even if it's only: "I agree with X".' (Julie Bradley). Julie stressed that women must have the confidence to speak up, that it was best to go with your instincts and not to worry too much about always being right:

Women don't value their own opinions, but their views are as valid as anyone else's.

Julie Bradley

Kate Barker proposed asking questions in meetings to seek clarification when appropriate. This will help you gain confidence (it is low risk if you start small). Next, enter the discussion by selling your ideas to establish your authority. Here it is important to be businesslike in presenting your case ('brisk' was Kate's preferred mode). Getting your ideas accepted and persuading others is about how you present information with confidence, how effectively you argue your conclusions, how carefully you read your audience. Remember, when you've been asked to present to a group about your field of expertise you have the answers your audience wants to hear.

Women are less confident about their own ideas. In debate they often follow rather than lead. Men are more forceful – even though they sometimes talk nonsense.

Martha Lane Fox

Ask for help

Among the women who emphasized the importance of not being afraid to ask influential people for help was Margaret McCabe:

Identify the person you think is most successful in your organization or profession and network with them or get them to be your mentor. It gets you where the action is. Ask them how they did it and what advice they'd give you. Flattery gets you everywhere but you have to mean it. At the top people can become very isolated – they like being approached for help, it confirms their importance and status.

Margaret McCabe

Louise Campbell also felt strongly that it was important to ask for what you want. Elsewhere in the world this is seen as normal, but in Britain this approach is sometimes seen as too direct, especially by women.

Kate Barker thought it was important to seek out influential people in your organization and find out what they think you should be doing. Through a mentoring relationship you can find out how others perceive you and your abilities.

Of course, the flip side of seeking help is to offer it by later becoming a role model or mentor and taking an opportunity to pass on what you have learned.

Get networking

Both Nikki Beckett and Rabbi Julia Neuberger thought it was helpful to find people with similar interests and aspirations ('people at a similar stage in the journey') in order to create synergy in the relationship. Julia Neuberger believes women do this instinctively (more so than men). Women are usually prepared to flex their agendas; men tend to have one ready to run.

Professional networks are helpful in building your confidence because you feel part of that profession and recognize its value. As well as gaining technical knowledge, there are opportunities to serve by running for office and this increases your self-worth and sense of achievement.

Julia Penny

But while networking is important, Judith Mayhew points out that in some sectors – law especially – some of the networks exclude women. She advises that we avoid wasting time storming such bastions of male supremacy. Better to focus on issues where we can get results.

Working successfully with others

Treat people well. Do as you would be done by.

Kate Barker

When you first join an organization or move to a new division or department you may be made aware of tensions and antagonisms between different departments and teams. Kate Barker advised that we avoid aligning along the traditional battle lines and maintain a degree of neutrality and integrity. On dealing with conflict, however, she was clear that when individuals become adversarial we might have to deal with them in the same terms. A very sound piece of advice was to act the emotion – it's much less draining. (This technique is used by many teachers when dealing with difficult pupils.) Jeanette Hughes agreed: we need to strike a balance between confidence and arrogance. But when dealing with someone who is cocky, for example, we may have to match their behaviour because that is what they understand. It is important, though, never to put people down and to endeavour always to see both sides of an issue. Margaret McCabe picked up this theme too:

Always be nice to everyone. Show good manners – even in the face of difficulties. Never tell the truth to people when you are angry; they can't take it. Always act on quiet reflection, when you're in control.

Margaret McCabe

On dealing with difficult people, Kate Barker remarked that problems often arise (more so in today's flatter organizations) as a result of people's self-perceptions. They often believe they are hard working and cooperative when in fact they are not. Correcting these perceptions takes time because they are often very deep rooted.

You can always take a second crack at it

Often, when we feel we have suffered an injustice – not getting a promotion we thought we deserved, being given an unfair appraisal, or receiving biased criticism – we allow ourselves to feel undermined because we are conscientious and vulnerable to having our competence questioned. Several of the women we spoke to said it is important to challenge statements and assumptions with which you disagree. Take time to reflect, gather your arguments and evidence and go back into the fray. Avoid being confrontational but seek clarification. Ask people to be specific in identifying improvement opportunities. Don't allow them to use woolly generalizations. One woman, when told she would not be ready for a senior role for two and a half years, went back to the panel and asked: 'What do you need to see from me and I'll do it within two years?' And, of course, she did.

When asked about dealing with criticism Professor Susan Greenfield advised not taking it too much to heart if your conscience is clear. Be true to yourself and trust your own judgement. Women at the top often have to put up with bitchiness and backbiting – and it's usually covert, so there is no direct way to answer back. Above all, she says, you need to be able to laugh at yourself.

Don't bottle it all up. Talk to other women. Find a mentor who believes in you and get networking. It will raise your confidence.

Professor Susan Greenfield

Become a leader

What makes a great leader? Often some stimulus event in childhood combined with some exceptional skills and

*characteristics. Many women who have succeeded have had an
unconventional upbringing.*

Leigh Woods

There was a high degree of consensus about the special qualities
that women bring to the workplace and to public life, particularly
their collaborative, less confrontational style and the way in
which this enables them to bring out the best in their teams,
their colleagues and their client relationships. It was also widely
recognized, however, that a consensual style of leadership could
(albeit mistakenly) be perceived as a weakness within some
organizations where it might be interpreted as an inability to do
the hard thing and take decisions.

*You need self-confidence to make the big decisions. Eventually
they come easily, by instinct. You then work back to find a
rationale to underpin them.*

Dianne Thompson

Many of the women who contributed to this book spoke of the
advantages that women have in being able to work harmoniously
with others. Our willingness to listen and learn from others without needing to impose our idea of how things should be done
enables us to lead teams very effectively.

Lena Bjorck thought it important to give your people the
individual attention they need and to tailor your response to
them. In this way you will be able to persuade and motivate your
team to do anything because they feel valued. Also, when
managing others we need to learn how to ask the right questions
and to leave people thinking they found the answers for themselves. In this way they take ownership for the work they do.

*Set goals with your team. I make them specific and achievable
– like winning a new customer. Reaching goals increases
everyone's confidence. We celebrate success by having a glass of
champagne or we all go out together. People need morale
boosters especially when things are hectic. Sometimes we switch
the answer phones on and take time out for half an hour just to
recharge everyone's spirits.*

Lena Bjorck

While it is important to engender team loyalty and to empathize with the problems of individuals you manage, Kate Barker warned against the temptation to take on their problems yourself. Make suggestions about how difficulties could be sorted out but don't feel you have to solve everything.

The challenges at the top

Work–life balance

The female advantage is having plenty of choices. The female burden is having to make them.

The women we spoke to were unanimous in emphasizing both the importance of establishing a balance between work and home life and the difficulty of achieving it within the framework of a high-powered career.

Don't keep juggling: choose some flexible work option. Women take on too much in combining work and home responsibilities.
Louise Campbell

'Having it all' was widely acknowledged to be a myth, but one that many women were still trying (with varying success) to live up to. Power requires sacrifice was the lesson we learned. And though there are examples of very high fliers seamlessly combining career and motherhood, women like the formidable Nicola Horlick are very exceptional and few of us could do what she does. Rarely can you have it all: combining a career and a family requires us to make choices and concessions.

We lack models of women who are sane and make balanced choices and don't listen to the sirens. I ascribe a lot of the blame to the media image of superwomen. We're overwhelmed with superwomen stories and profiles.
Avivah Wittenberg-Cox[3]

Kate Barker thought that schools, too, should make more efforts to accommodate the schedules of working parents. Sports days, parent's evenings and other school events are often timed unsympathetically, causing working parents to miss out. She urged us to recognize that the situation is not perfect and that we shouldn't grumble or beat ourselves up. We have to make our decisions and choices and live with the consequences. Recognize, too, that having a family may limit your work potential – you may not be able to network after hours because you want or need to go home:

> *The dilemma for many ambitious women is that of wanting to use your abilities and have a family. But the two jobs must add up to a package you can manage – though not always perfectly.*

Kate has been fortunate in having a very supportive husband (in publishing) who can flex his hours at times to cover the domestic front. This is in addition to a good support system of paid child-care.

And if you are going to attempt to scale the heights of your profession and have a family too, Dianne Thompson offered the following advice with which many others agreed:

> *Dedicate more resources to your support system on the domestic front. Have live-in help and learn to cope with the loss of privacy. Otherwise you put yourself under enormous pressure.*

Sue Slipman has been a single parent all her working life and feels strongly that it is important to have some balance – your life can't just be about work:

> *Your career should be about helping you grow and develop your skills. But you must have a life.*

She is also committed to family-friendly work policies, but would add the qualification that this cannot be all one way: people should be supported when necessary, but they should support the business in return. Rabbi Julia Neuberger also subscribed to this view:

> *There has to be give and take in emergencies. But women need to make up the time they take off. Employees must be work friendly.*

The importance of putting in place flexible and dependable childcare was constantly emphasized:

You need to take it year by year as the needs of the children evolve. You can't always second guess what will happen with childcare, so you always need a fallback.

Joy Kingsley

Many of the women we spoke to had either delayed having children until quite late in their careers or else decided not to have them at all. The dilemmas that arise when career and motherhood collide were eloquently described by Julie Bradley. Now in her late 30s, Julie feels she may have left it a little late to have children:

I'm not a superwoman and I don't want a trophy baby. Having children requires compromises and it has to be the right choice for you. I don't think women should feel pressured one way or the other.

Julie Bradley

Professor Susan Greenfield chose not to have children and is convinced that, so great is the commitment they require, she could not have achieved her present success had she become a mother. This is due in part to the norms of the scientific profession. Career advancement is dependent on having a continuous track record of research and publication – taking a break is not really possible. In corporate life career breaks can be no less damaging to your career.

I wouldn't have achieved what I have if I had married and had kids. Regaining your momentum after a career break is difficult. You need to be in the right place at the right time to capitalize on opportunities. Business is dynamic, things move very quickly. It's a case of out of sight, out of mind.

Carol Hambly

Leigh Woods has four children and opted not to take a career break:

If you want to rise to the top it's unrealistic to expect six-month career breaks. You've got to make some sacrifices. Some jobs are just not part time.

She feels the key to success is flexibility both in terms of the time you take off and in relation to the childcare arrangements you have in place.

CASE STUDY

Leigh Woods has in the past chosen some unusual patterns of work. For example, when she was working in the USA she commuted by air from Philadelphia to Ohio leaving on Tuesday and returning on Thursday each week. During this time she worked very intensively and was available to the office by phone when at home. When each of her children was born she treated it rather like going on holiday – she would be away a short time, but keep in touch and flex her schedule to accommodate whatever arose. She had a full-time nanny for some years, but as her career took off her husband decided to stay at home and look after the children.

Returning to work after a career break can be difficult though, Julia Barfield recalled how painful it was after her first baby:

I went back to work after four months and although I was determined to do it, it felt like I'd left a limb at home. And in a practice where an 8 p.m. finish was the norm, leaving at six felt like a half day. These days, however, some architects – both men and women – are working flexibly from home.'

Even when children are not yet in the equation, women face difficult issues. The younger generation of women (in their late 20s) who, academically, did better than their male counterparts and are now rapidly scaling the career ladder, are currently having to decide how to focus their lives:

Ten years on from university women seem to start wondering: 'Should I be with my boyfriend or should I be working long hours?' They feel guilty about wanting 'feminine' things like kids, family and travel. It's a real dilemma because it's difficult

*to talk to men about the range of needs, values and desires we
have as women. We want to express it all.*

Martha Lane Fox

*The issue is that wanting a career is about being able to shape
and control things – a very intoxicating feeling. This of course
vanishes when you have kids.*

Collette Graham

Fiona Reynolds felt strongly that the caring roles women take on
should be just as valued as their economic contribution. As
women we need to talk more positively about what we do. Senior
women, she felt, have a responsibility to show the way. For
example, she and her husband reversed roles for four years when
her husband gave up work to look after their children:

*It is very important to live the values you espouse and not to
play the man's game of hiding the fact that you have a family.
It's a personal challenge we all struggle to balance. We all need
to talk about it and recognize its importance.*

Many of the high achieving women with children were steadfast
in their view that you must not sell the family short by giving in
to the demands of a long-hours culture:

*It's been tough – a daily juggling act. But I've taught myself to
bite the bullet and decide: I'm leaving the office now.*

Senior accountant

Tessa Jowell strongly agreed with this approach:

*Be ruthless about making time for your children. I never felt I
had to steel myself to state my priorities. You can always sort it
out.*

Referring to the challenges she had faced over the years Sue
Slipman talked about the fact that she was often tired and had
little time for a social life. As a single parent her social life had
tended to revolve around her son for many years: 'Having a wife
would have been nice.'

Behind every successful woman . . . is a basket of dirty laundry.

Sally Forth

It is perhaps a measure of how far women have advanced that Rabbi Julia Neuberger recalls one of her greatest challenges as being pilloried for her progressive views on women's rights. In the early days her outspokenness made her very unpopular, but 10 years on her views are commonplace.

Choosing the right partner

The majority of the women we spoke to stressed the importance of having a husband or partner to whom you can look for support:

Choose a supportive partner who wants what you want out of life. Ensure you both have common aims and that he is willing to accept and work with your choices. He won't change for the better later.

Joy Kingsley

The problems of the dual career couple are not easily resolved, however. In many of the cases we looked at, the male partner had, at some stage, agreed that his career should become secondary – at least for a while – to allow the woman to pursue the opportunities open to her. But if your partner is not prepared to do this, then Julie Bradley offered the following observation:

Marriage is not a competition and you have to make compromises.

Sue Slipman added that even as a single parent, faced with the economic necessity of working, the problems were similar in striking the work–home balance. Her view was that it is always going to be tough for women, and from her personal experience and that of colleagues and friends she observed:

It always changes when children come along and you quickly have to develop different priorities. You have to make choices in your career, but unless men change it will not get any easier.

Lots of women fall by the wayside because they have a partner who can support them.

With reference to her marriage Rabbi Julia Neuberger remarked that there had always been a lot of give and take. At one point her husband left his job in the Civil Service to study for a Masters degree and was able to share the domestic workload:

Marriage, like management, is about negotiation.

We referred at the beginning of this chapter to the fact that women strive for balance in their lives – we derive our fulfilment from a variety of sources and when one aspect is unsatisfactory or missing, that is what we primarily focus on. Dianne Thompson warned of the potential consequences of allowing ourselves to be driven too much by ambition:

I always felt I had to prove things to myself – I'm a perfectionist. I chose intensive jobs, got the balance wrong and paid the price. I'd like to think my daughter won't have to work as hard as me. I don't want her to be driven. She's confident – not working class like me – and has more social ease than I had at her age.

Pay for domestic help

Do not do housework – pay for someone to do your cleaning.
                                                                Jo Hansford

A frequent warning from the women we interviewed was not to confuse having it all with doing it all. The further up the career ladder you progress, the more resources you need to devote to domestic help:

At home I like lots of support with housework and gardening. I work hard but not at home. I can't see the point of housework – it's a monumental waste of time. You've no sooner finished than it needs doing again.
                                                                Joy Kingsley

The downsides to success

One obvious downside to a high-flying career is the instability at the top of most organizations. Mergers, acquisitions, failing to meet targets, policy changes – any of these can mean you are out of a job. So how would that feel? Jeanette Hughes emphasized the need for resilience:

> *I'd be devastated, but I'm flexible and I'd get another job. And I always remember the wise words of one colleague: 'The hole you leave behind is the same as when you pull your fist out of a bucket of water.' No one is indispensable.*

And as you move up an organization, particularly if this brings you into the public arena, this can be 'significantly scary'. Kate Barker talked of how she felt about putting herself on the line every day as Chief Economist at the CBI:

> *It's a balance between the buzz and the burnout. When what you say is attributed to you personally you become a target for the media. You need nerves of steel.*

But this too can work to your advantage. Tessa Jowell found that her experience had helped her stick to her beliefs in the face of strong opposition:

> *When you have conviction people can agree or disagree with you. It doesn't make any difference.*

In addition to possible insecurities about your own future there are, when you are at the top, also the responsibilities of other people's lives and careers. Joy Kingsley talked of the pressures of her role. There are the day-to-day issues (500 e-mails a week), minor work problems and upsets, as well as the major difficulties brought on, for example, by a recession. You may have to take decisions that make you unpopular with your colleagues or which are seen as unfair. And then there is always the feeling of being pulled in two directions by work and home.

One of the great challenges at the top is simply being yourself. Professor Susan Greenfield, Dianne Thompson and Martha

Lane Fox emphasized how important it was to hold on to a sense of your identity and not to be seduced by media attention:

I am the same person as I ever was – I keep the same friends. But top jobs change people's perceptions of you. Society measures people against a hierarchy. Don't believe the publicity telling you you're important – it's just media hype.

Dianne Thompson

You must retain the ability to laugh at yourself.

Professor Susan Greenfield

It's the price you pay. You're always on show and sometimes it's hard to remember your real self-worth.

Martha Lane Fox

In this section we leave the last word to Rabbi Julia Neuberger who said with some satisfaction of her long and varied career:

There have been no downsides. I'm tired a lot of the time. But it's been great.

Know when you're beaten

Never quit when you're down. Pull the situation back and then leave them sorry to see you go.

Finance director

An issue that we will develop further in Chapter Seven is whether we are all suited to corporate life. Louise Campbell has observed many women reach burnout from trying every avenue to progress in corporate life, but finding their way blocked. Her advice is to remove yourself from an impossible situation, otherwise you end up contributing to your own loss of confidence. 'If you always do what you've always done, you'll always get what you've always got,' she quipped. We need to understand what we are dealing with (immovable objects) and recognize that not everyone is suited to corporate life. A better option might be to think creatively and to look for a career with some entrepreneurial involvement.

I want to look around after my MBA and perhaps set up a business or go into partnership with someone who has a business idea. I want to have a go and see how successful I can be as my own boss. If all else fails I can always get another job, but I wouldn't want to work in a big corporation again where you're just a small fish in a big pond.

Senior finance manager

The future of women in business and the professions

The New Economy

The difficulty within many technology and dot.com companies is that, while they are run by young entrepreneurs without gender-biased views, the fast-paced development and expansion rates of these enterprises makes flexible employment difficult.

People need to be able to give 150 per cent at times, so it's not easy to be flexible. But we try. I don't believe the technology world is easier for women – the fast pace and long hours in business start-ups make heavy demands. And people work harder with remote access – they're more easily available and forced to be productive even during their 'downtime', sending or receiving e-mails or mobile phone calls.

Martha Lane Fox

Accountancy

Julia Penny felt the promotion prospects for women are better in accountancy than elsewhere, particularly for those who don't have children. The long hours required within many firms, however, makes it difficult to combine a senior position with having a family. This stems from the culture of 'presenteeism' and the way in which accountants are evaluated – in terms of 'capacity' and hours booked on the time sheet. This leads to the perception that people are only doing well if they have worked lots of bookable hours. In this type of firm women are disadvantaged: they usually work smarter because their time is more constrained, yet because of this they are seen as less productive. This is further compounded by the fact that after hours informal networking is difficult for them and when they work flexibly and from home they are seen as less committed. The irony here is that, in London particularly, firms are keen to cut office overheads and exploit the cost savings of new technology. Yet there is considerable lack of trust in allowing people to work from home, despite the fact that giving people more control over their working life brings significant gains in productivity.

> *You need to make conscious choices. Flexible working arrangements don't really accommodate aspiring women because they can't hit the income generation or commitment criteria for promotion. But if you do take the flexible option, don't adopt a part-time mentality. Have the same domestic support as if you were full time.*
>
> Senior accountant

The up side, however, is that accountancy is potentially geared to women: it provides a structured training with flexibility since the introduction of part-time options for gaining qualifications. Relative to other types of jobs (witness the laddish cultures prevalent in the financial services and other sales sectors), accountancy is more egalitarian, offers good remuneration and accountants command respect regardless of their gender. Moreover, the long hours are not unique to accountancy and the high burnout rate for both men and women means that things must begin to change. Julia Penny expects that technology will force a paradigm shift and, as skills shortages increasingly bite, discrimination between core and non-core staff and part-time versus full-time working will become much less relevant measures of competence, commitment and potential for promotion.

However, in professional service firms the client's needs must come first:

> *Part-time and flexible options can be problematic. Clients expect commitment and consistency. If a woman is unable to give her full commitment to the client-serving role this hits women's ability to progress.*
>
> Senior accountant

One issue about which Julia Penny felt strongly, related to how the top jobs are allocated. She felt that part-time directorships should be open to anyone qualified for the position. The precedent is that, if the part-time option is open to those nearing retirement, then it should be possible at any career stage. We need to question the criteria for selection. Currently it seems to be the male paradigm of time served and perhaps we should rethink how we measure competence: do people necessarily get better at doing something the longer they do it?

The law

The two tiers of the profession – solicitors and barristers – are significantly different options from the perspective of employment for women and so we will look first at solicitors.

Solicitors

The skills shortages and the value many employers place on trained staff means that within some firms there is a genuine desire for women to continue working when they have children. Joy Kingsley explained that career breaks can create enormous problems for the managing partner, with some women out of the office for three out of five years while having their families. Part-time and job-share options – whilst good ideas in principle – in practice may not work so well for clients, who look for continuity of service. It also seems to be a commercial fact of life that it is more profitable for the firm to employ people full time rather than part time

> *Plan ahead. Before you decide to have a baby think about how you will manage. You must have a supportive partner who has respect for your career and achievements. Ensure you always make joint decisions.*
>
> Senior lawyer

There is also the issue of perceptions: full-time staff are seen to have greater commitment. Furthermore, although many firms are trying to get away from the long hours culture, to be considered for partnership people need to put in the requisite hours and to reach their fee-earning targets. There were several examples, however, of women who had achieved partnership on a part-time basis, but some of these women worked evenings and weekends to make up their hours. Law firms it seems don't want to lose well-qualified women, but keeping them is sometimes a difficult balancing act.

Some women want to work on after having children, but on their own terms – no evenings or weekends and fitted around nursery hours. This is not realistic for solicitors.

Joy Kingsley

Judith Mayhew added an optimistic note, however. She sees increasingly a blurring of gender differences – no one wants to work excessive hours any more and everyone is looking for work–life balance. Women are drawing support from their own networks (such as the Woman Lawyer Forum) and pressing for change. Meanwhile, the larger firms are recognizing that family-friendly policies improve the bottom line, and as both men and women in the City reach burnout, these economic arguments must prevail.

Hilary Meredith took the view that, while women are breaking through in the legal profession, significant changes were needed for everyone's sake. She believes the profession is perceived as stuffy, unapproachable and intimidating by many people, and that this must change. Women in her view have the communication skills to break down many of the barriers that exist. The problem is that no one likes lawyers – they are associated with life's traumas and, in order to survive, the profession needs to be more approachable and act as an advisory group.

Barristers

While recognizing that there are many difficulties for women barristers – getting a training being just one – Margaret McCabe was nonetheless encouraging to women who were seeking a career in the law:

Go for it, be intelligent. The legal profession is difficult to get into and you may have to take what you can get. Look for a Chambers that will be supportive. (Look at the partners and their assumptions about the role of women.) The great attraction of the Bar is its flexibility. You are self-employed and working part time is a viable option. Courts have terms and you can fix your schedule around them so that you take the school holidays off. But don't tell people that's what you're doing – they'll write you off as second rate.

Politics

It is widely acknowledged that there are too few women in politics, despite any number of initiatives aimed at remedying this situation. Tessa Jowell's view is that once women can achieve equal representation in Parliament then there will be a huge cultural change, not only in politics but also across the board in business and the public sector. But while the present situation continues: long hours and a House that is thoroughly women- and children-unfriendly – there is a risk that politics will increasingly become a career that women don't want to enter. Much of a politician's working life is unappealing to many women who can't bear to waste time or be part of a process with no tangible outcome. However, as work–life balance becomes less a women's agenda and more an issue that men too identify with, reform will follow. In time this will create government with greater diversity and a career option that is more attractive to many groups including women.

Sue Slipman offered the following insights into why too few women are breaking through in politics:

It's a tough business and a highly manipulative environment. The hours are long and the men are still very derisory about women. It's a secretive place and women generally do not like that way of working. Men are often reluctant to share information or good ideas while women prefer to share and work together.

Architecture

Julia Barfield, a partner with her husband in Marks Barfield (architects of the London Eye) has never felt disadvantaged as a woman and believes people in the profession are treated genuinely on their merits, having enjoyed an exceptional 'apprenticeship' working with Richard Rogers and Norman Foster.

The construction industry with which architects interface is still conservative and male-dominated, but women are well represented in architecture where husband and wife partnerships are common. She believes women's communication skills and their ability to see alternatives are advantageous in the profession, enabling them to anticipate and forestall problems relating to projects. Not infrequently male architects allow their egos to get in the way, and when they become adversarial with contractors everyone is the loser in the conflict that ensues. Men like to win by defeating others, but a woman's perspective on winning usually relates to the greater goal of ensuring a smooth-running project where there is a win outcome for everyone.

As more women are drawn into the profession, Julia expects that things will slowly change. She feels very privileged in being a partner in her own practice, where she has been able to set her own parameters and strike a balance between work and home. However, she did add that this balance is more problematic when you work for someone else, particularly where long hours are expected, and this is prevalent in architecture:

It's impossible to feel you've got it completely right. Women are in an impossible situation.

Corporate life

The ability to nurture and the ability to compete aggressively are not mutually exclusive as is often assumed.

Leigh Woods

Though every job has its own special challenges, Leigh Woods felt that being a woman boss in the UK was more unusual than in the USA and that there were fewer role models for women. She puts her success with her people in the UK down to her 'unique level of dedication'. She looks after and cares for them and makes visible her values and vision throughout the company. One of the problems with British business, she feels, is that it has long been male dominated with certain skill sets and experience being valued above others.

As business and the economy evolve, so the old skills will become less relevant and the talents that women bring – communication and people skills; nurturing; problem solving; team working and (above all) multitasking – will come increasingly to the fore. Companies need these qualities to provide greater balance and organizational strength. They need managers who can develop people successfully and this means being able to challenge and nurture them, motivating them to give more and ensuring they deliver effective customer interactions.

Carol Hambly agreed with this. Given the difficulty of changing male-dominated cultures, she felt that women would increasingly gravitate towards new forms of organizations with new cultural paradigms:

> *Why would women want to continue working for organizations that are male led? More female-led organizations will arise and attract talented women.*

Although things are getting better for women in corporate life, there is still a long way to go. Kate Barker mentioned how few women are represented at CBI member consultations – even though these groups are not drawn from the most senior levels of management. Many women, she believes, compromise on their ambitions because of the difficulties they encounter and don't therefore fulfil their potential:

> *Women's lives are often diverse and many prefer it that way. To a degree they self select out. The requirements of top jobs can seem too daunting.*

Jeanette Hughes, from the perspective of someone without domestic ties at present, commented that, though women are making progress, they are unlikely to achieve complete equality because of their biology. Some male bastions will not be broken down because many women will want to have a family rather than focusing uniquely on their career and this will inevitably prejudice their chances at work.

Starting your own business

Dare to dream

There's nothing that can't be achieved. You simply have to dare to dream it.

Margaret McCabe

Many of the women we talked to were passionate about their work, but those with the greatest enthusiasm for the job were usually women entrepreneurs. One such was the inspiring Lena Bjorck who took a fatalistic view of how she got where she is today:

I found what I was born to do. I believe in fate – we're all born under a star – I don't chase things. I had success purely because I concentrate 200 per cent on my customers . . . Believe in your vision and don't listen to those who say you can't do it.

Lena told us she rarely has bad days – she wakes up and can't wait to get to work at her catering company. Both she and Fiona Price (whose company provides financial services for women) agreed that work becomes what you make it when you run your own company:

You create your own experience every day.

Fiona Price

Another great enthusiast was Martha Lane Fox who admitted she was 'proud to have brought the Internet to people's attention', and particularly to have been involved in creating a new business paradigm showing how the next generation of entrepreneurs can do things differently. She hoped, too, that this model would be an inspiration to other women wishing to start up a new business:

Be tenacious. Don't assume you can't do it. Take the risk.

Her message was that the rewards of owning your own company are considerable: it can unlock your self-confidence and bring tremendous fulfilment. The downside, however, is that it can be lonely at the top (particularly in the glare of media attention) and that you need great reserves of strength to cope. But the scope afforded by the financial rewards helps to compensate for the drawbacks. Martha particularly likes having the freedom to put money into charities that she cares about in order to help out.

Running a business successfully

While we cannot, within the scope of this book, provide a comprehensive guide for a business start-up, we would nevertheless like to share some of the hot tips we gathered from speaking to successful women entrepreneurs.

Beware of seeking advice from men when setting up your business. Many of them think women are not really up to it. They are not good sounding boards – they like to be Mr Fixits: they leap in with a solution to a problem before they've even heard the full story.

Conviction

Aim for the top and be passionate about it.

Jo Hansford

Though the women entrepreneurs we interviewed came from different backgrounds – some had extensive business training, others had none when they started out – they believed passionately in what they did and were consequently able to inspire others and to make them feel part of something special. In fact nearly all the women we spoke to – whether in their own business or employed by an organization – had the happy knack of getting people to feel that they worked for *them* rather than for some faceless organization.

Goals

These can be huge or relatively modest but you must be focused on them. Nikki Beckett, for example, believes in having a BHAG – a Big, Hairy Audacious Goal: she wanted to run the world's number one retail software company. Allied to your goals you must have a clear business plan. But while it is important to do the financial and market analyses, the women we spoke to also relied heavily on their instinct and intuition:

■ Trust your intuition – it's your wisest counsel.
■ I'm very analytical, but I'm also highly intuitive.
■ Listen to advice but go with your instinct.

Get the people side right

It's commonsense – treat people as you want to be treated yourself.
Lena Bjorck

A common thread linking women who had started their own business was the desire to create an organization that embodied a new set of cultural values. These were often very different from the ones they had encountered in corporate life. Indeed, their hostility to the cultural norms they had experienced elsewhere was in many cases the stimulus that prompted them to break away and do their own thing. Feeling uncomfortable about unethical practices; disillusionment with corporate politics; frustration at the slow pace of change; impatience with poor customer service delivery; or being fundamentally opposed to policy changes – any or all of these issues had strengthened the resolve of the women entrepreneurs we interviewed that their people policies and practices would be different. They had opted for consultative and consensual management styles and processes, and developed businesses that were highly customer focused.

Women can experience immense freedom within enterprise cultures. It's very liberating because the traditional corporate constraints don't exist.
Louise Campbell

Follow the rules of thumb

Your greatest responsibility is to find a way of working that brings you joy.

Some simple but vital rules emerged from the interviews:

- Expect success.
- Don't waste energy worrying about the competition – it should keep you on your toes. Concentrate on your own business and focus on getting better.
- Recognize you are not indispensable and put systems in place to manage the business.
- Your role is to lead, motivate and support your staff – not to do everything yourself.
- Learn to empower and delegate so that you need to do less.
- As the business grows, recruit people who can grow with it.
- Go with your gut feel about people when recruiting – it's rarely wrong.
- Customer focus starts at the top, so share the vision of why customers are important.
- Never take no for an answer – keep trying.
- Plan. Set milestones and celebrate when you achieve them.
- Try to anticipate problems and have contingency plans to deal with them.
- Stay focused.
- Work hard but don't forget to have fun too.
- It's only work – keep your sense of perspective and draw your strength from within.
- Take a power nap in the afternoon if you can.

Starting your own business is a steep learning curve, but it's not hard. Women are often put off by the financial side. I advise them to take a chance – it's not that complex. As the whole process of setting up a business is demystified, so more women will do it. The Internet has changed how women see the possibilities – all the big dot.com stories are now about women.

Louise Campbell

A few final words of wisdom

Don't give yourself a hard time. Many women are perfectionists and their own most ardent critics. You can't always get it 100 per cent right, so admit this to yourself and others and try again …
Know you do most things well and with the best intentions.

Nikki Beckett

Disassociate yourself from negative people.

Louise Campbell

It's our time now. We have the essential communication and nurturing qualities. You can't fail if you bring those qualities to bear professionally.

Margaret McCabe

Men need to be encouraged to take on some family responsibility. Don't learn to iron and keep quiet about your ability to type until men have learned to do it.

Rabbi Julia Neuberger

Try using humour to defuse tension and debunk male chauvinism.

Professor Susan Greenfield

Be true to yourself and don't cast yourself in someone else's shoes because you lack confidence. There is no formula for success. Successful people are true to themselves, but without being dogmatic.

Collette Graham

I'm blessed with a close family and a strong group of women friends. They are my sounding board. First-class relationships are very important. Make sure you keep them in good repair.

Tessa Jowell

Work is work – it's not glamorous, in fact it's often mundane. It isn't like school or university – progression isn't automatic. It's down to you what happens to your career. It's up to you to make things happen.

Carol Hambly

Every day decide your own agenda of key items and don't allow outside interference. Wanting success is not enough. You must never give up and be prepared to pay the price.

Marissa Brambilla

Summary

The interview programme provided some invaluable advice. To sum up:

- Have your own roadmap with clearly defined goals and a plan for achieving them.
- Understand who you are and what drives you.
- Find your career niche and don't be afraid to do things your way.
- Seek help from networks and mentors.
- Don't be pigeonholed by others' expectations of you.
- Define success in your own terms.
- Choose to work for organizations that can be a vehicle for your career.
- Be professional at all times and don't be afraid of power.
- Accept that mistakes (your own and others') will happen. Learn from them and move on.
- Recognize you can't 'have it all': be prepared to make compromises and accept that balancing work and family will be difficult.
- Understand that it is often lonely at the top – it requires huge commitment and energy, and comes at a price.

In the next chapter we look at some issues that emerged from the research as critical to women's career development: how to manage your image and the impression you make, and how to heighten your visibility and improve your promotion potential.

Notes

1 *Financial Times*, 4 September 2000.
2 Ibid.
3 Ibid.

5

Personal image and impression management

Introduction

It is a commonly held view among aspiring women managers that getting on in your career is about keeping your head down and doing a good job. They have a touching faith that the simple virtue of conscientious hard work will be rewarded with career advancement. After all, it's only fair isn't it? Sadly, the world of work does not operate like school, where excelling earned you praise and prizes. In order to impress your manager (and other senior people who influence career progression) you need consciously to manage the impression you make. Not only must your dress, posture and demeanour reflect the organizational values, but your work behaviours must be focused on raising your profile, enhancing your reputation and creating value that is both visible and recognizable to the people that count.

(Much of the material in this section is drawn from the excellent research carried out by Val Singh and Susan Vinnicombe of the Centre for Developing Women Managers at Cranfield School of Management, and I am greatly indebted to them for making their findings available to me.)[1]

Your work persona

While some managers – appropriately labelled 'bystanders' – think it unimportant to consider what impression they are making, others actively try to regulate how influential people see them, in order to gain recognition or promotion. Many women are uncomfortable with these behaviours, having been socially conditioned to be modest and self-effacing. They generously share credit with team members and often down play their own contribution in order to give others the limelight. And though they may make special efforts for an interview or performance appraisal to create a favourable impression, they routinely neglect the range of executive skills necessary to manage how others perceive them on a day-to-day basis. But make no mistake, each of us needs a strong work persona that reflects the norms and expectations of the organization and signals to others that we have value to contribute at higher levels of responsibility and deserve the opportunity to do so through promotion.

When I worked as part of a team in a large international company I saw others getting on faster and wondered: 'Why not me?' Then I realized it's not really about intelligence, ability or even potential. It's about communication skills and how you affect people's perceptions of you and how you work.

Senior finance manager

When we join a new organization or take on increased responsibilities we face several hurdles in deciding how to present ourselves. First there is the dual agenda to decipher: formal systems, processes and norms for selection, development and promotion have unspoken, informal parallels. As a result of this, the perception or image of someone's performance becomes as important – or even more important – than the performance itself at appraisal time. So, the first task is to read carefully the organizational environment and decide:

■ What image or role identity would be most appropriate for you to adopt?
■ Who are the key players?
■ With whom should you be building relationships, especially upwards?
■ How are things done here in terms of personal managerial style?

A key disadvantage for women is the scarcity of female role models to whom they can look for clues about how to display potential for promotion. Even where such role models are present, the behaviours used by older successful women may not be those that younger women would wish to adopt, because they sometimes require women to behave like men. Many women are reluctant to appear aggressive and competitive, and feel more comfortable with more traditional female behaviours – building relationships, focusing on the task and nurturing others. In male-dominated organizations these behaviours can unfortunately carry with them the stigma of indecisiveness and be perceived as a lack of ambition and drive. Like it or not, impression management is the only game in town when it comes to career advancement. Those who fail to use it may find themselves at a significant disadvantage.

KEY RESEARCH FINDING: PERFORMANCE-RELATED PAY

In future, around a third of salary will be tied to individual performance.[2]

What is impression management?

Essentially, impression management is about influencing how others see us. It means taking control by ensuring the signals we give out are the right ones in the organizational context and that they are interpreted favourably by those whose good opinion is important. 'The "successful" manager is the one who manages the good opinions of others'.[3]

> *I hope to gain confidence by doing an MBA. If I'm to progress to Financial Director I must be seen to be able to compete with more experienced male self-promoters.*
> Woman MBA student

And if performance-related pay is to account for an increasing percentage of future remuneration packages, managing how our performance is perceived will be a critically important skill.

In this chapter several aspect of impression management will be dealt with:

■ **Self-presentation**: focusing on managing first impressions through appearance, style, voice, posture and body language.

■ **Self-awareness** derived from a personal audit of strengths and weaknesses, skills and competences, validated by reference to a trusted third party able to provide objective feedback.

■ **Self-promotion** by gaining visibility and by drawing attention to achievements, ambition and potential for greater responsibility. Also by enhancing our charisma and perceived leadership qualities.

■ **Self-monitoring** which requires us to continually reassess the impact of our style and effectiveness of our strategies for career advancement.

While managing your manager is dealt with in Chapter Eight, it is appropriate at this point also to mention the importance of 'influencing up'. That is, behaving proactively to gain the approval of those in the organization who control the resources and rewards to which you would like access. These behaviours draw on 'soft skills' including establishing rapport, for when people perceive similarities between themselves and us, they tend to like us more. This may, however, militate against women with male managers. If similarity of background and experience between managers and their direct reports is likely to result in higher performance ratings, then women may be disadvantaged by sex differences and role constraints when managed by men. Furthermore, some aspects of self-promotion may be risky for women, especially in traditional organizations where their role is primarily seen as contributing to the power and status of others – as in a personal assistant or secretarial capacity. So caution is advisable and we will consider later how best women can strike a balance by ensuring they are seen as competent without alienating those they seek to influence.

'Networking is creepy' . . . but necessary

A key form of upward influence is networking. The fact that women tend to have less powerful networks than men is well documented. Unlike their male colleagues, younger women particularly are less active in initiating and maintaining networking relationships. For while even senior women may wait to be invited into mentoring relationships this contrasts sharply with men, who actively seek out people with influence and power and initiate contact. And the evidence is compelling:

KEY RESEARCH FINDING

Where individuals network both within and outside their group, they are promoted more frequently.[4]

In a survey of 100 UK-based firms it was found that 'closed informal' systems of selection and promotion predominated.[5] In this way, names would be put forward and appointments agreed following discussions between the personnel function and line managers (often without candidates knowing). Formal assessment systems were often circumvented, with managers preferring to focus on candidates known to them personally. Furthermore, in evaluating promotees, more weight was given to general reputation than to what was formally recorded in performance appraisals.

Unfortunately, women put their trust in formal systems for career development, whereas men know the informal system – the grapevine – is what counts. Women ignore the importance of networking at their peril.

Style **and** *substance*

Finally, one sure way to impress and show commitment is through the quality of delivery in your work. But the problem here is that the high performance has to be observed in order to impress. With flatter organizations and spans of control extending from 5 or 6 to 20 or more people, the probability of a manager observing your accomplishments unaided are low.

Interestingly, achievement of results alone may not always result in high performance ratings. Managers also give high ratings to those who set high goals. So it is critical therefore to be proactive in making your manager aware of your ambitions and goals if you want a successful career. Too many of us, though, think our work should speak for itself. And our male colleagues would agree. But just in case their managers are too busy to notice, they ensure, through impression management tactics, that their performance is made more visible.

There is evidence that both men and women use impression management to influence upwards, but the tactics they use are different. Whereas women focus on developing relationships to establish contact with their managers, men take direct action to ensure, for example, that they ascertain and deliver their manager's objectives (as well as their own). And, not unexpectedly, this latter approach is more effective in drawing the boss's attention and approval.

Recipe for success

The route to career success is exemplified by the behaviour of young MBA graduate males. Compared with their female counterparts they:

- Use impression management tactics frequently and at an earlier stage in their careers.
- Build networks and take action to gain visibility.
- Ingratiate themselves by building relationships with supervisors.
- Volunteer for extra tasks (especially with the boss).
- Use keen, ready and attentive body language.
- Talk up their competence, contribution and achievements.
- Use self-promotion of their ambition and success.
- Look the part for the next promotional level.
- Move companies more often.
- Learn to be more adaptable and responsive to the corporate environment.

In return they are rewarded with an earlier start on their career path than young women, who are often reluctant to display these kinds of behaviours.

Women tend to begin to use impression management tactics around the mid career point, but, being late starters, they have difficulty catching up with their male peers who tend to deploy these tactics before the age of 30. Career breaks for motherhood and periods of part-time or flexible working may all conspire to

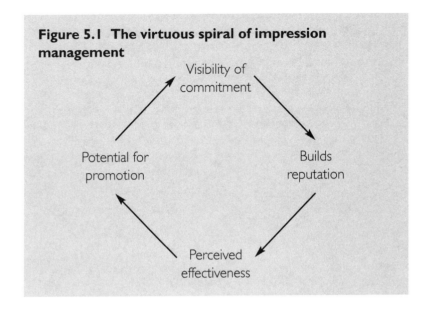

Figure 5.1 The virtuous spiral of impression management

Visibility of commitment

Potential for promotion

Builds reputation

Perceived effectiveness

hold back women's career development. And with informal rules within many companies about reaching a certain level in the hierarchy by a certain age, women who try to regenerate their careers by employing impression management tactics at a later stage may encounter resistance.

Pursuing impression management tactics can deliver significant career rewards and initiates a virtuous spiral of events (Figure 5.1). By increasing our visibility to the movers and shakers we enhance our reputation. Since this often gives us access to resources – because we have friends at court – our actual and perceived effectiveness as managers is enhanced. This in turn sends out clear signals about our promotability and differentiates us from the rest of our peers, which subsequently reinforces our motivation and effectiveness in employing impression management tactics.

By contrast, if we are unaware of the importance of self-promotion or are unwilling to adopt the required behaviours then this can create barriers to career advancement (Figure 5.2). Keeping our heads down and getting on with the job without making others aware of our achievements can lead to us being perceived as underperforming relative to our more proactive colleagues. This, in turn, is associated with lack of recognition for

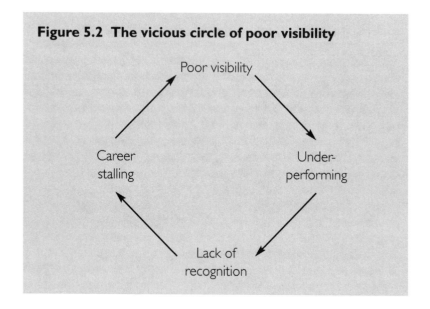

Figure 5.2 The vicious circle of poor visibility

our reputation and abilities, which disadvantages us in the next career round so that our progress stalls.

Self-presentation

Is climbing the corporate ladder a game? Absolutely. If you care about your career you should take these games seriously.[6]

The first key element in our impression management toolkit is to look the part, since the start point for business relationships whether with clients, with colleagues or with senior managers is the *first* impression we make. Like it or not they will quickly form a judgement about our professionalism, our credibility and the quality of work or service we are likely to deliver.

But, you may ask, how can someone decide these things at the first encounter? Quite simply, our professionalism is likely to be assessed on the basis of whether we are appropriately dressed – we need to be 'well turned out'. Confident posture and an intelligent and alert facial expression signal credibility, while careful grooming indicates attention to detail elsewhere – in our work and in the quality of service customers can expect. Finally, the way we shake hands, smile, make eye contact and greet the person helps them decide whether we are someone they want to employ or do business with. And all in thirty seconds or less.

The purpose of this section is to raise your awareness of self-presentation issues, suggest ways in which you can make a more favourable initial impression and help you formulate an action plan for improvement.

Why personal appearance is important

During the last decade numerous surveys were carried out among senior managers to determine what was important in career progression. Among the UK's top 300 companies, over 90 per cent of senior decision-makers agreed that personal appearance was the key factor in gaining employment. Companies expect their employees today to represent the culture and values in their marketing messages. An important employee role is to support promotional and public relations activity by demonstrating the company values through the way they dress and behave.

If you've taken the trouble to look smart and presentable, I'll know you will put the same amount of positivity and passion into the job.

Jennie Pailing, General Manager, The Sanctuary[7]

First impressions are derived from a combination of elements:

- Dress
- Grooming
- Body language and posture.

Dress

How we look in our business dress depends on the colour, style and fabric quality of our clothes. Some colours flatter our skin tone, giving us a healthy glow, whereas others make us look dull and drained. In order to determine your best colours, you might enjoy a session with an image consultant (details of how to find one can be found in the list of useful contacts at the end of the book), but you can also try the following do-it-yourself method: When trying on clothes, position yourself in good daylight and hold up some colours against your face (ask a friend to help)

- What is the effect on lines and shadows on the face (do they deepen or are they minimized)?
- Does the colour lift your complexion or make it duller?
- What do you see first – you or the colour?

Ideally, our best colours brighten our eyes and complexion and focus attention on the face (not on the clothes themselves), which is where it should be for business communication.

Colours for the business wardrobe

As a general rule, avoid the very deepest neutral and basic colours: black, deepest navy and charcoal, particularly with white. These tones can be draining on all but the strongest colouring, and it is a very high authority look (think of the police, judges, traffic wardens) that can be off-putting to those with whom we want to establish rapport.

Rather, to appear more approachable, choose mid-tones of navy, grey, stone or cocoa brown for your business suits worn with a lighter tone for coordinating tops.

Listed below are some qualities and the colours associated with them.

The psychology of colour – how to use its subtle power

It is beyond the scope of this book to explore in depth the full power of colour as it influences our lives. For the moment let us simply say that each colour has psychological associations that can reflect or influence our mood and frame of mind. For example, reds, oranges and yellows are warm and expansive and give a feeling of energy, excitement and joy. (Try adding a splash of yellow in your office or study as a mental stimulant.) Blues, indigos and purples, on the other hand, are cooler. They quieten the temperament and induce relaxation (and hence are excellent for decorating your bedroom walls). The psychology of colour is a language you can learn and use effectively in the way you dress in order to encourage certain responses from those with whom you interact.

Approachability

Signalled by pastels, soft pinks, peach and coral and by warm colours including tan, terracotta and rust. Avoid wearing all pastels or all pink, however, as this is a very low authority look.

Assertiveness/confidence

These are signalled by strong colour contrasts of black/purple/ red as well as black, grey or deep navy with bright or deep reds, berry colours or rich purple or violet; these can also convey glamour or drama, depending on the style of your clothes.

Authority

High contrasts of very dark with very light colours signal a claim to authority and control. But beware: in some circumstances this can appear threatening or it can look boring and conservative.

Businesslike

Dark blue, navy, grey or indigo with white or other light neutral tone but enlivened with some accent colour from any part of the palette (in a scarf, for example) give a businesslike impression, as can the basic blues, greens and purples, and the neutrals cream, stone, mushroom, slate and brown look good worn with richer pastel shades. Keep patterns fairly traditional (no flowers) and avoid anything wild.

Elegant

Deep, subdued and complex colours worn together suggest an understated elegance. Avoid anything too bright, garish or clashing. Staple colours will include ivory, charcoal, taupe, pewter, stone and oyster – all of which blend well and can be enlivened with rich colours like olive, jade, burgundy or crimson.

Sensitive

Colours in the purple, violet, lavender and periwinkle palette are perceived as artistic and intuitive. A touch of one of these colours can soften an otherwise hard or overformal look.

Negotiator

Deeper, softer tones of brown, warm beige, coffee and mushroom worn with other earth colours are comfortable and easy to relate to. Neutral greys have a similar effect. Ensure that you wear these colours in quality fabrics and that they are well tailored – nothing casual or unstructured or the look will be unprofessional. An accent of coral, brick red or a shade of turquoise or jade can break the monotony and add some dash.

Body shape – some guidelines

Anecdotal evidence suggests that the average woman has a worse body image than a disabled man. None of us is happy with our shape, but well-cut, well-chosen garments in the right fabric can hide a multitude of figure faults. So, next you need to assess your body shape:

- Wearing something close fitting (and in the privacy of your own room), look at your silhouette in a full-length mirror.
- Are you mainly angles or mostly curves – or, like many of us, a combination of both? (Look at your shoulders – are they straight or sloping? Do you have a defined waist or are

you more or less straight from shoulder to hip? Turning sideways do you have a curvy or a flat bottom?)

Angular body shapes look best in sharply tailored garments in crisp fabrics (poplin, wool gabardine, raw silk), which follow the lines and angles of the body. *Curvy figures* need softer tailoring with rounded shapes and lines, in drapey fabrics (wool or silk jersey, crepe). *The combination figure* – a blend of angles and curves – needs good tailoring executed in softer fabrics.

Shopping for your business wardrobe

Your business wardrobe is an investment in your career – having been an image consultant for some years I am still appalled that people fail to recognize this and consequently underspend dramatically on their personal appearance. Lack of self-esteem, and a readiness to find other priorities on which to spend money, prevent many women managers from looking their best. A quick glance across at our continental and transatlantic sisters should provide a lesson in dressing to impress: you need to show people what you think you are worth. And one of the most important lessons to understand is that our attitudes to ourselves – conveyed through our dress and demeanour – condition the way others respond to us. We touched on this in Chapter Three when we looked at female sex role stereotypes and the myths surrounding women at work. It just remains to reiterate that if we look like victims that's how we will be treated.

I always look my best. I've never dressed in grey business suits –
I love strong colours and dangly earrings and work them into
my business attire whenever possible.
                                        Leigh Woods, CEO at ntl

Before you start shopping, audit and organize your existing wardrobe:

■ Bag up everything you haven't worn for 12 months –
   because it's too small/too big, out of date or you hate it. (Put
   it in the attic if you can't steel yourself to give it away.)

■ Set aside whatever needs mending or cleaning and make an action point to sort it out.

■ Look at what you are left with and make a list of priorities.

TIP
To help you establish your priorities, keep a diary for a few weeks recording:
1. Where you went
2. What you wore
3. What you wish you had worn.[8]

Some ground rules

■ Always buy the best quality you can afford. Build a fund in a separate account to finance your business wardrobe.

■ Invest in fabrics with a high percentage of natural fibre – wool, cotton, silk or linen (with a percentage of manmade fibre for resilience), as these wear and dry clean better and creases drop out more quickly.

For a suggested shopping list, beginners should refer to the 'Levels of Dress for Women' sheet at the end of this chapter.

TIP
If you need help shopping, use the services of a personal shopper – a free service in most major department stores. Telephone your favourite store for an appointment. (Debenhams, House of Fraser and many other department stores offer this service.)

The suit is dead ... Long live the suit

Despite pronouncements by the fashion police in recent seasons, rumours of the death of the suit are grossly exaggerated. It will always be a must for business, except possibly in some media circles and within the fashion industry itself. So invest in some beautifully cut three-piece combinations – jackets with the option of trousers and skirts – that are good value and offer flexibility. Recent tribunal cases have, in theory, definitively established a woman's right to wear trousers to work.

However, there may be occasions – when you want to emphasize your femininity or when dealing with very traditional clients – when you need to wear a skirt. Ensure that it fits properly – can you get two fingers inside the waistband and does it move easily over the hips? If not, it is too tight and will cause problems by riding up when you sit down. This may expose more thigh than is appropriate in the business context – distracting attention from what you are saying and undermining your credibility. It may also cause you to sit very still and constrict your movements, which undermines your power. You must be free to occupy 'your' space and adopt powerful body language (of which more later). If your movements are overly restricted by your clothing, then you may appear to others as a low-energy person.

It is important to rotate your suits each day to allow the fabric to rest and air. Have them cleaned regularly. Invest in a good clothes brush and use it each day to remove dust and lint.

Shoes too need to rest between wearing to dry out. Invest in some shoe trees to help them regain their shape after wear and apply polish as you take them off, when the leather is still warm and can absorb the waxes more readily.

Accessories

To quote Patsy in *Absolutely Fabulous*: 'You can never have too many belts, bags and gloves'. The creative use of accessories is a clever way in which to enliven an otherwise ordinary business suit. Again, European and American businesswomen show great flair when accessorizing their outfits and to help you stand out from the crowd you need to follow their example.

Quality must be your watchword: silk for scarves, leather not only for shoes but also for bags, briefcases, wallets and watch straps (no plastic). Jewellery and other accessories state your worth to others, so avoid high fashion or romantic jewellery (lockets and hearts on neck chains, for example) as well as flowery hair ornaments and anything oversized. Keep the look subtle and in proportion. Avoid overkill – a striking scarf and earrings *or* brooch *or* necklace would be sufficient. So don't overdo it by wearing more than two 'statement' items at a time.

Stretching the budget

We have talked of having a special business wardrobe account, but how can you make your budget go further?

First, by pre-shopping before the sales to identify from your priorities list what you want to buy. Choose the clothes you want, try them on and make a note of them. Then later, when the sales start, you can simply take the clothes straight to the cash desk and avoid time-wasting queues at the fitting rooms. This also avoids panic and impulse buying (remember all that stuff bagged up in the attic).

Secondly, visit factory retail outlets (Bicester Village, Cheshire Oaks) where designer and quality labels are available at bargain prices. *But*, shop selectively and remember, a bargain is not a bargain unless it fits and feels right.

TIP
Ask friends and relatives for gift vouchers for Christmas and birthdays, redeemable at your favourite department store.

Personal grooming strategy

A business suit is not important (in my work), but good grooming is. Dirty shoes, greasy hair and chewing gum are my three pet hates.

Andrew Collinge, businessman
and celebrity hairdresser[9]

We are all familiar with some of the most common turn-offs – body and foot odour, dandruff, bad breath, tatty nails and scruffy shoes – so we will not dwell on the obvious, but move on to some more subtle issues.

Your hair and face

These are visible at all times and should count among your most valuable assets. You need to invest time and money in the cut and condition of your hair, so here are some dos and don'ts:

■ Have your hair cut regularly in a reputable salon by a stylist who takes time to get to know your personality, your lifestyle and how adept you are at managing your hair.

■ Never colour your hair at home – have it done professionally (it's expensive but the results justify it).

■ Avoid long hair hanging over your face and complicated styles that may collapse during the day.

Your skin should radiate vitality, so get into a routine of cleansing, toning and nourishing night and morning. Remember all the traditional advice about drinking plenty of water, avoiding too much coffee, tea, smoking and alcohol and getting plenty of sleep. Use a moisturizer with sun protection, keep out of direct sunlight and off the sun bed – UV rays are the prime cause of skin damage and premature ageing.

Facial hair should be professionally waxed, bleached or removed by electrolysis. Keep your eyebrows tidy, but avoid excessive plucking – if in doubt, see your beautician.

Keep smiling

Your smile is one of your most important business assets and to ensure you smile confidently your teeth must be in good condition. Visit a dentist regularly and, if you have discoloured, chipped or missing teeth think about cosmetic dentistry to remedy the problem. A couple of years ago I ran into one of the secretaries where I was then working. She had been absent for a few weeks and I was immediately struck by how different she looked. I asked her what the change was and she replied that she had recently had her front teeth capped. They had been severely discoloured, rendering her very self-conscious, to the extent that she rarely smiled and often put her hand in front of her mouth when she spoke. She had saved like mad for private dentistry and now she felt – and looked – like a new woman.

To spray or not to spray?

We take personal freshness as a given, but what about fragrance? If you love perfume (as I do) then use only the lightest fragrance

– try an eau de toilette without alcohol. Heat intensifies the smell of perfume, so be especially careful in summer or in central heating not to overpower people with your scent. I once read a survey of the perfumes people would least like to be stuck in a lift with. Imagine my chagrin when the one I was wearing was top of the list.

The great make-up debate

Some years ago, during my MBA programme, an image consultant ran a short session for the women students. At one point she asked us to take out and apply our lipsticks. Few of the women even had a lipstick and still fewer knew how to put it on. This raised my awareness of the fact that wearing make up is both a generational and a social issue. Younger, educated women tend not to wear make-up. It is not their 'thing', too girlie, anti-feminist. This is a pity, because there is strong evidence that women who wear make-up earn more and get promoted faster. So perhaps some of us need to rethink our stance on this one. In relation to business dress, the unmade-up face looks inappropriate. Next to the deeper colours and formal lines of a suit it seems unfinished. This can lower your status and lessen your impact. Therefore, if you don't already do so, think about a discrete touch of make-up as the finishing touch.

TOP TIP

If you lack confidence in choosing and applying make-up, visit a department store or larger branch of Boots for a free make-up lesson and advice on what to buy. If you set some priorities and assign a budget, you won't be intimidated into buying things you don't need.

Corporate entertainment

If you can't dress for success, at least dress for trying.
Lyn Alpern and Esther Blumenfeld[10]

Whether you issue the invitation or receive it, attending a corporate event still has broadly the same purpose: it is an opportunity for both parties – host and guest – to project a different image and move the business relationship on to a new level.

One important note: the apparent informality of these occasions is only superficial. You are there representing your organization and you are still on duty. So resist the temptation to indulge in too much alcohol – however freely it may flow – in order to maintain your control and dignity.

A few other ground rules:

- **Dress to impress**   Your business 'uniform' looks safe and unimaginative and may give the message that you haven't made an effort. Remember: the way you look is the way you will be treated.
- **Don't wear anything too formal**   You are trying to create rapport on a new level.
- **Don't economize**   These events are important to your career, so show a little subtle panache with some stylish jewellery or other accessories.
- **Wear something you feel good in** so you appear confident and at ease.
- If the invitation does not specify a dress code and you are uncertain what to wear, telephone the host and find out.

Avoiding the pitfalls

Earlier I referred to the fact that you might sometimes want to emphasize your femininity. I feel that some of you may have winced at the thought. But many successful women would argue that your femininity can work for you and that therefore you should not shrink from using the fact that you are a woman to get what you want.

Now it is important here to clarify this and to differentiate femininity from sexuality. Being feminine is about being aware of your power as a woman: your communication skills, your ability to win people over, your intuitive capabilities and your concern for the feelings and wishes of others. And an attractive appearance is no handicap. Again, research shows that good-looking people have a natural advantage, and so you need to be aware of and to capitalize on the fact that your appearance can influence people's decisions.

Using your femininity is about getting what you want without letting others feel they've been cajoled. Being easy on the eye doesn't hurt either.

Moya, senior teacher

Being professional though means not sending out the wrong signals to clients and colleagues. Short skirts, stilettos, plunging necklines, flowing hair, elaborate jewellery, heavy perfume and dramatic make-up are all to be avoided. Displaying your sexuality at work (even unconsciously) discounts your credibility and makes you undervalued. Male colleagues and clients will be distracted (and get the wrong idea) while women may feel resentful.

You have to be so careful about the perceptions of your behaviour. Unscrupulous men will deliberately misread your intentions and accuse you of flirting so they can undermine your professionalism.

Ruth (24), training to be a barrister

Some years ago I ran a training programme for middle managers. The time came for presentations after a particular syndicate exercise and a young woman got up to speak on behalf of her group. The content was excellent and her delivery very polished – she was obviously a person of considerable ability. But the attention of the predominantly male audience was focused throughout on her (very shapely) legs. She was wearing a tight lycra mini skirt, which completely undermined her performance.

To summarize then, looking attractive and professional means focusing on the fit and quality of your clothing and building a core wardrobe of stylish, contemporary items. This means that your clothes and accessories make a passing reference to fashion but do not follow it slavishly. Interestingly, the fashion icons of the 1950s – Grace Kelly, Audrey Hepburn – who epitomize timeless elegance and femininity, are now back in style. Dressing like a lady is 'in'. For some of us it was never 'out'.

To conclude this section we quote the commonsense advice offered by Rabbi Julia Neuberger, CEO of The King's Fund:

Go to a personal shopper or image consultant. Get your hair cut regularly. Find your own style and stick with it.

Self-awareness

'Know thyself' should perhaps be the watchwords of every aspiring manager. Self-knowledge and a clear understanding of what makes us tick are essential if we are to be happy and successful. One of the key issues, of course, is what makes us truly happy and how we define success. Insight into these things is a prerequisite if we are to achieve fulfilling lives. One of the best pieces of advice I was ever given was: 'Before you start climbing the career ladder, make sure it's leaning against the right wall.'

If we unpick this there are several implications. First, are you doing the right kind of work that closely matches your competences and temperament, enabling you to shine? Secondly, are you in the right kind of organization with a culture and values you don't simply accept, but strongly advocate and identify with? And finally, how important is it to you to have a high-flying career? Do you want your life to focus primarily on work or are there other priorities in your life – family, friends, travel, hobbies, etc. that you don't simply want to accommodate, but would like to devote significant time to?

Some of these questions are dealt with in the next chapter, when we consider the major challenges for women at work and how to deal with them. But at the end of this chapter I have included some exercises to set the scene for your overall action plan. The first requires you to take stock in terms of your attitudes to personal growth and the barriers preventing it. The others relate to raising your self-awareness through self-knowledge and feedback from other people, and assessing the match between your skills and competences and the work you are currently involved in. I hope you find them helpful.

Self-promotion

Seeking to impress one's manager regarding one's commitment may seem unnatural to many women, as well as unnecessary, but managers are busy people, and competitors may be making sure that their extra efforts to deliver the manager's goals are being noticed and rewarded.[11]

We have already discussed how difficult many women find this issue. At work we tend to underplay our achievements both through the way we attribute them to others – 'It was a team effort' – and through our self-deprecating language: 'Oh, it was nothing'; 'Any one could have done it'; 'I was just lucky'.

But if we want to get on in our careers we need to tackle this activity and become skilful at it. We have to recognize that women are perceived to be less committed at work than men, despite there being no evidence to support this view. So how do senior managers – the people we need to impress – define work commitment and what are women doing wrong when they try to communicate it?

Everyone's career is their own job.

LeighWoods, CEO at ntl

What top managers expect

In addition to readily observable behaviours – delivering quality work, getting involved and putting yourself out – senior managers list some less tangible qualities: being proactive/using initiative, being ready for challenge, being creative and being business aware. Interestingly, men's definitions of commitment are more closely aligned to those of senior managers than are the definitions given by women.[12] Our 'organizational citizenship' – whereby we conscientiously follow the rules, 'go the extra mile', are courteous and behave with sensitivity and consideration – though worthy, is less visible to managers than the tactics employed by men. They deliver their managers' goals and publicize their own achievements. Not all men, however, are innately gifted self-promoters (despite appearances to the contrary). Some men find it difficult, but most learn to overcome their reluctance because, early in their careers, they are made aware that self-promotion is the way forward. They quickly assess how decisions are made in the organization and where the real power lies. To ensure visibility they regularly speak to their managers about their work and their achievements.

Visible commitment
means faster development

Women may also be reluctant to advertise their commitment because to do so may seem cynical and self-serving. But whether people genuinely want to do the right things or simply want to be seen to do them, the end result is the same and both sets of behaviour are identical to an observer – they both signal commitment and only the motivation is different.

If you do things well, do them better. Be daring, be first, be different, be just.

Anita Roddick

Getting your commitment noticed would be less critical were it not for the fact that visibility is directly linked to getting the right kind of development assignments. Many women readers will be aware already that if you don't tell your managers explicitly that you want to be involved in challenging projects or new areas of work, they will assume you are not interested. (Even when you make your interest clear, however, you may not get the work you want if you have not already established you are ready for a challenge by making your manager aware of previous achievements.) The experience of successfully completing challenging work in turn builds your career capital, enhances your reputation and raises your profile. This puts you in pole position on the promotion track. So the importance of visibility is not in dispute. It only remains for women to decide what they want to do about it.

Women are often too cautious – they won't speak up and ask challenging questions. They are conditioned not to offend.

Professor Susan Greenwood,
Director of the Royal Institution

Some strategies to consider

Ultimately the decision whether or not to start demonstrating your commitment in more visible ways is entirely yours. But listed below are some of the strategies that have been found to be effective in raising managers' awareness of the commitment of their people:

■ Be aware of how decisions are made in the organization – both through formal and informal channels – and know who holds the power.

■ Talk to and show your manager your results.

■ Ask questions to establish a dialogue and stimulate discussion so that you can express your views.

■ Push for career development and make it clear you are ready for promotion.

■ Stand up and say what you think to get yourself noticed.

■ Take credit when it is due to you and do not understate your contribution.

■ Monitor the impression you are having on others by asking for feedback and modifying you behaviour accordingly.

■ Do not rely too heavily on your manager being able to recognize your talent without some help – he or she may be too busy.

I mentioned earlier the importance of establishing rapport with your manager and that this is easier if there is some common background, experience and interests on which to build. In organizations dominated by traditional male values this may be difficult for women, who lack the time or inclination to network by playing golf or nipping down to the pub after work to talk football and 'bond'. Though women are good at forming relationships, the degree to which your boss and other influential men will feel comfortable with you may be limited, and so you may need to resort to other tactics to win their approval and support.

Effective self-presentation is about treading a fine line between fitting in with the group and differentiating yourself sufficiently from your peers to ensure that the organization spots your potential and pushes you forward on the career track. One approach to helping you stand out from the crowd is to develop your charisma.

Developing your charisma

If you have it [charisma] you don't need to have anything else;
and if you don't have it, it doesn't much matter what else you have.
J. M. Barrie[13]

Charisma is notoriously difficult to define – like nailing the proverbial jelly to the wall. Barrie's statement seems to imply that people are born with charisma, that it's a talent some are lucky enough to posses while the rest of us look on in awe and envy. There is certainly a grain of truth here, but each of us has the capacity to influence others through the force of our personality and enthusiasm, if we can only learn to unlock our inner power.

An analysis of how charismatic people behave is helpful in identifying ways in which we can heighten our own appeal. Think of someone you regard as charismatic (and, like beauty, this is in the eye of the beholder). We can probably predict with some accuracy that the person you have chosen will be:

- More animated
- More outgoing and interactive
- More emotional and passionate
- A natural actor.

Animation

Charismatic people expend more energy than the average person. Showing more animation gives them a greater chance of influencing their audience favourably.

TIP

Develop a more animated facial expression to show enthusiasm. Make sure your diet and exercise regime is keeping you well supplied with energy.

Interaction

They listen more eagerly and respond more enthusiastically to others.

Emotion

They do not hide their emotions because they know that human connections are made more easily on the emotional level than on an intellectual plane. Injecting emotion into your argument makes it more compelling to others.

Acting

Charismatic people use their natural gifts to captivate attention. They are powerful speakers, unafraid of an audience, who use their voices to great effect.

From general characteristics, let us move to the particular. What specific behaviours and attitudes can we identify among charismatic people? A useful article appeared in *Fortune* magazine some time ago and we draw on this for the next section.[14]

The message: simplify and exaggerate

Charismatic people know that messages must be simplified in order to travel. We live in the era of the sound bite. Few people have time for detail and many do not have the intellectual capacity to absorb it. If you want to make your mark in meetings and presentations, you must learn to distil complex ideas into simple messages that everyone can quickly understand and remember. Symbols, analogies, metaphors and stories are powerful aids to understanding and help you get your message across to a wide audience – from senior managers to the caretakers and cleaners.

Do it once. Get it right. Go home.
Kate Barker, CBI quoting her former boss
whom she much admired for not
perpetuating a macho long hours culture

It is basic principles and simple messages that motivate people, not masses of detail, so keep your communications succinct and memorable.

Romanticize risk

Charismatics are optimists who relish challenge and are prepared to put themselves on the line. They are evangelical about their cause and speak, not only to people's minds, but also to their hearts to enrol people to their mission.

It's better to try and fail than to do nothing.
Lena Bjorck, MD Inn or Out

Challenge the status quo

A risky one this for many women, but charismatics are rebels who fight convention. Their behaviour may be seen as idiosyncratic, but stems from their intense passion and belief in what they do. By asking original and penetrating questions when listening to the views of others they show they are not afraid to speak out, even when this goes against the flow. Their success comes from their ability to pull the emotional levers that get people on board.

Speak out. Take the risk – if they don't want you as you are, go elsewhere if your value isn't appreciated.

Martha Lane Fox, Joint MD of lastminute.com

Set challenges for others

Leadership and managing teams is about challenging others to test their intellect, courage and mettle so that they stretch themselves to achieve.

Everyone on the team has to do well through the support, opportunities and frameworks created by the manager ... But I have zero tolerance for people who don't care and can't be bothered.

Colette Graham, Head of International
Communications, Centrica plc

Walk a mile in someone else's shoes

This is where women score over men, in their ability to empathize and see things from another's perspective. They readily adopt the mindset of 'If I were X, how would I think about this?'

Treat people as people, not as machines – be aware of their personal concerns. Small gestures go a long way.

Joy Kingsley, Managing Partner, Pannone solicitors

No compromise

So how should we put all these things together to raise our game? And how can we do so without compromising our integrity? Orit Gadiesh, former Chair of Bain & Co., a leading US consulting company, refers to her internal compass and the nautical concept of 'true North' (as opposed to magnetic North which varies around the globe). The key is to hold firm to a set of guiding principles that direct you to what is 'true and right'. Charisma can be a positive or a negative force. To benefit ourselves and others it must be anchored in what we believe to be right and good.

Charisma without substance is a dangerous thing.

Kim Campbell[15]

Body language

'Body language' in this context refers to all the forms of non-verbal communication that human beings engage in. And it is a fact that more human communication is made through gesture, expression, posture, position and distance than by any other means. Human beings are essentially visual animals – we receive nearly 90 per cent of the information about our environment through our eyes. What we refer to as perception and intuition derive from the gut feelings engendered by our observation and interpretation of the (often unconscious) non-verbal clues we receive from others.

So finely attuned are we to the behaviour of others that we can quickly spot any lack of congruence between gestures and the spoken word, between what a person says and the signals they often unknowingly give away. What is more, if we are aware that the words do not match the accompanying gestures, then we always believe the non-verbal signals. They carry five times the impact of the spoken word when the two are in conflict.

All this is, of course, interesting in itself, but what has it to do with personal image and impression management? The purpose of studying body language – both in theory and in practice – is twofold:

1 To improve our personal style by ensuring we practise open, positive gestures and eliminate negative signals.
2 To make us more sensitive to the non-verbal signals of others.

So, by raising our awareness of how our own body language may be interpreted, we can take steps to ensure we project a positive image and make ourselves more acceptable to others. We also become conscious of other people's behaviour, enabling us to detect positive or negative signals and respond appropriately.

Creating a professional presence through positive body language links back to the previous section about charisma, since signals, like confident eye contact and animated facial expression, are part of the charismatic's toolkit.

Some words of caution are necessary before we proceed with the topic. Gestures must be viewed in the context of time, place, circumstances and any other accompanying gestures – the person giving a limp handshake, for example, may be disabled or arthritic rather than simply ineffectual.

We are also trying to understand a language not decipher individual 'words', so we need to look at groups of behaviours – 'gesture clusters' as they are called – in order to understand what is going on. And we need to be aware of congruence – do the gestures and words match or conflict in terms of the message they are transmitting? For example, beware of anyone who adopts a very judgemental pose (steepling the hands and looking down the nose) while at the same time telling you he or she sympathizes with your viewpoint.

Can you fake it?

During impression management workshops we are often asked whether it is possible to fake body language. The answer is: not really. Trying to fake it is an exhausting process (ask any actor) and certain 'microgestures' – pupil dilation, breathing and heart rate, blushing and sweating – conspire to give you away. These are controlled by the autonomic nervous system, and we cannot override this.

Creating a professional presence

The purpose of studying body language is to learn to use positive gestures and eliminate negative signals in order to make others more comfortable. We also need to be more sensitive to the non-verbal signals of others if we want to project a positive image and establish rapport. This is extremely important in business communication and listed below are some positive and negative signals to be aware of:

Positive signals	Negative signals
■ Sustaining eye contact	■ Fidgeting with the face
■ Open palm gestures	■ Nervousness
■ Relaxed posture	■ Fiddling with objects
■ Being still	■ Pointing
■ Using 'your' space	■ Not using 'your' space.

The ability to make and sustain eye contact – without of course staring people down – is an important component in making a striking first impression. Our eyes are said to be the windows of our souls and if we can make our expression open, intelligent and friendly this shows confidence.

Body movement is important in signalling how much you are in control – it is said that powerful people move more slowly and speak more slowly. They are also not afraid to occupy their rightful space. Some women are inclined to sit or stand in a rather constrained fashion – sometimes because of their clothing or because they are shy and uncomfortable being on public view. But remember: the ability to present yourself as someone special can convince other people that you are and encourage them to treat you well. So practise an upright, confident posture and move with assurance. Avoid standing or sitting with arms folded or with your arm diagonally across your body (to protect your vital organs). These gestures are defence mechanisms.

Confidence tricks

To build your confidence, wear your best colours with at least a splash of something bright to draw attention, especially in a group of men. You want to be noticed, not overlooked and you are making a statement about what you are worth, not saying, 'Don't mind me'. We have already emphasized the importance of wearing something you feel good in (eventually all your clothes should feel like this) and avoiding anything too tight or too short (that constrains movement and prevents you using strong positive gestures).

Before entering a room – and especially after a journey – practise some deep breathing and relaxation exercises to get rid of tension, especially around the shoulders and neck, so you do not appear awkward and embarrassed.

On entering a room, avoid defensive gestures (arm across the body) even if you feel a little threatened. Stand straight, chin lifted slightly to show confidence and as you walk, allow your arms to swing gently (rather then holding them stiffly at your sides). Wearing shoes with a small heel (especially if you are petite) will give you poise and help you hold yourself elegantly.

It is important to practise your business handshake and make sure it says the right things about you. You can do this with friends or colleagues and get some feedback so you can improve. Your handshake is a powerful non-verbal introduction and you need to be able to use it confidently.

The business handshake signals:
- Who you are
- Your status
- Your intentions (professional).

Open gestures

In meetings, practise open palm gestures (palm up) to signal credibility, openness and honesty and look for similar gestures in others that show they are opening up to you. By contrast, concealing the hands (in pockets, under arms) can signal concealment, deceit or withholding (information, cooperation, etc.).

Mirroring

A great way to show empathy and agreement and to establish rapport is by using mirroring techniques, both in your body language and in your spoken language. We mentioned this technique earlier, and reflecting back the other person's feelings and emotions verbally can be supported by copying their positive gestures. Leaning forward eagerly when they do so, nodding and active listening, returning a smile or an eyebrow flash all help to make others feel more comfortable by signalling that we like them and *are* like them. Mirroring positive gestures in this way puts people in a relaxed and receptive frame of mind during both social and business interactions.

Women rarely use gestures of dominance or superiority either with peers or subordinates, and it is important not to be intimidated when men attempt to dominate using these tactics – bone crushing handshakes; spreading out their body and possessions beyond their own legitimate space; leaning back, arms folded to disconcert; sneering; looking superior; interrupting and talking us down. These issues are dealt with in Chapter Eight where we suggest some coping strategies you may care to adopt when you encounter such challenges.

Putting it all together

Finally, when you do observe negative body language in others, take steps to relax their negative posture. Unless you do so you will not be able to deal with the negative thoughts and attitudes that lie behind the gestures. Negative physical behaviour reinforces and locks in the negative mental state. So, when, for example, we meet resistance signalled by a person's arms being firmly folded, the body leaning back and the prospect literally 'looking down his or her nose', we need to find some way to involve the person physically. For example, we might take out a report, a brochure or other documents and lean part way towards the person – taking care not to invade his or her space. The document is kept just far enough away so that the person has to unfold his or her arms and lean forward to see what it is we are pointing to. Once we have lured the person out of the negative posture we can start to interact and ask questions to find out what is causing the resistance. But we cannot begin this process until we unlock the body posture.

The key issues to remember about body language are:

- Remember to look for gesture clusters not isolated clues (arms folded can signify cold, for example).
- Refer to the context before making a judgement (the person who stays very still may have difficulty moving, rather than be lacking in energy).

■ Unlock your own negative postures and open up to others.

■ When you observe negative signals in others take steps to relax the negative posture.

■ Do not be intimidated by archetypal male body language – it's just a game they play and you don't have to take it seriously.

In Chapter Eight we build on this section when we discuss some interesting tactics for making yourself 'irresistible' to others.

Summary

The need to manage the impression we create at work is inescapable. To ensure you make a greater positive impact:

■ Know that the way others perceive you is as important as how you actually perform.

■ Take positive steps to influence how others see you through careful attention to your appearance, style and body language.

■ Practise self-promotion through strategies to gain you greater visibility and credibility.

■ Continually reassess the effectiveness of your personal and leadership style and career development strategies.

In the next chapter we look at some of the big issues and challenges confronting women in their career and lives, and examine some of the work/life options you might consider.

Pause for reflection

Workbook Exercise I A framework for change

The focus of this chapter is change. For some of you this may imply a fairly fundamental re-think about your frame of reference and the way you behave. This, in turn, requires you to move out of your comfort zone and overcome some barriers to change. These barriers usually fall in to two categories:

Self	*Others*
▧ Lack of time	▧ What will they say?
▧ Cost	▧ How will they react?
▧ Effort	▧ Will they reject me?

Of course, when you change it requires others to move out of their comfort zones too in order to adjust to the new you. But, to what extent do we create our own constraints? The way we raise objections to change is defensive: though they appear logical and rational (cost and time), they also invite sympathy and deflect criticism. We need to unpick what's happening here. Take the word 'can't':

When I say 'I can't' I really mean
▧ I don't like the idea.
OR
▧ I can't be bothered.

Recognize that you can do it if you want to
▧ If other people can build empires, you, too, can find the time, money and motivation necessary to realize your potential.

Enlarge your comfort zone

- Feel the fear and do it anyway[16]
- Feeling uncomfortable means you are pushing at the barriers holding you back from learning new behaviours.

New behaviours are vulnerable so:

- Be positive and set goals for yourself.*
- Visualize what you want to achieve.*
- Practise positive self-talk.*
- Reward yourself for your achievements.*
- Don't give up when you experience setbacks.*

Change the way you see yourself:

- See yourself as someone with a successful and positive professional image and you will become that person.*

As your comfort zone enlarges, so the time, effort and commitment required to practise effective impression management will no longer limit your behaviour.

Workbook Exercise II   Gaining greater self-awareness

Exercise 1   Knowing yourself

Take a sheet of paper and write down the words and phrases you think best describe your personality, temperament, behaviour and preferences.

Re-read the list, refining what you have written and remembering to include the detail as well as the general picture.

The next stage is to get feedback from a trusted source – but be prepared to be criticized as well as flattered.

Exercise 2   How others see you

Ask a friend to help by writing down what comes to mind when they think of you – they may interpret your qualities negatively or positively since there is no such thing as total objectivity.

*Sports champions and other high achievers use these techniques.

Getting a second or third opinion will allow you to compare notes and gain a balanced perspective.

Finally, compare your notes and the feedback from others and decide the priorities for your change action plan.

How I see myself:

_____

_____

_____

_____

_____

How others see me:

_____

_____

_____

_____

_____

Priorities for change:

1. _____

2. _____

3. _____

4. _____

5. _____

Workbook Exercise III   Auditing your skills and competences

Take some time to reflect about your skills, experience and qualifications and list out:

What you excel at	What you are good at	What you get by on

Underline or highlight the competences you are majoring on in your current work.

Draw up a list of action points to ensure that, in future, you major on what you excel at:

_____

_____

_____

_____

_____

Levels of dress for women

Level one

▓ Skirt suit in deep colour with matching skirt and jacket, styled conservatively or on simple contemporary lines. Worn with classic court shoes and tights, simple jewellery and light or contrasting blouse or top.

Level two

▓ Skirt suit in stronger colour or sharper cut.
▓ Classic, matching dress and jacket.

■ Classic trouser suit in deep colour.

■ Coordinating jacket and skirt in classic style.

Level three

■ Skirt with shirt, blouse or classic twin set (matching top and cardigan).

■ Deep, tailored trousers with shirt or top.

Level four

■ Casual sweater/blouse/top with casual skirt or trousers.

■ Sleeveless dress.

■ Sporty tops and pants.

It is the convention in business always to try to dress one level higher than your clients, in order to show respect and to demonstrate that you have made an effort. Levels one or two are the norm in many business environments – though, increasingly, there is a move to dress down within the office and to adopt a more casual approach. 'Dress down Friday' is gradually becoming acceptable from Monday to Thursday as well, though many find it difficult to adopt a less formal style for work. As a woman, it is important to remember that dress still denotes authority. So avoid the sleeveless look – even in warm weather: more flesh on display equals less credibility I'm sorry to say. For formal meetings, always have a jacket handy to slip on when you want to command respect.

Within your own organization, look at those in authority and power. How do they dress? If you are unhappy with them as role models or there are too few women to give the lead, then develop your own look, one that singles you out from the crowd as an individual with taste and discrimination. You don't have to look like one of the herd, but you do need to look stylish and well groomed.

Notes

1 Singh and Vinnicombe, 'Managing the promotion of high commitment/high performance through impression management strategies: a study of male and female managers', 16th EGOS Colloquium, June 2000. And Singh and Vinnicombe, 'Gender and impression management strategies: managing the good opinions held by others for career success', British Academy of Management Conference, September 2000.

2 Kelly Services research, Graeme Leach, *Tomorrow's Work – A Report Into the Future of the Way We Work*, Kelly Services, September 2000.

3 Gowler and Legge, 'Rhetoric in bureaucratic careers: managing the meaning of success', in *Handbook of Career Theory*, Cambridge University Press, 1989, cited by Singh and Vinnicombe.

4 Susan Vinnicombe and Hilary Harris, featured in *People Management*, January 2000.

5 Ibid.

6 M. A. McCormach, *What They Don't Teach You at Harvard Business School*, HarperCollins, 1986.

7 Quoted in *Cosmopolitan*, November 2000.

8 With acknowledgements to Mary Spillane, *Presenting Yourself – A Personal Image Guide for Women*, third edition, Piatkus, 1996.

9 McCormach, op. cit.

10 Cited by Carol Turkington, *The Quotable Woman*, McGraw-Hill, 2000.

11 Val Singh and Susan Vinnicombe, 'If you've got it, flaunt it. Is visibility through impression management the key to unlocking negative perceptions of women managers' commitment?' presented to the 8th International Women in Leadership Conference, November 1999.

12 Ibid.

13 Cited in *What Every Woman Knows*, Act I.

14 Patricia Sellers, 'What exactly is charisma?' *Fortune*, vol. 133, no. 1, 1998.

15 Cited in *The Quotable Woman*, op. cit.

16 Susan Jeffers, *Feel the Fear and Do It Anyway*, sixth edition, Random House, 1997.

6

The big issues

Introduction

'What do women want?' is a question frequently asked in the media these days. Any attempt to answer this at the start of a new millennium is no easy task, when women's attitudes, lifestyles and expectations are rapidly changing. Avon – the international cosmetics company – however, commissioned a Global Women's Survey,[1] the key findings from which were that, in confronting their life challenges, three factors would significantly improve women's lives:

- Greater financial independence.
- Equal job opportunities.
- The ability to start up a business.

The consensus among the women interviewed was (unsurprisingly) that women are more valued if they earn their own money: they command greater respect within the family and their husbands seek their advice and offer help with the housework and childcare. It was apparent that women's working and professional lives were closely linked and that this was causing their expectations to rise with respect to:

- The need for greater flexibility at work to accommodate family responsibilities.
- Their desire for employer/employee partnerships and some shared vision.
- Opportunities for women to exploit their personal characteristics (organizational skills; creativity; people orientation; communication skills).

The research feedback showed that women everywhere possess high levels of self-esteem, and are therefore ready to play a more significant role, both in business and in society. One conclusion the report drew from this is that businesses today must reinvent themselves to take account of the fact that the world is increasingly defined by women's changing needs and their growing economic power.

But the other side of the coin is that women themselves need to define what form they want this 'significant role' to take. Which brings us back to our opening question and the answer it begs: what women want depends on which women you talk to. Some want to focus single-mindedly and to go as far and as fast as they possibly can in their careers. Others want greater diversity and the option to combine some form of paid work with bringing up a family. And then there are those who want to be full-time mothers, at least while their children are small.

In this chapter I want to offer readers a framework for thinking through some of these career–life choices. These are the big issues that confront women today, and I would like to try to help you decide your best options by exploring the implications of those issues and the possible consequences of the choices you might make.

Career versus job

Given that women's hopes and expectations for their careers vary widely and that their capacity to fulfil these may be constrained by many factors (including childbearing, dual career issues and wider family responsibilities), what kinds of career patterns do most women follow and how will these match the world of work in the future? What choices will be open to us and how far will our need for diversity and flexibility disadvantage us?

The issue of whether women are prepared for the demands of a modern career is considered in a research paper by Maureen Wood.[2] She proposes the view that typical female employment patterns – flexible; part time and temporary; characterized by transferable skills – are what are required in today's economic climate. Restructuring in the workplace, the need for greater employee flexibility and transferable skills that are constantly updated, as well as the shift to flexible working, are accelerating change on many fronts and redefining our understanding of the word 'career'.

As Wood points out, most definitions of 'career' are based on a male employment model: a (normally) continuous sequence of work, experience and advancement. Many women, however, move in and out of employment according to their changing circumstances. So Wood suggests an alternative view, that of an 'individual' career, comprising separate but related experience and including unpaid work (like being a carer), but excluding the idea of advancement. With considerable insight she has encapsulated the way women's needs, values, attitudes and aspirations change over time by formulating a more relevant definition of 'career'. She calls this personal perspective the 'career in the head'.

... Important differences in career paths and patterns between men and women mean men represent the past and women the future.[3]

We have seen in Chapter Three and elsewhere that, because male work values and roles predominate in most organizations, women are seen to lack commitment and loyalty, and are therefore perceived as less promotable. Wood argues that the diverse roles from which many women derive their identity are complementary to the way they see career fulfilment and may ultimately make them a better employment investment. As we have established, what is important for many women is the challenge, autonomy and development opportunities associated with their jobs. Most men prefer high earnings, job status and security. But it is difficult for organizations to sustain the traditional patterns of pay rises and promotions in today's competitive economy. Since the employment patterns of women do not lead them to expect lifelong careers, they are better able than many men to cope with the uncertainty and change that are the norm in organizations today.

Patterns of employment[4]
▨ **Transitory**   frequent change, unstable.
▨ **Steady state**   consistently follows one occupation.

■ **Linear**   chooses a field early and pursues it upward.
■ **Spiral**   develops one field then moves on to a related/
unrelated field on a cyclical basis.

Most of us recognize that very many women find themselves with either transitory or spiral work patterns. We will consider later in this chapter the concept of the 'portfolio' career, whereby individuals draw on a variety of skills, periodically reinventing themselves to take up work opportunities that best fit their situation and aspirations. But for now we will merely refer back to the evidence we have shown in previous chapters of women trained in one field who have opted to leave or change direction because their ambitions were frustrated, or their needs and values no longer coincided with what their organization could provide. Following these unconventional career paths need not be seen as the lesser option because you never know where they may ultimately lead.

From her research evidence Wood draws some important and heartening conclusions for women. The zigzag nature of careers today means that, increasingly, women will find greater equality of opportunity in the workplace. Because, as more firms move to flexible working to meet customer needs, so the same work options will be open to (and required of) everyone. No longer will careers be strictly linear, continuous and upward. Rather, they will take on the transitory and spiral patterns women have always created for themselves. Wood calls this a shift from 'career dependence' to 'career resilience'. And rather than being seen as less committed, women will be seen to lead in accepting flexibility, managing uncertainty and juggling priorities. In effect they will become more attractive employees. And men may have to play catch up.

The disappearance of the 'job-for-life' concept and the emergence of more fractured career paths will benefit women. More flexible, variable careers will play to women's strengths and to the way they want to run their lives.
Julia Budd, partner at Egon Zehnder
(recruitment consultancy)[5]

But if in the future we will no longer be constrained by traditional definitions of what it means to have a career, what new benchmarks will we use to measure our success?

Defining career success

You need to let go of other people's definitions of success and their timetable in which you should achieve it.

Jayne Buxton[6]

In some ways this section heading is a misnomer: for many women success in their lives is not solely about what they achieve in their careers. As well as fulfilling work it includes satisfying relationships (with a partner, with family and with friends), non work-related interests, personal development and, often, activities that 'put something back' to compensate for the many advantages from which they feel they have benefited.

In her research paper Jane Sturges establishes that women are 'less inclined to define career success in terms of hierarchical and career progression'.[7] Previous research had represented career success as something that can be defined objectively and measured through external criteria such as status and salary. Her findings, however, show that not all individuals see success in this way, not least because, in today's flatter organizations, working up the hierarchy is less available as a means of advancement, delayering having removed many levels of management jobs.

It is important, therefore, at the outset of your career (and at periodic intervals thereafter) to assess where your own orientation lies: how do you, personally, define career success? As a start point, ask yourself which of the typologies described by Sturges you most closely resemble:

Climber

▪ I am driven primarily by external criteria (job grade, progression through promotion and pay level).
▪ I have a strong desire to get to the top because of the status I would acquire.

■ I am goal orientated (I set stretching targets for myself relating to pay and position).

■ I have strong positive feelings about the organization (my own ideas of success are closely allied to those defined by my company).

■ I enjoy working in a corporate environment

WHERE TO FIND YOUR CAREER NICHE

Large, international companies where scope exists for movement both vertically for career progression and laterally for breadth of experience.

Expert

■ What I value most is achieving a high level of competence and being recognized personally for what I do.

■ Respect from others is very important to me (positive feedback; gaining colleagues' respect; getting thanks and praise).

■ Job grade is less important/unimportant to me.

■ I value job content over status or position in the hierarchy.

■ I would not sacrifice job content or enjoyment to gain promotion.

■ Responsibility and autonomy are important success indicators to me.

WHERE TO FIND YOUR CAREER NICHE

Small- to medium-sized companies and sectors where a high degree of technical expertise or subject specialism is valued: accountancy/finance, law, science, consultancy or high technology, for example.

Influencer

■ It is important that what I do has a tangible and positive impact.

■ I want to leave my mark.

- I like to get involved in activities outside the normal remit of my job in order to influence outcomes.
- Progressing up the hierarchy means I can exert greater influence.
- Having a good reputation builds my influence in the long run.

WHERE TO FIND YOUR CAREER NICHE

In roles where measurable outcomes or tangible results are possible, such as product development, project management or corporate communications, and where cross-functional involvement is possible.

Self-realizer

- Defining career success is difficult.
- Achievement is a very personal matter to me.
- Personal fulfilment is more important.
- I want success in my own terms.
- I get a sense of achievement from being good at what I do.
- I need to find my work personally challenging in some way.
- Meeting a challenge and personal development are what I value most in my work.
- Balance between home and work is essential.
- It is important to me to enjoy my work – it must be interesting.
- I set my career goals in relation to personal achievement, not organizational landmarks.

WHERE TO FIND YOUR CAREER NICHE

Gain experience and work towards a role where there is a high degree of autonomy, such as divisional or business unit manager. Important to gain entrepreneurial experience with a view possibly to starting up your own enterprise. (Many women who have set up dot.coms have this mindset.)

Acquiring critical skill sets

Whatever our 'career anchors' may be, in terms of what we find important and fulfilling, we need to ensure that we are appropriately qualified to pursue our work goals. In previous chapters we referred to the importance of acquiring a set of core skills and then layering upon these experience and competence. This is key to building your value, since your employability derives from a mix of these elements, as well as from your track record. And if we are seen as employable, then scope for career development is determined primarily by the structure and culture of the organizations we choose to work for. Let us first look at the critical skill and knowledge sets that have been identified as the basis for career success in the 21st century,[8] before considering how to assess whether or not a given organization will facilitate, our career development:

- **Technical specialism**   including computer literacy and the ability to manage and use information. (Note that, though people management skills are important in some contexts, on their own they are not an automatic qualifier.)
- **Cross-functional and international experience** in order to manage multidisciplinary teams and projects, managers must be able to understand how other functions and business units operate. (You may recall how this type of experience was invaluable to many of our successful women, including Nikki Beckett and Dianne Thompson.)
- **Collaborative leadership**   future projects will be both temporary and ongoing, so having the ability to integrate quickly into new or existing teams will be crucial. (Women's higher emotional intelligence enables them to do this with greater ease than men.)
- **Self-managing skills**   delayering and the rise of the knowledge worker will mean that more people will need to be self-managing in terms of continuous learning, juggling the work–life balance and developing their careers. (Many women find self-management of their careers problematic because they hold back from asking for the opportunities they want.)

■ **Flexibility** including the ability to lead on one project while acting as team member on another. (Women generally are more comfortable with this type of ambiguity in status and hierarchy than are men.)

ACTION POINT

If you feel you are deficient in any of these skills areas then where can you find opportunities to develop them? The career-life planning framework in the Chapter Nine should help you to formulate a personal development strategy.

Finding career opportunities

As we work to acquire these desirable skills, how can we identify organizations that will facilitate our career development and encourage us to enhance our skill sets further? The kinds of organizations we should, as women, be working for are those where a virtuous spiral of support, challenge and development opportunity can be identified.

Some of the criteria we need to consider include:

■ **Scope offered for lateral growth** Are there schemes in place for job swapping, cross-functional project work, job shadowing and secondments?
■ **Established career paths and development practices** Is there a systematic management development programme and succession plan in place? Has it been communicated to you and where do you sit within it?
■ **Managerial commitment and support** Will your boss enable you to acquire the experience needed to move to the next level by involving you in challenging new work?

ACTION POINT

When applying for new jobs/transfers/promotions ensure you tackle these issues with the interview panel and your proposed line manager. In your current post, if the organization is not meeting these criteria, what can you do to help bring about change?

Avoiding the career cul de sac

Women are at risk of their career stalling on two fronts. First, the majority of women (as we have seen earlier) prefer to pursue their careers within one organization rather than job-hopping. And if they fail to take up the challenge of self-management they may fall behind their more proactive male colleagues. Additionally, where organizations are slow to facilitate internal mobility, it is individuals in specialist roles – and many of these are women – who are most at risk. For, while employers are keen to attract and retain knowledge workers, the scope for technical and professional personnel to progress their careers via conventional routes is limited. As we have demonstrated (in Chapter Four and elsewhere), it tends to be the generalists within a company who are promoted, since the way up is via man management rather than through specialist knowledge.

If you have chosen to be a specialist, because this is what you find fulfilling (see 'Expert' above), then you will need to seek out companies that offer a wider range of career development opportunities. If these are routinely offered primarily to those who generate new business or fee income, what measures are there to ensure that back-office personnel are not disadvantaged in the promotion stakes? Are there alternative roles (internal or external consultant, for example) that would be similarly fulfilling for you, but allow you better access to promotion opportunities?

Evaluating the
fast-track potential of your job

A key factor in determining whether your job could lead you to the top is what Kelly and Marin term 'position power'.[9] According to their observations, even when women 'do all the right things' – change their attitudes; seek counselling; undertake management training – they still lag behind their male counterparts in gaining career progression and pay rises (even when issues like career breaks, etc. are factored in). They conclude that some external issues must be at work – including structural challenges like the informal networks we looked at in Chapter

Three – and that women's career strategies must change in order to overcome them. They helpfully point to a number of ways in which women can evaluate the fast-track potential of their jobs in relation to four critical factors:

- Power
- Networking
- Recognition
- Personal control/autonomy.

They remind us that it was Rosabeth Moss Kanter who first established that it is, broadly, job position that determines power and not the characteristics of the jobholder. Today, positions of power are still less likely to be held by women, and so men continue to have greater access to authority.

KEY RESEARCH FINDING

On the FTSE 100 list of companies, women hold only around 5 per cent of directorships. In the USA, by contrast, 97 per cent of *Fortune 500* companies have a woman on the board. This is seen as indicating a strong correlation between profitability and having women at the top.

So where are the jobs with power likely to be located in an organization? They are to be found:

- Within the central flow of work.
- Clustered around tasks rather than social activities (i.e. strategic or financial planning rather than PR or HR).
- Where there is hierarchical position power (line management).
- In roles with access to resources (sales manager, production manager etc.).

(There will be some variation in the types of roles associated with power, depending on the business sector and the organizational culture, but the above holds generally true.)

ACTION POINT

Audit your job for power potential.

Finding a job with power potential is only half the story, however. Where power is concerned perception is everything. You need to act like a leader by taking charge. What problems exist in your organization that are crying out for a solution? Take responsibility for a key issue, work out a project to resolve it and you can showcase your skills and demonstrate leadership. This will earn you a reputation for tackling difficult issues and getting results. It will also help you build some exceptional skills and expertise that are perceived by your organization as delivering real value.

Finally, the true leader is a visionary, so you must define some stretching goals and have a passionate belief in your own and your team's ability to achieve them, and then make your vision a reality.[10]

We return to the theme of leadership and teambuilding in Chapter Nine.

Keep marching continuously in the direction of your dreams and one day you will be leading the life you have imagined.

Thoreau

Your company: friend or foe?

We have already established how important it is to your career progression to get yourself noticed by key decision-makers and influencers through networking and mentoring. So, the first question to ask yourself about your current or prospective company is whether there is observable segregation of the sexes. Are women channelled away from jobs that make them visible, where they are allowed to display their competence and have it recognized? What is the composition of project groups, committees and working parties that report directly to senior management? How many women can you count? Fewer than 30 per cent and there is no critical mass upon which to build, and you won't – unless you truly are a superwoman – change things single-handed.

ACTION POINT

If you are trapped doing work that is mainly routine, move on and broaden your portfolio.

Next, what scope for autonomy and flexibility does your current or potential job provide? Is your job comprised of routine or repetitive tasks requiring precision and accuracy? If this is the case, you are less likely to acquire the skills you need to get to the top. Also, the more efficient you become at routine tasks, the more you are seen as indispensable in that role, and the less likely you are to be promoted. The key is to gain experience in decision making and risk taking to hone your judgement, as well as budgeting and resource management. You could also carve a niche by serving in roles where you are seen to reduce risk for others in the organization by providing important information, whether financial data, marketing feedback or competitor tracking.

Recipe for managing your career successfully[11]

■ Plan your next move: always be looking for a new job using your network of contacts (men do it all the time).

■ Know your value by benchmarking yourself against professional and other networks/associations that monitor pay.

■ Is the ladder up against the right wall? Why are you doing what you are doing? If you don't really like it then reassess your portfolio to gain new skills and experience so that you can move into something new.

■ Put your career first and avoid being selflessly loyal to any company. Monitor your company's progress in terms of profits and share price. Be aware of threats and opportunities and have a contingency plan.

■ If you get to burnout because you are frustrated, then deal with the situation and stay in the job until you have another. However tempted to throw in the towel, you are much more attractive to new employers when in a job than out of work.

■ To build your skills portfolio look for opportunities outside your organization. Volunteer: get on to committees and decision-making bodies for charities, professional associations or other groups to gain extra experience.

*Stay in the game. Don't drop out. Keep learning and maintain
your contacts. Expect some highs and lows. And some of the
lows may be very low.*

Jayne Buxton, co-founder of Flametree Key Management

Gaining international experience

KEY RESEARCH FINDING
Only between 3 per cent and 5 per cent of UK expatriate
managers are women. Misconceptions about women's abilities to
handle international assignments and their willingness to accept
them are the key barriers.

We showed earlier that it was important to gain international
experience to ensure advancement. Yet, as global competition
intensifies and more women move into lower level management
roles, women in overseas assignments are still very few. The
gender stereotyping by senior managers (discussed in Chapter
Three) relating to women's availability, suitability and preferences
effectively debars women from international management. This
has led to the phenomenon known as 'the glass border'. Of
course, the double bind for women is that a prerequisite for
secondment to international assignments is senior management
experience in your home country – unless you are a man, in
which case the criteria are less strict, according to research by
Lineham and Walsh.[12] Their findings were that women needed to
be better qualified, more ambitious and more mobile than male
managers in order to succeed.

*The bottom line is that these stereotypes – one on top of the
other – make it less likely that decision-makers are going to
think of women managers when they build executive global
teams. This is doubly destructive because, as it turns out,
women want these assignments, they do well abroad and they
told Catalyst they would seize the opportunity again.*

Sheila Wellington, President of Catalyst[13]

But some women have broken through. So how did they do it?

According to the 50 respondents interviewed by Lineham and Walsh:

- They persistently asked for their next career move (rather than waiting for it to be offered).
- They showed themselves better than their male counterparts at multitasking and balancing different functions simultaneously.
- They got themselves known, and communicated their aspirations openly.

> *You must let your intentions be known. I constantly keep saying what I want.*
>
> MD of a manufacturing company[14]

Many respondents were emphatic about the need for sacrifice in your personal life if you are to break through. They spoke of the loss of leisure and the possibility of remaining unmarried or risking divorce through career pressures. Some felt it better to remain unencumbered if international management is your goal. This is simply because it is easier to relocate if you are single and have no ties – resettling a family is notoriously traumatic. For those who were married (31 out of the 50 interviewed), there were the stresses of juggling work and family remotely, of sustaining a commuter relationship or of having a 'trailing spouse' that marked them and their partners as 'the odd couples'. Those who had divorced referred to the inability of many men to accept that a woman should have an equal or more successful career. All these factors impacted adversely on their quality of life. One respondent (divorced), speaking of the strain of taking on too much responsibility both at work and at home said:

> *My career was a big threat to my husband. I was the major money earner, and it came to a point where I did everything. When I look back on what I have done, no woman in her right mind should ever contemplate doing all of that.*[15]

The respondents were almost unanimous in their belief that it was much more difficult for women to have an international career than men. Role conflict, time pressures, lack of geographical mobility, poor support from a partner and long hours all conspire to force women to choose between a career and a family.

However, should you be committed to working internationally, and succeed in gaining the support of your partner (if you have one), then Lineham and Walsh suggest that you make it clear to your employer that your partner's career does not necessarily take precedence over your own, and that your career aspirations are not subordinate to his. And a word of warning: be prepared to be seen as 'the odd couple' if your partner, rather than yourself, is the 'trailing spouse'. In many countries managers are still predominantly men – in southern Europe less than 5 per cent of managers are women and, even in Switzerland, men whose wives work are seen as unable to provide adequately for their families.

Recipe for a successful overseas assignment and repatriation

■ Make it known you want a career in international management.

■ Choose a mentor who can help, and network with the right people.

■ Get involved in international women's networks and talk to other women about their jobs and how they got international experience.

■ Ensure your employer allows sufficient training and preparation time before the relocation. Will your spouse be able to participate?

■ Clarify the duration of the secondment and the scope of your responsibilities.

■ Seek help finding employment for your spouse if appropriate.

■ Before you leave, make sure a support system is in place so that you can access regular contact with your networks whilst away.

■ Find a senior mentor locally.

■ Secure your exit route and make sure there is a plan for your repatriation and reintegration.

■ Check out the area to which you are moving. Do other wives work there as a rule? (There are places even in northern Europe where this is not yet the norm.)

▉ Forestall integration problems by ensuring your new neighbours don't assume you're too busy to socialize or get involved in the community.

▉ Get everything in writing where relevant.

So, let us assume you are prepared to make the necessary sacrifices required by high office, and that you have been proactive in building the skills and experience needed to qualify you. What else must you do to ensure your place in the upper levels of the corporate hierarchy?

Getting to the top

Listen to yourself. Decide on your own whether you want to put career or family first. I could not have had the career I have if I had had children – or someone would have had to suffer.
Women have tremendous opportunities today and have earned the independence to choose their path.

Barbara Kux, executive director,
Ford Motor Company[16]

Getting started

We have established that there are often significant differences in the process of career development between men and women: women tend to occupy 'specialist' support roles, while men tend to become 'generalist' line managers with associated higher status. Yet despite these apparent disadvantages some women – as we saw in Chapter Four – have attained positions of significant authority and power. Some of the factors that contributed to the success of the women we interviewed included:

▉ **Parental encouragement**: being brought up to expect to succeed, and to have self-belief.

▉ **Success breeds success**: some early challenge that allowed them to prove themselves and gain confidence.

▉ **Building a broad foundation**: through development programmes and wide-ranging experience.

■ **Finding a mentor**: someone who would believe in and champion their careers.

Here we provide a more structured framework for understanding the process of how women get to the top, drawn from the work of Vinnicombe, Singh and Sturges.[17] Based on in-depth qualitative research with six male and six female directors at BT they identified three interrelated factors (closely paralleling my own research findings) that contribute to a successful career:

■ Finding a mentor
■ Taking on challenges
■ Becoming visible in the organization.

These were found to be equally crucial for both men and women, but the factors operated differently according to gender.

Mentoring

We have referred elsewhere in the book to the benefits of finding a mentor, including the opportunity for greater visibility through high profile assignments and access to senior networks. The research findings showed that men were more likely than women to identify and cultivate mentors, though the women reported there had been no shortage of people offering unsolicited help to them. 'Cultivating' mentors for men is about finding opportunities to socialize and interact with influential people, and they are more proactive and selective in doing this than their female counterparts. Men would 'buddy up' with 'useful' people for work purposes then, move on when the contact was no longer valuable. Women, by contrast, saw their (usually) male mentor as a fatherly sponsor – they sometimes spoke of having been 'adopted', of being offered protection that allowed them to grow. This had had a profound influence on their future careers.

So what are the roles of a mentor that have such an impact? Career advice and counselling is one area, linked to a second – coaching in management techniques. Acting as an advocate on their protégée's behalf was another (and we have seen how this can help raise an individual's profile and credibility). Finally, 'executive mirroring' was identified as helping to show the often politically naïve younger manager how to forge an appropriate managerial identity and a style congruent with the norms of the organization.

The mirroring process may be by passive observation of what works and how the senior person deals with organizational politics. Opportunities for shadowing were also beneficial in enabling individuals to absorb business etiquette and decision-making processes. A really critical advantage of mentoring was the access it gave to information not in the public domain: where the organization was moving strategically and what, as a consequence, would be a good career or development move.

ACTION POINT

If you have not yet found a mentor, take steps to do so. Choose someone who is not only influential, but has a track record of ensuring newcomers are given opportunities and encouragement.

Challenge

We cited earlier the importance of having a supportive boss in order to gain opportunities for challenging work. We have to recognize that there is a degree of risk involved for male mentors supporting women. In male-dominated organizations a woman manager is often seen as a 'test case'. If things go wrong this can be publicly embarrassing for the male mentor because of the high visibility of the woman. Finding someone who will take the risk – when you are relatively inexperienced – of involving you in challenging work can be problematic. How can you overcome the barriers?

1 **Have you established a good track record?** What previous achievements can you point to that would reduce the perceived risk? (Remember the importance of keeping your career portfolio up to date.)
2 **How does your mentor see your potential?** Have you made clear your aspirations and what you are prepared to do to achieve them?

3 **When offered a challenge, how do you respond?** You
need to do so confidently. Don't express a lot of self-doubt
(men don't). Your crisis of confidence may spark the same
response in your mentor.

Next, what kinds of challenges should you look for in order to
make your mark? The projects in which you should lobby for
involvement are those with visible outcomes where you can
achieve measurable results. Seek out challenges in:

■ Heading up a project
■ Managing a department/division/business
■ Pioneering a Greenfield area
■ Handling a crisis or turnaround situation
■ Taking on new responsibilities beyond your previous
experience.

*I was appointed Head of Communications at 29 (in a major
pharmaceutical company). But I'd earned my spurs through
facing off difficult problems in damage limitation campaigns
over product recalls, investment policies and the cost of
drugs.*

Colette Graham

Visibility

Whom you report to and your job role are critical in raising your
profile. One of the women in our study told us she was sure she
was regarded as more important and influential simply because
she reported to the managing director. A good start point,
according to Vinnicombe, Singh and Sturges is the role of
personal assistant to a senior manager. This will bring you
into contact with senior personnel much earlier than would
otherwise be the case. The network of contacts you form will
help you develop an overview of the organization and provide
intelligence about opportunities as they arise. Acting as
Secretary to a senior committee is also invaluable in getting you
noticed by the inner circle and allowing you access to strategic
information.

Getting the right reputation is critical for appointment to corporate boards. Our research into impression management (upwards influence) indicates that women managers do not tend to use such strategies as early in their careers as their male peers, and hence may not gain the visibility, reputation and networks needed for later access to board level positions.

Val Singh[18]

ACTION POINT

If your current job role does not allow contact with senior managers consider which projects, working groups and committees you might want to get involved in. Take this up with your line manager as a development opportunity during your periodic one-to-one meetings and ask for his or her help.

Vinnicombe, Singh and Sturges point out that being mentored, getting challenging work and gaining visibility is part of a cyclical process: your personal qualities and track record can attract an influential mentor, who then earmarks you as having high potential. This leads to opportunities for challenge, which in turn gets you visible to other influential people and allows you to draw on higher-level support.

Developing an acceptable style

We saw in Chapter Three how women can be held back by gender myths and stereotypes, and in Chapter Seven we look at the day-to-day issues impacting on women at work, particularly how these gender issues affect their interactions with male colleagues and senior managers. At this point we need to consider how women can best adapt their style of interaction as part of their career development strategy.

Catalyst, a not-for-profit research and advisory body that works to advance women in business, published an important study in cooperation with Opportunity Now.[19] Across the UK, the USA and Canada they found that successful senior women used two primary strategies to advance their careers:

■ Consistently exceeding performance expectations.
■ Developing a style with which male managers are comfortable.

KEY RESEARCH FINDING

In all three countries senior women identified male stereotyping and preconceptions of women's roles and abilities as a top barrier to women's advancement.[19]

Mary van der Boon, director of the international management training company Global TMC speaking at WIN 2000 had some helpful insights and advice to offer to women who want to be able to interact more effectively with their male colleagues:[20]

■ Closely observe male colleagues to see where their comfort zones are (for example, they don't like displays of emotion or discussions about feelings).
■ Keep your behaviour businesslike to signal that you are a professional on the same level.
■ Practise active listening by slowing down and focusing on the other person to establish empathy. They will be flattered by your attention and become well disposed towards you. This breaks down barriers and establishes trust. (We often distrust and dislike what we don't understand.)
■ Practise positive self-talk and if you are nervous when presenting, rehearse and use relaxation techniques to help your credibility.
■ Be approachable and avoid using your expert power too heavily. Avoid seeming always to know the answers – let others be clever too. Draw them out and allow them to shine.

Again, this advice may seem counter-intuitive to some women, while others may rail against the need to adapt their style in order to avoid antagonizing men at work. But as we have said elsewhere, we don't want to force anyone to change. We merely show what other women have found to be effective in advancing their careers, and counsel you that refusing to adapt may have adverse consequences for your progression.

Moving from middle to senior management

What it is hoped our readers have gathered from this chapter so far (and from the book as a whole) is that there are few, if any, overnight successes in getting to the top. Rather, it requires a long, sustained effort and lots of self-discipline. But what marks out the role of the senior manager from that of the middle manager is that she focuses more on the bigger picture rather than on the detail. This mind-shift does not come easily to many women – we tend to be perfectionists and like to protect our credibility by paying painstaking attention to every detail. As you move up the hierarchy, so the scope of your responsibilities broadens and there simply is not time to attend to everything. This is where the art of delegation is important: ensuring your team knows what's expected, but leaving them to get on with it in their own way, within the parameters you have set. (Delegation is covered in detail in Chapter Eight.)

Our ability to act as leaders by tackling big problems is constrained by the other demands on our time. Through effective delegation we can free ourselves to be innovative, to propose new ideas and to capitalize on opportunities – all of which raise our visibility and signal our value to the organization. Add a measure of self-belief and the ability to use the culture to your advantage (rather than being a victim of it) and you are on your way.

Developing a sustainable career

As we saw earlier, all the indicators are that more and more women will in future want to get to the top and be prepared to forego having children or even getting married in order to fulfil their potential. They will be well qualified for life at the top, and society's expectations are rapidly changing in relation to women's roles. But where women want to have a career and a family is it possible to find a flexible option that allows them to balance work and home, if not perfectly then at least manageably?

The issue of building a more creative career path was the topic presented by Jayne Buxton[21] at the WIN 2000 Conference. She spoke of her experience in switching from a high-flying career to a less exhausting role after she became a mother:

CASE STUDY

'In 1992 I was a management consultant. But when I had my first baby I fell in love and my priorities changed overnight. I knew I would continue to need work challenges, but also that I would no longer be able to work a 60- or 70-hour week. My employer was supportive and I worked flexibly three or four days a week. I recognized there was a trade-off to be made, that I couldn't always have the best projects and that there would be a degree of sidelining. But I still wanted to try for partnership. I was persuaded to take on more work and ended up doing 12-hour days, six days a week. My health suffered – I couldn't work for about 8 weeks. When I did go back it was to a new role – still intellectually challenging but no longer mainstream and I learned to enjoy the job for what it was. My subsequent career as a writer – and ultimately founder of Flametree – was born directly out of my experience of coming to terms with not having it all. I wanted to support other women in meeting their challenges and help them find their own equilibrium.'

Jayne's experience demonstrates clearly the potential dangers of striving too hard to be a superwoman and failing to acknowledge our physical limitations. It also shows us that no ignominy attaches to recognizing that few of us can do it all – high-flying career and motherhood – and that fulfilling and challenging employment alternatives are available to us.

KEY RESEARCH FINDING

Nearly half of all senior women managers surveyed in the UK said commitment to family responsibilities was a top obstacle to career progression.[22]

Avivah Wittenberg Cox has researched the issue of how women reconcile the demands of work and family by interviewing a number of high-flying women MBA graduates, and her findings were published in an issue of *Salamander*, the INSEAD Alumni newsletter.[23] She has kindly given permission for the interviews she conducted to be summarized below.

Julia Budd, who recruits at board level for headhunters Egon Zehnder was quoted as saying that though the playing field has been levelled for women, they still have to be prepared to play the game according to rules set by the men:

Women who want to make it to the top are expected to work the same hours and sacrifice the same things that men traditionally have. So the onus falls on the women to make the trade-offs and establish a balance that they can live with.

She makes the point that this often results in women choosing career compromises, because they refuse to make the personal sacrifices getting to the top requires. To a degree, in her view, women themselves are responsible for the glass ceiling. And perhaps there is an issue here we must confront. Achieving balance in some roles is almost impossible. As Julia maintains, there will always be jobs that require body and soul commitment. These will be filled by individuals who are driven, ambitious and single-minded enough to do them. And the majority of those individuals will be men. But does making those career compromises necessarily mean we have failed ourselves? Not if the experience of the following women is anything to go by.

Sandrine Tézé, an MBA graduate from INSEAD, has enjoyed a 20-year career with consultants Bain & Co. and during much of that time she has worked flexibly: after her first child she worked part time, after the second she worked a four-day week and after the third child she decided to take a two and a half year career break in order to take stock and think what to do next. Her decision was to go back into consulting because it allowed her to stop and start and to opt for part-time working. She now works a three-day week – but very flexibly – and was even appointed partner while on a part-time schedule in 1996. This may seem like an ideal arrangement. But, she admits, she still feels the need for special support from time to time. Every year she is tempted to quit because juggling her priorities means always neglecting something, even with the benefit of a supportive environment both at home and at work. She draws support from her mother, a psychologist, who says that she has seen too many women of 40 and 50 regretting that their only role has been that of wife and mother. They are unhappy that they never took the opportunity to prove themselves in the world of work.

*There are no superwomen. They just don't exist . . . Unless you
are very strong and have an amazing support network you
burn out. You really have to like competition. I do.*

Sandrine Tézé,
Vice President, Bain & Co.[24]

Another INSEAD graduate facing the dilemma of choosing
between a high-flying career and a more family-friendly option
was Jane Sommers-Kelly who, at 36 found herself at a career
crossroads. She was an investment banker with two children
under two, and was forced to reassess her options when her
next career move would have taken her overseas. The prospect
of working in a high-powered environment like London or
New York proved unacceptable. She and her partner then drew
up a matrix of personal and family goals and priorities
mapping their income needs, together with issues like job
satisfaction and preferred geographical locations. Having
identified the geographical and industry sectors where she
wanted to work, she then tapped into her network of contacts
and subsequently became a corporate fundraiser for the
INSEAD Alumni Association in North America. She and her
partner had by this time saved enough money to enjoy a
degree of financial flexibility and so were able to make such a
move. She adjusted her expectations, particularly of herself,
and made a new rule for herself that she would leave the
office each day feeling happy with 75 per cent of what she
had done there. She had some advice for other high-flying
women:

*Make your mark as fast and as early as possible. Get your CV
and financial security established, then as soon as possible
break away and do your own thing . . . Keep as your measure
the day-to-day rewards that you get from work – not the
identity and status that society attaches to it. Try to limit the
guilt.*[25]

Is there any good news for the future of women who want to
combine a high-flying career with having a family? Julia Budd
suggests there is both good news and bad news:

▉ Companies with a strong female customer base and those with large numbers of female employees will have to make it a priority to promote women to the board.

▉ Through sheer weight of numbers and the calibre of their qualifications women will increasingly get themselves promoted to senior positions.

▉ The men/women split is unlikely to reach 50/50, however, because the work–life balance issue is so difficult to resolve.

▉ Increasingly men will have to face the same work–life balance issues.

▉ The rise of the 'portfolio career', combining flexible and varied work will play to women's strengths and the way they want to run their lives.

So, what advice would she offer? First, if you want to climb the career ladder pick your partner carefully:

Successful women inevitably have supportive husbands. Men ready to take a back seat on the career front – with no reservations. It's extremely hard, if you have two people shimmying up the greasy pole of corporate ambition.

Secondly, consider entrepreneurship as an option. Remember that women-owned enterprises now account for 50 per cent of new business start-ups in the UK. Julia sees this as a very effective way for women to reject traditional career development models and to create their own vision of life and work.

Helena Dennison, Chair of the Women's City Network (WCN),[26] echoed this theme when she commented that 40 per cent of the WCN membership is composed of women entre-preneurs. In Helena's view, women progress as far as they are allowed in the corporate world before either leaving to start up their own business, or getting totally frustrated as the system fails to meet their needs.

UK employers need to assess what they can do and what programmes they can put in place to meet the needs of men and women who are trying to juggle work and home commitments. It just makes good business sense.

Norma Jarboe, Executive Director of Opportunity Now

Recognizing burnout

Tired? Distracted? Has your interest in work flagged? Do you have a growing sense of futility? Then you could be reaching burnout. But you should not worry: these signs are increasingly common among professionals who work long hours, are highly dedicated and push themselves too hard. In addition to losing your perspective and ability to focus, though, you also risk incurring health problems, and so it is important to take immediate remedial action. Do not get caught in a downward spiral of trying to work harder to compensate. Everything will simply take longer, you will accomplish even less, and your frustration will increase.

On their website,[27] Advancing Women suggest the following steps:

- *Acknowledge the symptoms and take action.*
- *Reduce your hours and start working smarter by raising your productivity through focusing on key tasks. Delegate.*
- *Take a break – whether a weekend away or even an afternoon off.*
- *Take exercise to relieve stress – a walk in the fresh air is invigorating.*
- *Plan some leisure activities that will change your perspective.*
- *Recharge your batteries by meeting new people and learning new skills unrelated to your work.*
- *Take charge by managing your reactions to situations that trigger stress and anxiety.*
- *When you react positively and constructively then you feel in control.*

Towards a better balance

Overall here a picture of British business has been presented that is less than edifying from the perspective of women- and family-friendliness. But, thankfully, this picture is gradually changing and there are some heartening examples of best practice. Cathy Cooper has highlighted a number of organizations that have brought work–life balance policies into being and reaped significant benefits in terms of retaining skilled employees.[28] At Glaxo Welcome the board comprises one-third women with children. The intensive competition for knowledge workers has brought about a revolution in its working culture that has impacted on every aspect of work practice. Cooper cites as evidence the way a board meeting was rescheduled and the agenda adjusted to allow two board members (one man and one woman) to attend their children's nativity plays. By embedding new flexible practices into the line management process Glaxo Welcome has almost eradicated presenteeism. When people work too long they are told to go home, and if they persist they are counselled to manage their workload more effectively.

BT is well established as a best-practice employer in respect of work–life balance. But, so effective have their policies been in raising awareness of the damaging effects of presenteeism, that men are now as likely as women to reject a promotion because it threatens their home life.

Meanwhile, in response to employee feedback that made work–life balance a top priority, Price Waterhouse Coopers now monitor employee hours via timesheets. Presenteeists are told to take time off in lieu or to adjust their workload.

So how can you help to ensure that your organization becomes more employee-friendly? If you want to gain greater flexibility for your team then you will need to put forward a business case that demonstrates there would be no negative effects on your work or that of your colleagues. The National Work–Life Forum provides guidelines and details of schemes for introducing flexible working that you might like to consult.[29]

Recycling yourself

We have already seen that at certain points in their lives women may find themselves unable to pursue their careers in a linear fashion. The needs of children, a partner's career taking precedence, ageing and dependent parents – any or all of these factors may at some time unavoidably interrupt our working lives and force us to rethink how we can earn money and find some fulfilment of our own. Joanna Parfitt[30] presenting at the WIN 2000 Conference spoke of her experience as the 'trailing spouse', who had spent many assignments in places where she was unable to work in an orthodox way. As she was keen to point out, this does not necessarily mean that you are debarred from doing any paid work. It simply requires a little imagination to find a new niche where your skills and experience can be put to good use – and turn you a profit.

Much of what Joanna recommends for expatriate wives applies with equal relevance to women taking a voluntary or enforced career break, especially where they would like to work part time, but this is not possible within their normal profession. For many of us, our identity is closely tied to our careers, and when we don't earn we feel undervalued and often become frustrated because so much of our capability is underutilized.

She suggests as a first step that you take an inventory of your skills – you may have to think laterally here, because you need to focus on things you could perhaps pass on to individuals or small groups (e.g. keyboard or computing skills, a language or making presentations). What could you use to earn money and keep your self-esteem?

Listen to what people grumble about: 'What we really need is a . . .' Could you offer a product or service that meets people's needs or link up with others to do so?

Some of the things that Joanna herself did included co-writing, publishing and marketing a book called *Dates* while living in the Middle East. Later she worked with her Indian cook to help her augment her income by providing a takeaway food service and party catering.

Letting others know about your offering these days couldn't be easier or cheaper – simply create your own website. It is completely mobile and widely accessible. Joanna recommends giving incentives to encourage people to revisit, such as updates of valuable information, hints and tips, etc.

If you are stuck with skills that are non-transferable (perhaps, like a German woman I recently met, you are a lawyer living abroad and unable to practise locally), then acquire some new skills by distance learning or via the Internet.

Even when there is no financial necessity to work you can still find fulfilling outlets, perhaps by doing something creative. An excellent example of this is Jane Asher, who is married to the successful political cartoonist Gerald Scarfe. Having taken a break from her acting career to have a family, she made a commercial success of her skill at producing celebration cakes by writing a book on the subject. This in turn led to TV appearances to demonstrate her talent, and on into other work as a presenter. She is now one of several celebrities to have her own grocery line on the supermarket shelves. It is very important to have a portable career to meet the life changes you are likely to encounter. This will be drawn from your diverse experience, skills, contacts and training. In order to establish yourself quickly in any new situation you need a portfolio of evidence to show prospective clients. If you are relocated overseas it may not be possible to transport your reputation – your portfolio will have to speak for you:

Draw up a portfolio of clippings, thank you letters and testimonials, brochures and business cards to create a picture of your past reputation. Have some visible evidence to show people.

Joanna Parfitt

Some hints and tips for the portfolio careerist[31]

- Wherever you are it is vital to keep in touch with your old contacts (easy enough via e-mail) and you never know when they might be helpful.
- Regarding networking, be a giver – whether of information, of an idea or of a useful contact.
- Don't thrust your business card at everyone. Build relationships and wait to be asked for your card. The business will follow.
- Club together with others who share your interests to form a group or association for mutual support if there is nothing already in existence.
- Take part in 'virtual clubbing' on the Internet with women's and other networks.
- Share your passions with others who share your interests – it is infectious and builds rapport.

*Don't worry that you are doing all the giving – it will come
back in the end. And when you give willingly the return may be
higher than you imagined.*

Joanna Parfitt

CASE STUDY

'I was an expatriate Shell wife for 26 years – a trailing spouse as
we are now called. But behind the scenes we were our husbands'
guides, and helped overcome misunderstandings with the local
culture or work environment. We have lived in Brazil, Canary
Islands, Singapore, Malta, Oman, Qatar, Scotland and Nigeria. Our
children went to boarding school in Holland. In the past I have
organized children's parties for 500 and other big events, and
been involved in charities – one of which I set up in Nigeria.

'Eventually Shell introduced a scheme where wives could be
sponsored on training courses and I attended The School of
Colour to become an image consultant. We settled back in
Holland two years ago and I am gradually getting my business
started, though the Dutch market is very resistant to new ideas
about personal image. But I don't let that put me off. I have
organized a fashion show and got involved in other events to
promote my work. My brain always tries to get ahead and do
something out of the ordinary.'

Geraldine Wijsbeck, image consultant, The Netherlands

Summary

A range of career/life choices is now available to most women.
But each entails choices, compromises and possibly sacrifice.
How do we decide which option is best for us?

- Redefine career/life success in your own terms, setting your own goals and milestones.
- Build a skill set for the twenty-first century.
- Audit the fast track potential of your job and, if it's going nowhere, move on.
- Delegate in order to concentrate on high profile work.
- Focus on exceeding performance expectations.
- Develop a style with which male colleagues are comfortable.

■ Don't be afraid to downshift when circumstances change.
■ If you take a career break maintain your skills and networks.

In the next chapter we focus down on the day-to-day issues that confront us in our careers, looking at how we can manage our tasks and our interactions with others, in order to have a successful and fulfilling working life.

Notes

1 Marissa Brambilla, Area Vice-President Avon Products Inc., Presented at WIN 2000 Conference.
2 Maureen Wood, 'The move towards a different career pattern: are women better prepared than men for a modern career?', *Women in Management Review*, vol. 14, no. 1, 1999, MCB University Press.
3 Nicholson and West in Marsland (ed.), *Women Managers Moving On: Exploring Careers and Life Choices*, Routledge, 1995, cited by Wood, op. cit.
4 M. J. Driver, 'Career concepts – a new approach to career research', in Katz (ed.), *Career Issues in HRM*, Prentice Hall, 1982.
5 Quoted in *Salamander*, INSEAD Alumni Association publication June/July 2000.
6 Speaking at WIN 2000, September 2000.
7 Jane Sturges, 'What it means to be successful: personal conceptions of career success held by male and female managers at different ages', *British Journal of Management*, vol. 10, 1999.
8 Derived from Allred, Snow and Miles, *Characteristics of Managerial Careers in the 21st Century*, Academy of Management Executives, 1998. Quoted by Linda Holbeche in *People Management*, 8 June 2000.
9 'Position power and women's career development', *Women in Management Review*, vol. 13, no. 2, 1998, MCB University Press.
10 With acknowledgements to Advancing Women, 'Your first workplace resolution: take the steps necessary to succeed', www.advancingwomen.com
11 With acknowledgements to Mary van der Boon's presentation at WIN 2000. Contact her at: www.globaltmc.com
12 'Senior female international managers: breaking the glass border', *Women in Management Review*, vol. 14, no. 17, 1999, MCB University Press.
13 'Passport to Opportunity: US Women in Global Business', *Catalyst*, November 2000.
14 Advancing Women, op. cit.
15 Ibid.
16 Quoted in *Salamander*, INSEAD Alumni Association publication, June/July 2000.
17 Susan Vinnicombe, Val Singh and Jane Sturges, 'Making it to the Top in Britain', Centre for Developing Women Business Leaders, Cranfield School of Management.
18 Quoted in *Reflections – Review of 2000*, Cranfield School of Management.
19 'Breaking the Barriers: Women in Senior Management in the UK', December 2000, www.catalystwomen.org
20 www.globaltmc.com
21 Co-founder Flametree Key Management and author of *Ending the Mother War; Starting the Workplace Revolution*', Macmillan.
22 *Salamander*, INSEAD Alumni Association publication, June/July 2000.

23 Ibid.
24 Ibid.
25 Op. cit., note 9.
26 *Human Resources*, May 2000.
27 www.advancingwomen.com
28 *People Management*, May 2000.
29 www.worklifeforum.com
30 Editor of *Woman Abroad*. E-mail: www.womanabroad.com
31 With acknowledgements to Joanna Parfitt's presentation at WIN 2000.

7

Coping strategies for your working life

Introduction

When I was 11, my mother told me that when I played games with boys I must let them win ...You really have to apply yourself to lose and I just wasn't good at losing.

Andrea Dworkin[1]

In the previous chapter we turned our attention to the major decisions we must make in our careers and lives. We now consider how best women can manage the day-to-day challenges they encounter at work. Many of the issues we discuss have perplexed women everywhere for decades, but one of the most insidious problems is that women have frequently taken responsibility for difficulties and constraints imposed on them by others.

As Avivah Wittenberg Cox has found from her research among MBA women, in organizations defined by male values we are foreigners in hostile territory: we don't speak the language, so at first we keep quiet and learn to fit in. Later we become competent and, gaining confidence, we integrate into the culture, (though it often feels alien still). Finally, some women gain enough assurance to affirm themselves and their needs by moving on to companies that are more person-friendly, or start-up their own enterprises.[2]

The purpose of this chapter is to help guide women through the minefield that is learning to fit in, and to enable them to do so without compromising their integrity too far. We want women to play these games to win, but to recognize also that not all battles are worth fighting single-handed. Sometimes discretion is the better part of valour and, in the face of overwhelming difficulty, we simply have to find an exit route and retire gracefully.

Establishing credibility

The first rungs of the ladder

In Chapter Five we discussed the importance of personal presentation and impression management. At no time is it more vital to make a good impression than in the first few days and weeks of a new job, and in order to capitalize on the initial honeymoon period, you need to plan your strategy.

Step 1 Check your facts

Before you even begin the new job, review the information you have gathered about the company and take the opportunity to acquire more – from your new boss to ensure you are fully informed. You can also glean information from other sources, such as report and accounts, general and financial press reports and trade papers. Many of these are available via the Internet.

Step 2 Start building your network

When new recruits first join a company there is usually a round of formal and informal introductions to team members and colleagues. This is the perfect time to identify those people who can help you get established and on whose experience you may be able to draw. But be aware, too, that this should be a two-way process: look for opportunities to reciprocate support in order to build strong working relationships.

Step 3 Know what's expected of you

Ensure you focus your energies on areas that add value. Spend time finding out what's important in the company and in observing the culture ('how things are done'). If unsure about how to proceed, check with your boss to clarify the position. If you have problems, however, always present your boss with some options and ask which would be the most appropriate.

Step 4   Meet targets and deadlines

To establish your credibility it is vital to deliver on key tasks. If this is new to you then follow these steps, particularly for complex jobs:

■ Break down the task into its component parts.
■ Working back from the deadline, fit the parts of the task into a time frame, estimating how long each part will require.
■ Work out the tasks to be completed daily or weekly, keep a checklist and stick to it
■ If completing your work is dependent on inputs from others, ensure that their input will be available when you need it.
■ Manage your time effectively.
■ Ask for help when you need it and don't waste time searching for information that colleagues may be able to provide. Determine beforehand your list of queries and make sure you choose a convenient time to approach people for answers.

Step 5   Show measurable results

Always try to find some way to measure the results of your work, perhaps using past performance or the achievements of others as a benchmark. Record what you do and, if it is good, send a brief report to your manager. Show that you are doing more than is expected of you.

QUESTIONS TO CONSIDER
To what extent are you able to influence:

■ cost savings
■ increases in sales
■ customer service
■ number of transactions processed
■ budget spending.

What sort of improvements could you make? List some action points you could implement over the next three-, six- or twelve-month period.

Coping with criticism

Women worry more about what they are not achieving – even those who perform well are often very self-critical and look for improvement opportunities by seeking feedback on their performance. Men tend not to behave like this – even when they are failing. They tend to go into denial and would certainly never seek to discuss it.

Senior woman lawyer

None of us likes to be criticized. We all have an idealized self and we don't like to fall short of that ideal. Many of us are highly self-critical and tend to perfectionism, so very little that anyone else says when we have failed to reach our own exacting standards can make us feel worse than we do. This may mean that we find taking criticism quite stressful. We already feel bad enough; having our mistakes pointed out can often undermine us further. These facts require us to rethink the way we cope with such occurrences. It is an integral part of having responsibility and, since we all make mistakes, we are bound to receive adverse feedback at some time.

In order to re-frame some of the criticism you receive, try the following:

1 Avoid focusing too much on its negative aspect: what can you learn from it and how will you move forward? If you can develop as a result of the criticism, this is a positive outcome.
2 Don't generalize the criticism so that it becomes a reflection on you as a person. It is a learning opportunity not a condemnation of who you are. Don't dwell on it – learn and move on.
3 Don't react immediately to what is said. Take time to reflect on the feedback rather than getting angry and defensive. Take a few deep breaths or even ask for time out to consider the comments before responding.
4 Put your response calmly and coherently. If you feel the criticism is unjustified or too unspecific, ask for clarification or an example.

Putting criticism into perspective is essential if you are to have a balanced working life. Worrying about it too much will make you fearful, nervous and risk averse in decision-making. And this is not the stuff that successful managers are made of. Developing resilience to criticism (and other forms of adversity) is a key managerial skill. Sometimes, however, we need to stand up for ourselves in the face of unjust criticism or when we suspect that the truth is being distorted to undermine us. (And this will happen.)

At my last interview I was told I didn't get the job because I came across as aggressive. I was very upset by this and don't know what to do about it.

Lee, hotel manager

Lee made the mistake of not asking for clarification when she was given this feedback. What was it about her manner that led the interviewer to that conclusion? Can he give examples of what she said or how she said it? How could she adjust her behaviour? When criticism is not given constructively we are entitled to challenge it, rather than simply accepting it and worrying about it later.

Dealing with difficult people

In the early stages of your career, coping with people who make you uncomfortable or angry or make unreasonable demands can be very stressful. What should you do to manage the situation?

Most women prefer to pacify, soothe and smooth over the water. But, Princessas understand chaos creates chances. Forcing a showdown means you are challenging the accepted order. It reflects your power.

Harriet Rubin[3]

1 You must tackle it – and sooner rather than later. Letting unacceptable behaviour go unchallenged allows it to get worse and makes it more difficult to deal with subsequently.
2 Reflect on past feedback given to you by others (see Workbook Exercises in Chapter Five) and ask yourself

whether anything about your behaviour could have been misconstrued or caused friction, leading to the present situation. Is there anything you could do to make yourself easier to work with?

3 Stepping back, how would an outsider see the situation? Are gender, ethnicity or differences in background contributing to the situation? Do you always treat others as you would like to be treated or do you tend to change your behaviour towards those who irritate and annoy you?

4 In confidence (avoid gossiping), approach others you work with to find out if they share your problem with the individual in question. Have they any coping strategies they can share with you?

5 Having taken stock you need to confront the situation by talking directly to the person involved. To make this easier, plan what you want to say and choose your moment carefully. Find somewhere private to have a talk – possibly outside of work – to ensure you have the other person's full attention. Think about the person you are dealing with, and adjust your style and approach for maximum effectiveness. Think about his or her body language and about how he or she communicates with others.

6 Be professional and don't fight fire with fire. Strive for an atmosphere of cooperation by showing concern and by asking open, non-threatening questions about problem areas. Listen attentively, follow the nuances of what is being said and check your understanding before you reply. Maintain eye contact and control the pitch and tone of your voice.

7 If the situation has become very acrimonious, or you fear the other person may become aggressive, then seek out a mediator who can help control the discussion and facilitate a workable outcome. In some circumstances it may be appropriate to involve your union representative (if you have one).

8 Should the problem remain unresolved or if you really cannot confront the person, keep a log of all incidents that cause you distress or difficulty, listing times, dates and the names of any witnesses. Write down how you felt after each incident. This will act as useful evidence should you need to take the matter further.

9 Before the situation becomes too stressful, talk to the human resources team or your head of department. State why you find the behaviour unacceptable, put forward your evidence and state clearly how this is affecting your work and what you would like to see happen.

Finally, you may have to recognize that, though you can't change other people, you can change your approach to them. Whenever you are dealing with confrontation state the problem clearly and avoid tagging on distracting side issues. Be firm: 'If you don't stand for something, you'll fall for anything', so decide what you will and will not accept. Try to ensure that you reach a solution and then reflect on the lessons you have learned and move forward.

When all else fails

There may be times when you feel like giving up. Perhaps there are insuperable problems with your boss or with a colleague; perhaps you feel your promotion is blocked; or perhaps you are simply no longer fulfilled by your work. Before you resign, however, reflect on the other options available.

■ Have you made real efforts to resolve any conflicts or difficulties? Or, fearing confrontation, would you rather move on than deal with the situation? Tempting though this may be, you can't keep running away from conflict, you must learn to deal with it constructively.

■ Could you ask your boss for more responsibility, or are there new projects that you could get involved in? Does your company have a coaching or mentoring scheme from which you could draw support in developing your career? Be assertive in asking for what you want and set your sights high.

■ Have you explored all the promotion possibilities? If you have been told you are not yet ready or there is no vacancy at the next level, what about job shadowing? Could you start to learn another job while waiting for an opening?

■ What about a lateral move or a job swap to acquire new skills? Think about the gaps in your portfolio (see below) – if, for example, you have no finance or IT experience, how could you acquire some?

■ If you feel you must leave then begin your job search, but don't tell your colleagues. Remembering that your next employer may ask for references, continue to do your job conscientiously – even during your notice period – and make sure you leave on good terms with everyone. Do not see this as an opportunity to settle old scores – you never know when or under what circumstances you may meet people again.

CASE STUDY

Anne and Sharon were account managers in a large international company. Both were ambitious and when an internal promotion came up they both applied. After the interview and assessment panels had been held, Sharon was called in to see the head of department and told that, it had been a close call, but it had been decided to appoint Anne. Sharon faced a difficult dilemma at this point, since she knew that Anne had applied for and been offered a job elsewhere, working for a competitor in fact. Should she tell the head of department at this stage or wait to see what Anne would decide? She liked Anne and was reluctant to betray a confidence, but she had her career to think of too.

This story illustrates the dangers inherent in taking others into your confidence once you decide to move on. Apart from the risks to your own position should someone betray your confidence, it may also create a dilemma for the person in whom you have confided. In this case Sharon has very little thinking time in which to decide what to do. She could hint that Anne is moving on or even tell her boss outright what's happening. The problem with this is that if he then confronts Anne she may deny everything (saying that Sharon must have misunderstood). If Anne then goes on to accept the promotion, Sharon will still have to work with her and that could prove very awkward, particularly if Anne is in a more senior position.

The only course open to Sharon is to keep quiet and see what happens. If Anne takes the promotion perhaps Sharon would be best advised to seek a transfer or look for new opportunities elsewhere in the medium term.

Handing in your resignation

Telling your boss of your intention to leave can be nerve-racking and the best way to minimize the stress is to prepare beforehand what you intend to say and then stick to the script. You may need to be quite agile in avoiding giving more information than you wish to – your boss may well probe for details.

Attempts may be made at a counter-offer. You should have prepared your response beforehand. What is your bargaining position in relation to what might be offered (more money, promotion, a transfer)? Would you entertain a counter-offer or are you set on moving on? Decide a game plan and stick to your guns.

Your boss may get upset, overreact or even become confrontational. Keep control and without appearing obstructive, simply reiterate your prepared points and do not be drawn. Dwell on the positives – the opportunities you have been given and the things you have learned. Be as helpful as possible in leaving everything in good order and in handing over to your replacement. Try to leave on a good note, ensuring that the last impression is as positive as that first one you strove so hard to make.

Lastly, keep the door open. Maintain your business contacts and relationships with mentors and influential people as well as your friends. They are part of the network that should underpin your career throughout your working life.

Grace under fire

So far we have talked about establishing credibility. In order to sustain and build it further we need to be aware of the importance of maintaining control. Work pressures and stress can lead to loss of control at times, but if we can be aware of the triggers likely to push us over the edge then we can take timely action to avert an inappropriate outburst.

Symptoms of a loss of control include:

- Bad temper
- Bad manners
- Swearing
- Being late or disorganized
- Being hypercritical.

So we need to maintain a professional demeanour at all times, controlling negative emotional responses and being always well presented and well prepared. Being controlled is a little like playing poker. Both require practice to achieve competence and in both we must control our reactions (the poker face) so as not to give too much away inadvertently. This is distinct from the considered displays of emotion linked to charisma that we advocated in Chapter Five.

TOP CAREER TIPS

When confronted with the unexpected:

- Keep cool; do not react immediately.
- Do not make snap judgements.
- Get the facts – ask questions to clarify the position.
- Take time to reflect.
- Make a considered response.
- Never side against superiors or peers or gossip about them with your subordinates – you teach them bad habits.

Decisions, decisions

Decision making is an important managerial skill that we all must acquire. But many people find this hard through:

- Fear of making a mistake
- Reluctance to take risks
- Lack of confidence in their own judgement
- Excessive eagerness to please others.

As a consequence they put their career development in jeopardy. For the ability to be decisive draws admiration and raises our credibility: leadership and decisiveness are synonymous.

When dealing with contentious issues, sound people out
beforehand. If they have taken an entrenched position, offer
them some options: 'If we did this ... would your view change?'
Julie Bradley, managing partner Devonshires

How can you make that vital next step towards being an effective
manager?

▪ Realize that having perfect information is impossible and
   make the best possible choice based on the data available.
   Having reached a decision, focus on a positive outcome and
   see it through.
▪ Seek advice by consulting those whose opinions you value
   and run your solutions past them. (This is not an
   opportunity to abdicate responsibility; it is about using
   others as a sounding board.)
▪ Be sure you have the appropriate authority for the level of
   decision you are taking. Check whether the matter should be
   referred up.
▪ Draw on the skills and experience of your team. Though this
   takes time, it gives you access to a wider pool of ideas. Do
   not dismiss out of hand suggestions you do not like – you'll
   stifle initiative. Be prepared to consider everyone's view
   before you reach a conclusion.
▪ Have the courage of your convictions and once you have
   formed a view you can substantiate, then stick with it. You
   will respect yourself and show others what you are made of.
▪ Do not be afraid to follow instinct and intuition. This way of
   thinking taps into our understanding at a deeper level – the
   more experience you gain as a manager, the more you will
   learn to trust your 'gut feel'. It is usually possible to work
   back from an intuitive idea to support it with rational
   arguments acceptable to other, more analytical, thinkers.
▪ Do not be panicked into the wrong decision. Take some
   small actions to move the issue along while you reflect on it
   calmly. 'Sleep on it' is sound advice.

Hindsight is a wonderful thing and, unfortunately, it is often
impossible to foresee the outcome of our decisions until after the
event. So do not angst about what you have decided: even if

the outcome is not what you wanted, you have the right to make mistakes – it is part of the learning process.

Interacting with senior managers

Meeting senior managers can be nerve racking because they have the power to influence your career progress. Naturally you will want to make a good impression. But how does one do this without appearing to try too hard?

Plan and prepare

Efficiency always impresses. So whether you are interacting with a senior manager from your own or a client's organization, do your homework and be up-to-date with:

■ The current state of your own/your customer's business.
■ The state of the client's account where relevant (research the history).
■ The manager's organizational role and responsibilities.
■ Key issues of the day – read a quality newspaper and have a view.

Have an agenda (if you have requested the meeting) or be aware of his or her priorities and purpose, and rehearse what you want to say. Check in advance you have all you need – documents, facts and figures, brochures and other material. (But beware of information overload.)

First impressions count

So be on time (a few minutes early). Dress smartly and avoid fashion statements. Make sure nothing about your appearance could be seen as girlish – you need to establish credibility (refer to Chapter Five). When the meeting opens, wait for the senior person to extend his or her hand. Shake it firmly, smiling pleasantly and greet him or her formally ('How do you do?

Thank you for agreeing to see me.') Make confident eye contact to establish rapport. Being prepared is crucial, since it is easy to become tongue-tied when meeting the great and the good. An American friend of mine was once introduced to Eisenhower (twice President of the USA and Joint Allied Chief Commander in the Second World War). He was so overawed that he only managed to stammer: 'Thanks to meet you, Sir.' He has never forgotten the quizzical look with which the great man met this salutation.

Try not to show intimidation

Avoid looking tense and apprehensive by practising some relaxation and breathing exercises prior to the meeting. You must not mumble or speak too quickly. Be confident – you are well prepared and have a valid contribution to make.

Make a good beginning

Wait to be invited to sit and respect his or her personal space. (Do not, for example, put your briefcase or papers on the desk.) Wait for the senior person to open the dialogue ('What can I do for you?'). Be respectful in your manner, but not sycophantic. When asked, state your purpose and check how much time you have and mentally allocate your priorities accordingly. Never use first names unless invited to do so or if you know this to be the organizational norm. Avoid trying to impress or to seem to know more than you do – that way lies disaster. Fight shy of making jokes – you may be nervous and you do not want to sound inane. Also, you are unlikely to be able to gauge the other person's sense of humour at this stage.

Try to think before you respond to questions. Nothing wrong with a brief pause, it shows you are giving the matter your full attention. Beware of giving more information than the person asks for or requires. Keep to the point, stay focused and do not let your concentration lapse. Listen actively and make notes if appropriate. (But don't write everything down verbatim unless you are being given detailed instructions.)

Making an effective close

Should the discussion still be in mid-flow when your time slot is nearing its end, pause to confirm whether you can continue. Leave enough time to review and summarize your action points and timescales. Offer to minute the meeting and send a copy. Thank the person for their time and say how much you have enjoyed meeting them. This will sound more sincere if you can mention something particularly interesting that you learned from the encounter. If there is follow-up activity make sure you keep your promises and fulfil your action points promptly.

Moving up

Seek out other women

Earlier chapters have stressed the importance in career planning of seeking out women-friendly companies in order to avoid some of those more likely to hold you back. In order to be well informed you need to do your research (newspapers, financial reports and the Internet), not only by counting the number of women in senior management and on the board, but also by scrutinizing company policies and by talking to women inside the organization to check that it delivers on its stated values.

I have constantly emphasised the need for networking, and your primary one should be drawn from other women. They have years of experience in dealing with many of the challenges that will confront you. Move quickly up the learning curve by drawing on that experience. Though male mentors can sometimes be helpful, research shows that it is predominantly women who support other women in their careers.

There are also problems inherent in older males mentoring younger women because of ingrained gender stereotyping:[4]

- It is difficult for male mentors to identify with their protégées.
- They may be tempted to lapse into a father–daughter relationship and become overprotective.
- It lays both participants open to accusations of a sexual liaison.

■ In addition, the woman may become ensnared in the time-honoured role of handmaiden/assistant, or even find herself relegated to token protégée as the company strives to be seen to be women-friendly.

CASE STUDY

'While I was doing my training I went out after work with my boss and a group of colleagues. He began to recount a favourite case involving the Obscene Publications Act. He described in graphic detail, and with apparent relish, the pornographic material he was required to look at in order to gather evidence. I was horrified. I felt undermined and very vulnerable because of the power imbalance. I wanted to protest, but my livelihood depended on this man. I don't know if he was aware of the effect this had on me, but I was very upset.'

Elizabeth, barrister

Unfortunately, in some instances, it also allows the man to abuse his power and authority, often in quite unsavoury ways. Did this man realize the effect he was having? Can there be any doubt? But, of course, when you are young and inexperienced you are totally unprepared for this kind of behaviour. That is why you need to draw on the support of other, more experienced, women who are wiser in the ways of men.

Building an effective network

Behind every successful businessperson is a strong network of powerful and influential people able to open up a wealth of business and other opportunities. At the earliest possible stage you must begin systematically to build your own network. However busy you think you are it is time well spent. Banish images of manipulation, insincerity and 'selling' yourself. This is not about judging everyone in terms of how useful they might be: it is more about giving than receiving. The best networkers start by generously sharing whatever favours are at their disposal: leads, contacts, referrals or helpful ideas. They are the archetypal 'resource investigators' who put themselves out as facilitators and matchmakers to those they meet at business and other events. This is 'relationship networking', and it's about building connections with people and collecting rather than distributing business cards.

Networking is about finding people with similar interests in order to create synergy. Women do it more instinctively than men, without necessarily having a clear agenda. Men always have an agenda ready to run.

Rabbi Julia Neuberger, CEO The King's Fund

What goes around comes around

Once a connection has been made, the skilful networker will constantly find ways to renew it: whether by e-mailing interesting news or by posting off clippings and other useful information. It is also important to see your network as a whole – who could be helpful to whom – rather than simply who could be helpful to *you*. By doing favours without expecting an immediate return you store up credit on which you will later be able to draw when you need help. Taking this selfless approach will build your reputation and repay you many times over. 'But,' some of you may say, 'I don't have the confidence at big events to approach people I don't know.' (And the temptation at conferences is always to 'find a friend' as a security blanket.)

Here are some suggestions to help you overcome your shyness:

- Visualize having the confidence, charm and friendliness you aspire to (think of a role model you admire) and then *act as if* you were that person.
- Find someone who looks as lost as you feel and offer to introduce him or her to someone you know. You will quickly forget your own nerves if you focus on putting someone else at their ease.
- Get involved in the organization of the event if your company is hosting, so that you have a formal role in greeting people and showing them round.
- Be proactive in meeting others; don't just huddle with a group of colleagues the whole time.

■ Introduce yourself to put the other person at ease, ask questions to draw them out and listen closely to their replies. (Chapter Nine discusses listening and communication skills.)

■ Target people you want to meet by obtaining a delegate list beforehand, and prepare what you will say to them.

Building your career portfolio

As we have seen, in the world of employment today we can expect to have several jobs and career changes, requiring us to retrain and acquire new skills.

There is no such thing as a career path – it's more like crazy paving and you have to lay it yourself.

With the need to move upwards or laterally, or to change jobs to advance our careers we need constantly to prove our employability. Having a career portfolio is a means to demonstrate why we should be selected ahead of others. The portfolio has been described as 'an imaginary briefcase full of evidence of your talents and experience'.[5] The more you can pack your portfolio with impressive evidence of your skills and competences the more valuable it will be. Employers look for two sets of qualities in employees: attributes and skills.

1 The key attributes sought by today's employers are:
   ■ Enthusiasm for learning
   ■ Good communication skills
   ■ Flexible team players.

2 The critical areas of skills and experience include:
   ■ Marketing and PR
   ■ Leading teams
   ■ Financial control (managing a budget)
   ■ IT literacy.

As you develop your portfolio, you need to look for opportunities to build your experience in valued areas and to collect evidence of the skills you acquire. Tangible evidence includes certificates of study and proof of attendance at conferences and seminars. In addition, ask for written feedback from managers in whose projects you have been involved, as well as from customers and colleagues, if appropriate. Include everything in your portfolio.

Top career tips

- Be proactive in information gathering and goal setting.
- Be alert to new opportunities to learn, develop and progress.
- Take on new responsibilities and extend the parameters of your job.
- Volunteer for tasks that make you more valuable (but know when to say no and do so pleasantly but assertively).
- Make time to study.
- Constantly update your CV and monitor the gaps.
- Look at the competences required at the next level up the organization (see the job description and talk to job holders) and plan how you will prepare yourself for promotion.
- Understand the key elements of your boss's job and be prepared to act up.
- Show enthusiasm for your job and tell others what you enjoy about it.

Volunteering: The single most important thing to do if you want to develop professionally and intellectually.[6]

The trick is to identify the key issues at work (in your sector as well as your company) and to find tasks you could perform or get involved with to influence decisions about those issues. Finally, remember that if you raise your profile at work some people won't like it. But don't let them sabotage your efforts. Don't be oversensitive: women are particularly anxious about what others think. Remember: act powerfully and people will treat you accordingly. If you are to be successful, you need to worry less about being liked by everyone and more about being effective in what you do.

Opportunities are usually disguised as hard work. That's why so few people recognize them.

Anne Landers

SOME PERSONAL ASSESSMENT QUESTIONS AND ACTION POINTS

1 What additional practical skills do you need to acquire (e.g. IT, making presentations; personal image)? What could you do at work or in your own time to acquire those skills?
2 What aspects of your job could you expand by taking on new responsibilities (e.g. by innovating new systems and processes)?
3 Thinking creatively, how could you link your job to work that interests you or broadens your profile?
4 What shape is your portfolio in currently? Make an action point to review and update the evidence in it.
5 Write out a 90 day CV for yourself:
   - Set some goals and timescales
   - Review it regularly to assess progress
   - Decide on new achievements
   - Constantly re-evaluate to improve.

Getting a salary increase or promotion

We saw in Chapter Two that women are notoriously bad at asking for the salary increases and promotions they deserve, compared with their male colleagues. We also saw in Chapter Five how important it is to communicate your ambitions and goals to your boss if you want to be seen as promotable. A little planning and a few simple steps will move you in the right direction:

1 Book an initial meeting with your boss to explain that you are keen to add value in your work. State clearly your career goals and ambitions. Ask what you have to do to get a salary increase or promotion within a reasonable time span.
2 Find out his or her objectives and ask for special projects that will develop your skills and help you make a greater contribution to those objectives. Demonstrate your willingness to support him or her and the department through your work.
3 Ensure you diarize progress meetings with your boss to get and give feedback

4 Check the appointments pages to see what other companies are paying for the same work that you do.
5 At the progress meetings be ready to show the evidence in your portfolio of your achievements relevant to the tasks set.
6 If your boss will not help or 'company policy' stands in the way of your progress, think about moving to a more lucrative job elsewhere.

Although line managers argue that assessments are made on objective criteria, they will admit, when pressed, that perceived ambition and networking play an important role at higher management levels. Since gender stereotyping labels women as less ambitious, and since women are seen as less able to participate in informal networking than men, we can see how women can be disadvantaged in the pay and promotion stakes. This is another reason why it is critically important for women to develop more political savvy and to use it to their advantage at work.

Barriers to moving up

Gender stereotyping

There is a danger that what follows in this section may be dismissed by some younger women, who may think that what we have to say on the subject of male behaviour no longer applies. In the face of media hype about the 'post-feminist era' they may have been lulled into believing that problems faced by women in the past were peculiar to their mothers' generation, and that since then men's attitudes have changed dramatically. Where once there was sexism among men, now there is thought to be admiration for women's confidence, financial independence and educational achievements.

> *Young women think they have got it made, and men are inclined to agree. The best of all possible worlds is on the horizon, in which women are independent and men have all the sexual partners they could desire. For make no mistake about it, men still see young women as sex objects, and those same*

young women are not entirely sure they are unhappy about that. Today's young women do not feel hostile, they feel friendly towards the men they meet . . . and are convinced that their refusal to engage in hostilities and their unambiguous friendliness allow men to see them as equals.[7]

In her brilliantly researched and wittily presented book,[8] Elizabeth Mapstone has explored the psychology of argument and shown that gender is central to the meaning of the exchanges that take place in both our social and working lives. What we are talking about here is not the language we use or our conversational style – we reflect on those issues elsewhere – but about how the experience of 'arguing' is perceived and remembered. One of the key issues for working women is the way in which gender stereotyping militates against them in any argument at work. For, as Mapstone points out:

Because argument in practice is often seen as adversarial and inimical to feelings of warmth and friendship, arguing has traditionally been construed as a masculine occupation, while women have been expected to avoid it by conciliation.[9]

Mapstone's research shows that gender stereotypes allow men to discount women's disagreements. That is not to say *all* men discount *all* women's arguments, but gender roles provide a framework within which women's arguments can be interpreted in such a way that the man is not required to modify his position. Of course, as many of us can testify, men will take advantage of this. But this is not the worst of it: the real threat lies in the all-pervasive assumption that women are incapable of rational and logical argument.

It will be another twenty years before most elements of unconscious stereotyping can be eradicated.

Helena Dennison, founder of
the Women's City Network[10]

We saw in Chapter Three some of the gender stereotypes applied to women in order to control them, and how the common denominator is that none of the stereotypes requires men to treat women as equals. And this, as Mapstone so clearly demonstrates, is what happens when women and men interact at work.

Meetings, bloody meetings

At the first partners' meeting I attended there was silence every time I spoke. Men don't like to challenge a woman in front of other men in case they lose – they won't risk a public confrontation.

Senior woman lawyer

Attending and performing well at meetings is critical to your career advancement, since they provide a forum where you can showcase your talents to a wider audience of peers, influencers and decision-makers. The scenarios women encounter in meetings are well documented and the issues are all about how to get yourself heard and your agendas recognized. Typically, when women try to take the lead in meetings the men shift uncomfortably, look away and appear not to have heard. Whatever suggestions a woman makes are met with silence. And if the ideas are any good, they subsequently resurface, put forward by a man as his own.

Last week I had the wonderful experience of having one of my ideas stolen by a male colleague. The thing is that my project was presented to the whole group while I was not there. Everyone thought it was great and the company president approved it. Now I don't know what to do to get back credit for the whole idea.

Paola, recruitment manager, Italy

So, we see the same reaction to competent women everywhere. In Paola's case it seems the act was conscious and deliberate. But men routinely exclude women from decision making and refuse to listen when they speak because this might require them to amend their view of the world: first by admitting that women have a valid, rational contribution to make, and, second, by possibly having to act on it.

The red thread

We will return to Paola's specific problem shortly, but for now let us consider what to do when our ideas are 'stolen' in meetings. Harriet Rubin talks about the 'Red Thread' we can use to reel our ideas back in.[11] She suggests we open with the phrase: 'When that first occurred to me . . .' and then elaborate on the idea in a way that only its originator would be able to do.

In the old order, decision making is men's work and they feel threatened when their role is usurped:

Men always try to talk over you. It deteriorates into a real free-for-all sometimes and you can't make yourself heard.

Pamela, finance manager

Sometimes the following approach can be successful in dealing with this:

■ Drop the pitch of your voice; speak more slowly and more loudly.

Harriet Rubin also suggests the physiological technique of lowering your heart rate so that, by a kind of echo effect, it occurs in others and you influence and control them by the pace of your heart rate and breathing.[12] This technique, of course, requires practice if it is to be used with confidence. But, Rubin assures us, if you use it you will begin to be heard.

Above all, avoid entering the fray. You won't be heard. Better to speak more quietly, become the eye of the storm, so that others strain to hear. When interviewing Martha Lane Fox we were intrigued by how quietly she spoke, but her undoubted intelligence and business acumen make you want to listen closely to what she has to say.

Branded as a troublemaker

One way that men may reject women's ideas is to brand them as 'idealistic' for which read 'unrealistic'. This is because women's ideas often mean uncomfortable change for men – remember how we like to find new ways of doing things, requiring them to move their thinking or their actions outside the box.

I have the results on my budget, but they (senior management) don't accept my way of doing things. I'm always seen as creating problems because I want to change the way we do things.
Susanne, sales manager, Austria

In the last century the concept of woman as the power behind the throne was commonplace. Indeed some women even argued that the emancipation of women was unnecessary. What need had a woman for the vote when she could influence the way her husband cast his? Today it runs against the grain for younger women to countenance anything but plain speaking in business – after all, modern assertiveness training encourages us to ask for what we want and to state our views openly. But apparently this is just the way to antagonize the men we work with:

Women who display high status behaviour will be threatening to a male audience unless they also communicate that they have no desire to usurp male status.
Linda Carli, American Association for
the Advancement of Science[13]

High status behaviour includes speaking loudly, rapidly and with conviction, as well as making frequent eye contact. So we need to avoid emphasizing our competence – the normal default pattern for contemporary women trying to establish their credibility:

I seem to be the main target of a lot of aggression – I'm a woman and I'm American. It's a constant negotiation to get agreement or approval for my proposals from senior management. I give my opinion and I'm personally attacked – they tell me I don't know what I'm talking about. And when I try to defend myself by citing my experience and training they tell me my MBA is worthless.
Christine, an American working in Switzerland

Instead, it would seem that, in order to influence men we need to avoid coming on too strong. We must make them like us rather than getting them to acknowledge our competence. For, as Mapstone points out, when we think we are being knowledgeable, competent, confident and intelligent, we are perceived by men as unlikeable, condescending and threatening.

KEY RESEARCH FINDINGS
Women who are effective in arguing with men are usually careful to signal their awareness that they are dealing with a man.

In a one-to-one situation a possible approach might be:

- A soft, gentle voice
- A suggestion of self-deprecation.

But this can be just a front – the iron fist in the velvet glove. And remember, it's just a technique to get you what you want.

As Harriet Rubin maintains, rational strategies don't always work and they are not every woman's natural style. It doesn't matter that the tactics are manipulative: they can be fun and take us outside the confines of inhibiting rules, allowing us to use our inherent strengths.

Now I've learned an important lesson: even with people who don't trust you or feel threatened, you can form alliances and join together to deal with a common enemy. Then they let the barriers down and accept you.

Karin, HR director, Italy

Getting your share of voice

To be successful in meetings we need some different approaches. Again we need to downplay our competence as a reference point when we are discussing or negotiating, and focus instead on projecting warmth. One technique you might try in seeking to establish credibility for your ideas is to refer to a third party – to an article or report you have read – and draw on that as an independent validating source. ('According to a report in the *FT* last week . . .')

Prior to meetings we need to use some political skill to sound people out about our agendas and try to form alliances. Women have resisted this in the past for fear of being seen as ganging up against men ('the monstrous regiment of women') or as gossiping. But we need to join with other women in a common cause and recognize that collectively we can achieve more than if we act in isolation. As we mentioned in Chapter Six, it is important not to be naïve about organizational politics – they are an unavoidable fact of office life and we must learn to use them to our advantage. If we try to ignore them, others may use them against us.

The great and almost only comfort about being a woman is that one can always pretend to be more stupid than one is, and no one is surprised.

Dame Freya Madeleine Stark[14]

Language and labels

A common way for men to control women and diffuse the threat they pose is through abusive language and name-calling. Who hasn't heard a female politician referred to as 'a cow', 'a bitch', 'a ball breaker' or 'an old dog'? The former prime minister of the UK, Margaret Thatcher, herself the frequent target for such epithets, reportedly said that it always cheered her up immeasurably whenever the criticism got personal, because then she knew that the other side hadn't a single political argument left. The purpose of name-calling is to discredit women by labelling them with some gender stereotype that, though irrelevant to the matter in hand, emphasizes once more that women are not to be taken seriously. As an example, older women will be described as 'old bags' or 'menopausal'. For if a woman is no longer a sex object then it's legitimate for the man to dismiss her.

Men are in denial about their sexism, but in private they like to undermine women colleagues. They play the game of 'Who is the ugliest woman lawyer you have to deal with?'

Senior woman lawyer

At the Woman Lawyer Conference in April 2000, Mo Mowlam talked eloquently of the backlash against women. In her experience, when women achieve equal representation, men feel disadvantaged because this challenges their natural assumption of power and dominance and they become antagonistic, undermining women of all ages by referring to them as 'girls'.

Strong women, who strive to push through their agendas, are usually perceived as 'strident' (a man would be 'firm', 'strong' and 'decisive'). Mapstone suggests that rather than running away from them, we should embrace the words used to criticize us and make them our own. Remember again Margaret Thatcher. Years ago she was described by a Russian newspaper as the 'Iron Maiden' (an instrument of torture). Thatcher immediately turned this to her advantage by changing it to the 'Iron Lady' and claiming it as her trophy.

It's hard to be heard. We adapt our vocabulary to the language
of men and when we talk their language we are less convincing.

Avivah Wittenberg-Cox[15]

Coping with male colleagues

One of the unavoidable conclusions in Mapstone's book is that men feel under no obligation to agree with their female colleagues. Women on the other hand recognize the need to reach a win : win outcome in negotiation – we want to get our point across, but understand we must compromise sometimes.

Because women are now skilled at presenting their viewpoint logically and cogently they rarely see a problem with their male colleagues. They generally believe men are willing to listen and accept their arguments. But in the diaries kept by men of their exchanges with women colleagues in the Mapstone research, they consistently recorded that their arguments with women were unimportant (and could therefore be ignored) or that the women became emotional and took things personally.

By contrast the women recorded that these same arguments *were* important and that they succeeded in being heard because they were calm and rational. Men have problems hearing the content of a woman's argument when she speaks logically because of the gender myth that holds women incapable of rational argument. As a result, men try to work out what the woman *really* means when she is speaking, and because they have a vested interest in declaring her incompetent, if she persists in her argument – because she doesn't think she is being heard – then she is seen as overreacting. They see her as emotional and difficult. Further, men reported that three out of four times their female colleague did not listen, but this too was deemed unimportant.

Dirty tricks campaigns

Conveniently forgetting

The previous section begs the question: Why are men so indifferent about convincing women? The answer is that men think they can get around the issue anyway. Two scenarios often ensue from arguments between men and women at work:

- Women find their views have been ignored and the men do what they want anyway.
- Men agree a course of action and then win by letting the matter drop or by not implementing the changes agreed.

How to overcome these attempts at sabotage?

I write everything down. I minute everything and I copy everyone in. That way there can be no arguments about who agreed to what.

Sharon, account manager

Writing things down is your insurance against memory lapses ('I'm sure I never agreed to that!').

Over your head and behind your back

A common ploy used by men to clip a woman's wings and some-times to get rid of her is to approach her boss and complain about her, either directly or by innuendo. Mapstone describes how women are a visible and direct challenge when they hold power and, because they are seen as usurping men's role, they are considered fair game. In the face of conflict with a woman, roll out the gender assumptions again:

■ She is clearly incompetent (I disagree with her decision).
■ She is offensive and rude (she put me down and I feel offended).
■ Her personality does not fit (she is a woman and should not be in a position of authority).

Men will say things about you that are not true; they'll try intimidation and bullying. I just stay completely deadpan and refuse to react. They can't cope when you don't respond.

Account director, IT company

The resentment and anger men feel is because a woman is in power and she shouldn't be. That's their prerogative.

If a woman succeeds in a role, it's put down to good luck; if she fails, it's because she's not competent. It's the reverse for men. If they succeed, they're competent; if they fail it's down to bad luck.

Helena Dennison[16]

Whispering campaigns too are often waged behind women's backs, with allegations ranging from incompetence and emotional instability to promiscuity and even lesbianism.

When my old boss and I left the States to take up new jobs together in Europe, a colleague warned me: 'Just be aware that people will say you followed John as his mistress.' And they did.

Marcia, fund manager

As with bullying and other forms of harassment this can almost induce paranoia, making the victim feel powerless and ashamed. So how do you deal with it? The first thing is not to be surprised by it. Vicious and unpleasant though these attacks may be, they go with the territory. They are a male response to the threat of incursion by competent female rivals, especially if those females (as is often the case) are campaigning for change.

If you put your head over the parapet, expect to get the flak. In this business professional jealousy is rife. When my profile appeared in the trade paper a male colleague got very huffy with me. When I asked him what the problem was he said he didn't like the article because it made me look more important than him.

Beverly, chief accountant

Next, brazen it out. Accused of sleeping your way to the top? Laugh it off: 'If only it had been that simple.' Hold your head up and prepare to raise your profile both inside and outside the organization:

TOP CAREER TIPS

■ Get involved and get elected to office – particularly within a high-profile professional organization.

■ Get into print – write something for publication to demonstrate your expertise.

Establishing your competence and status in another, public arena will widen your support network and enhance your credibility at work. Though this may not always have the desired effect:

Some years ago, a colleague with whom I had previously worked was brought in as my boss. Soon after we attended an industry conference together, where I was presented with a major award in recognition of my achievements. At the conference itself my new boss began running me down to my colleagues and others – much to their surprise. They were quite shocked that he was unable to express pride in the achievement of his team member. I was hurt and felt terribly undermined – I couldn't understand what I had done wrong.

Jennifer, computer training specialist

So what is going on here then? Professional jealousy of a woman competing on equal terms (and winning) has sparked a game of 'blemish', a power play adopted by people when threatened, in order to discredit the achievements of others. Interesting, too, that this particular male – though he misjudged some of his audience – must have believed he could make the accusation of incompetence stick *even in the face of overwhelming evidence to the contrary.* How could he attempt this if not by implicit reference to the widely held gender stereotypes of female incompetence?

Stealing your ideas

We have not forgotten Paola, whose colleague stole her project and presented it as his own. We have suggested below some strategies you might find helpful in her situation, depending on the precise circumstances, your objectives and your preferred style:

- **To win back the high ground and take back the project** Tell your colleague that you have rechecked the project details and some vital information was missing or incorrect. Ask him when he would like to go over the project with the team and the president to explain the omission or discrepancy. (If there are no discrepancies you can say later that they were an error in calculation.) Or

- **Take back the project and stay on good terms with the colleague** Approach your colleague and say how disappointed you were not to present the project yourself and that you feel the relationship of trust between you has been seriously damaged. You will therefore need to explore this with senior management and/or the HR department. Perhaps you are being oversensitive, but you feel that an objective perspective on the problem might help you work through it. Or

- **Marginalize the colleague and take the project back** Send out a memo or e-mail about the project to the whole team and the president – again referring to some important detail or making a comment that shows some in-depth knowledge about the work. Ensure, in a subtle manner, that there can be no doubt it was your project. Do not copy in your colleague.

- **As a last resort** If you cannot get any support and if you feel strongly enough, explain to your manager that you feel this is a resigning issue if you can't trust colleagues to give you credit for your work. Of course, you should not make such threats unless you are prepared to go through with them. But if this kind of behaviour is characteristic of the organization and no one else is prepared to take a stand against it, you may want to reconsider whether this is a company you should continue working for.

Some years ago, when I was teaching in a university, I initiated a ground-breaking project. An important meeting with an external body was called, for which I wrote a paper, having understood it was an opportunity to present my work. The day before the meeting my boss, who until then had not been involved, told me that he would attend in my place. Making sure he did not have a copy of my report, I deleted it from my PC and took the next day off. Frantic calls were made to my answering machine – where was the report? When I returned to work I behaved completely innocently and said I was very sorry, I had no idea he needed it.

Catherine, trainer and consultant

Revenge is a dish best eaten cold

In the previous section we looked at ways in which we can manage difficult situations, particularly how not to let others get the better of us by stealing our ideas, taking credit for our achievements or other dirty tricks. At this point we would like to add a few words about revenge. It is a fact of business life that every one of us at some time may be the victim of bad behaviour, unfair treatment or even treachery. And we will be powerless to fight back. However, you can take some comfort from the saying: 'What goes around comes around.' The following example illustrates the point nicely.

CASE STUDY

Sue worked briefly for a three-man training partnership in a business development role. It proved a testing time. The partners could not agree priorities, but gave her huge responsibility to deliver additional revenue without any authority to make things happen. She felt isolated and constantly undermined. Finally, close to a breakdown, she was made redundant. The damage to her self-esteem and to her confidence in her professional judgement was enormous. However, she negotiated three months' pay in lieu of notice and took some time to recover and look for work. She was fortunate to get the first job she applied for – a temporary post developing training materials for a large public company. Very quickly she was given a permanent senior role with a significant budget to design and commission training programmes. One day, to her surprise, as she crossed the reception area she passed one of her former employers waiting to see one of her team to sell in some training. They passed the time of day and he asked what she was doing now. Realization dawned when Sue told him of her new role: 'Well,' he said, attempting jocularity, 'I suppose we can kiss goodbye to any hope of selling training here.' 'Oh, you're absolutely right on that one, Peter,' she replied smiling sweetly.

Our message is that, in the face of adversity, you pick yourself up, dust yourself off and move on. For sooner or later, in our experience, ill-doers get their just deserts, and in ways that are more apt and satisfying than anything you could hope for or imagine.

Managing your manager

I used to challenge my boss and tell him directly that he was wrong. If you do that, watch out! He gets really angry and switches off.

Karin, HR director, Italy

As Mapstone found, men get very angry with their subordinates and don't hesitate to show it, particularly when their instructions are questioned or disregarded. This can cause severe problems, for while men are comfortable within hierarchies and work to perpetuate them, women find them alienating and prefer to break them down. As a consequence women's behaviour is wide open to misinterpretation:

■ Men expect subordinates to obey orders promptly. But women, for whom cooperation and equality are important,

prefer to be *asked* to do things and may want to discuss the
how and why.

■ Women like to change things and break down hierarchies (to
get things done quicker). Men are uncomfortable with this
because it shifts the emphasis to personal relationships and
informal ways of doing things.

■ Women think it silly to be obsessed with status. Men like to
see people observe the correct form and are socialized to
strive to be insiders.

The female subordinate who disregards the formal hierarchy
of authority – however well meaning her intentions – will incur
the wrath of her bosses.

> *The low status woman who appears not to acknowledge the*
> *status of her male superior by arguing with him, almost*
> *inevitably incurs anger.*
>
> Elizabeth Mapstone[17]

The question then arises: How can you present your point of
view without provoking anger? The key is to anticipate the issues
that may arise and to:

■ Incorporate these issues into the work situation by initiating
a discussion about how things might be done and providing
information about how best to accomplish the task (e.g. a
benchmarking report).

■ Let it appear as though you are using your knowledge and
skills to support your boss and to promote him and his
department.

In short, present the benefits to him of the proposals you want to
move forward. Show how they will help him achieve his broader
objectives and enhance both his reputation and that of the
department.

Double talk

In our experience of coaching women managers, a problem often
arises between female subordinates and their male bosses over

the discrepancy between what the boss says he expects of her and his conflicting behaviour when the woman tries to meet those expectations:

Boss's stated expectations

- She needs to get her views heard in meetings.
- She must learn to say no and restrict her workload.
- She must not set herself up to fail.
- She should ease up on perfectionism.

Boss's behaviour in practice

- His failure when chairing meetings to exercise control when people attempt to drown out others (especially women).
- His refusal to reprioritize when additional urgent work arises.
- He allocates unreasonable workload.
- He is highly critical of mistakes.

There is often, too, a failure to recognize that some of the behaviours the male boss asks for are very difficult for women, owing to the prevailing gender stereotypes. Typically a boss might give feedback on the need for a woman to be more 'dynamic', to show greater 'drive' and to be more assertive. Not until we work with the manager to unpick the implications does he realize the problem: dynamic in a male equates to 'pushy' in a woman; having drive and being assertive transpose to being bossy and strident.

CASE STUDY

Earlier we quoted Christine, an American woman working in Switzerland. In her company the hierarchy is dominated by men with a 30-year history in the organization. Most of them are archrivals, fighting for resources and power, and passing down to their subordinates the same attitudes of rivalry and non-cooperation. People are told not to talk to those in other departments. Losing your temper and shouting are seen as legitimate ways to get what you want (if you are an alpha male). This creates a tense, stressful work environment where it is very difficult to get anything done and dissent is seen as rebellion and disobedience. After 18 months Christine is negotiating her way out. And rightly so, for this is an organization where bullying is not only practised but legitimized, and this should not be tolerated.

The boss from hell

None of the books about dealing with difficult people is very helpful when it comes to the really difficult boss. Like many people, I have worked for bad tempered, vain or egocentric men. Perhaps the best I can say is that I survived. In retrospect, though, what would I have done differently if I had known then what I know now? (And it is, I assure you, a case of: 'once bitten twice shy' – I would not want to go there again.)

In the early days of my career (in the 1960s) the Service was very hierarchical and the boss inhabited a huge office on the top floor. One day I was carpeted for a mistake made by one of my team. I have never been so frightened in my life. He was utterly scathing and literally threw the offending file at me. I was devastated by his anger and contempt for me and I was shaking like a leaf. I'll never forget the feeling of terror he inspired.

Margaret, senior civil servant

The precise nature of the boss from hell varies widely. At one end of the spectrum are the 'mad, bad and dangerous to know', exemplified by the mythical tales of press barons publicly lambasting employees who fall short of their exacting standards for dedication and hard work. Few, however, see this behaviour as bullying ('I just like to push my ideas through'), particularly in an industry where such tactics are not unusual. At the other end are the incompetent and ineffectual, those indifferent to challenge and incapable of leadership. In between is every shade of character from the combative and distrustful to the ruthlessly ambitious and opportunistic.

At one point I worked for a director who had no thought or interest in the motivation of his team. His main concerns were his own status and power, and having an easy life. He came into the business when it was expanding and rapidly outgrowing the premises. At a time when everyone was clamouring for space, his first action was – very insensitively – to have his own office enlarged.

Finance Manager

CASE STUDY

'When I worked with the senior partner I hoped to progress quickly, but he never briefed me properly and I was always afraid of making mistakes. I should have set some parameters. I worked hard (until 2 or 3 a.m. some nights) and a partnership was always dangled but never materialized – I was never the right person at the right time. But I loved the kudos of the work and got a kick out of people thinking I was a good lawyer. But I was an idiot to put up with the stress. I wish it had never happened and I'm glad I got out of it – I enjoy life much more now.'

Senior woman lawyer

How best to deal with your particular monster? The first step is to know your enemy by learning to read his (or more unusually *her*) moods and anticipate his or her behaviour. The most disagreeable bosses are those who are apparently indifferent to the good opinion of others and don't hold back on being aggressive, pushy and demanding when they want to get something done.

KEY RESEARCH FINDINGS

Bullying bosses fail to make the most of their employees' talents and kill innovation.[18]

For women, dealing with a difficult boss requires a mental juggling act. Like our male colleagues we must learn to:

■ Try to objectify what is happening by seeing the job title rather than the individual person ('respect for the office').

■ Recognize that some men like to exercise coercive power and draw on their hierarchy status rather than take our preferred cooperative approach.

■ Not take personally behaviour that arises from basic character defects (lack of control, egotism etc.): we are the *occasion* of the behaviour, not the *cause*.

■ Remember: we cannot control the behaviour of others but we *can* control our response to it.

If you can learn to be a chameleon, matching your response to the boss's moods – keeping away when he or she is bad tempered and charming him or her when the opposite is in evidence – then you can learn to survive. But beware: spending your life treading on eggshells can be exhausting and stressful and is usually possible only in the short term. If you do not have or cannot develop the requisite mental toughness and resilience to put up with it, plan your exit route early before you burn out. There is no shame in knowing the limits of what you can tolerate. Fortunately, the demand today for skilled and experienced business people is such that no one is forced to cope indefinitely with a hellish boss. And as more people vote with their feet to join more people-friendly organizations, so we can expect these monsters to die out.

So, what would I do differently? I hope I would have the courage to stand up to unacceptable behaviour by refusing to be bullied and shouted at simply because someone else thought they could get away with it. I would never again think I had to stay in an unpleasant work situation because I *ought* to. I would leave for something better, 'because I'm worth it'. Everyone has the right to be happy at work and to be free from the oppressive tyranny of bosses who do not know how to use power fairly and compassionately.

Women managing men

One of the earliest problems women managers meet is the challenge to their authority from younger male subordinates. As Mapstone shows,[19] these confrontations arise when men cannot accept the idea of equality: they are secretly annoyed at having to compete with women, especially one who appears to be winning because she is the boss. Their resentment sometimes takes the form of subtle aggression, whereby they close ranks and resort to 'locker room' language and horseplay.

Clichés about female bosses still abound to the extent that even some women subscribe to them:

> *I've heard she's a right old battleaxe.*
> Female character in a coffee advert,
> referring to her new female boss

- Women get promoted on their looks.
- They sleep their way to the top.
- They behave like bitches, especially to other women.
- They are dictatorial and don't listen to what others think.

The traditional role of women has been to service those who get to the top, not to get to the top themselves. The real work of decision making belongs to men. To help them cope with this reversal, men fall back on gender stereotypes:

- The woman boss is portrayed as 'nanny' or 'matron' scolding her 'little boys' (Margaret Thatcher).
- She is depicted as emotionally weak and liable to burst into tears.
- She cannot take criticism.
- She is illogical.
- She uses unfair tactics (back to the tears again).
- She nags.

Women managers report that men constantly question their decisions to test whether they are up to the job. As a direct consequence of having to justify her decisions a woman manager, however, is in danger of appearing incompetent. She can be drawn into this kind of discussion because her style is generally more cooperative and consultative, but the old adage holds true: 'Don't complain. Don't explain.' Dealing with these onslaughts can be exhausting so, again, recognize what is happening and don't allow yourself to be undermined. Obliquely and humorously remind them of your authority when they overstep the mark: 'Well, if you are going to persist with this, perhaps we should take it up at your appraisal?' They also need to recognize your power to help advance their careers. If you have established strong networks within and outside the company, then your power base and influence will be much stronger. Also, let off steam by talking to other women who have experienced similar problems. Tell stories and share strategies.

Women near the top deny discrimination in public. But in private they speak out about the fact that they are kept down, have to work harder and be better than the men. Don't pretend you're satisfied if you're not. Men battle for the top as if they have a god-given succession right. Women prepare by collecting qualifications. But these won't open the doors of power.
Dr Eva Latham, human rights specialist
speaking at WIN 2000

But the trouble does not stop here. The real danger is when male subordinates think they can bypass a woman's authority by persuading her (male) boss to override it. Now here we have to be very sure of our ground. It is crucial to establish your competence early in the job, and to make sure your hard work and commitment are made visible. In this way you establish your value to your boss. After all, he appointed you because he had confidence in your ability to do the job and he would be very unhappy to be seen to be wrong. Therefore when younger men challenge they are unlikely to be successful because your boss knows he must support you or risk losing face.

TOP CAREER TIPS
- When challenged be cool, be dignified.
- Keep a written record of what has occurred and, if required by your boss to give an account of your actions, remain calm and recount the facts unemotionally.
- State clearly what you think should happen and how you intend to move it forward.

Managing other women

The women in our research held very positive views of other females. They cited honesty, openness, integrity, loyalty and fair dealing as qualities typical of working women. But women have weaknesses too and those include: a reluctance to say no or to delegate; difficulty in focusing single-mindedly (because of the constant temptation to multitask); and a consensual management style that is often mistaken for an inability to take decisions.

It is these perceived weaknesses that can sometimes lead female subordinates to see their women bosses as incompetent. They can appear muddled, indecisive, disorganized, overworked and lacking authority. And some women simply don't think a woman should be their boss. Since they themselves have low self-esteem, they can't see how a woman can be up to the job. Gender stereotypes are at work again: how can a woman be as bright as a man? She cannot have the same degree of authority and status: women are mothers/nurturers and, as such, not very clever.[20]

Women subordinates need careful handling. Because of their tendency to see instructions as either wrong or unnecessary (especially when issued by a woman), they may not always carry them out. Now, because a woman manager generally takes pains to check understanding when issuing instructions, she becomes quite aggrieved when things are not done to specification. This can lead to friction, especially if she takes a tough line. Women need to be ruled by consent, not coercion and it is important to remember that women managers (but rarely men) may get fired for being abrasive.[21]

It is important to demonstrate to women that you are on their side, to give a sympathetic hearing to their complaints and problems (work and non-work related). At all costs avoid asserting your power and authority. Being authoritarian is male behaviour. Non-nurturing behaviour in women is often seen as domineering. You are expected to be caring. You're a woman – it's your job.

Will you be mother?

Women who adopt warm, motherly personas are more likely to reach and hang on to powerful positions . . .

Elizabeth Mapstone[21]

Young single women (as well as many of us who have children), will baulk at the idea of being seen as motherly. Naturally, having worked for our qualifications and experience we want to be recognized for our competence. But as Mapstone's research clearly demonstrates, gender always handicaps women unless they are prepared to adopt a nurturing role.

Women who appear competent are often perceived as dominant and scary and consequently fail to win people over. We are acceptable to men either as sex objects or as someone to solve their problems (den mother). Should we care about playing the gender game if we can work it to our advantage? Reconciling this issue is very difficult for most women.

I was interviewed for a promotion couple of years ago and was dismayed to realize that the (male) interviewers had not read my CV. They asked me whether I had any sales experience, so I pointed out that I had sold at board level to some of the largest companies in Europe and gave some examples. I didn't get the job, although in the objective tests I achieved higher scores than the other candidates (all men). The feedback they gave me said I came across as passive–aggressive.

Julie, senior manager

In Chapter Five we drew a distinction between femininity and sexuality. We emphasized the importance of not renouncing your femininity to become indistinguishable from your male colleagues. Being able to draw on your female power is a key part of being a woman manager. At the WIN conference in September 2000 a recurring theme was the need for women to stand out rather than trying to blend in. Harriet Rubin even advocated the power of dressing all in white to make a real impact among dark-suited males. This may feel a little extreme to many of us, but a bright splash of colour can certainly enhance both confidence and visibility. It is assertive and makes a statement of independence, disarming our opponents.

In order to succeed in a man's world you can't be plain vanilla.

Linda Marcelli[22]

The WIN keynote speakers were also keen to encourage women to explore the intuitive and playful side of their characters by being provocative, disruptive and challenging the *status quo*. We need to acknowledge gender differences and turn them to our advantage. For example, by using our ability to touch people – physically and emotionally – to make connections.

> *There is a saying: 'It's nothing personal – it's just business.' But business is personal. You manage with your head, but you must lead with your heart and get involved emotionally in order to get the best out of others.*
> Marissa Brambilla, VP Avon Italy, speaking at WIN 2000

Keeping our heads down, doing a good job and being one of the boys may seem a viable strategy, but we are actually more successful when we allow our true nature to shine through by being warm, charming, demonstrative and personal in our working lives.

As we saw earlier, the management style of the future encapsulates many of the qualities embodied by women. But the value of those qualities is not yet fully appreciated in practice (though it is widely acknowledged in theory).

CASE STUDY

A woman engineer was involved in a major project where there was some friction between the different teams participating. She suggested sending thank you notes to the team leaders to say their work was appreciated under difficult circumstances. Although this tactic worked in defusing a potential communication problem, no one recognized it as a valid business contribution. It was merely seen as the sort of 'nice' thing that a woman would do.[23]

As Avivah Wittenberg Cox maintains, we must teach men our language and our ways of doing things and get their legitimacy accepted.

From coping to winning

Perhaps some of the most helpful advice for dealing with the challenges of being a woman in what remains largely a man's world comes again from Harriet Rubin who proposes three core strategies:

Strategy 1   *Ask for everything*

We need to have the courage not to compromise by negotiating only for what we believe we *might* get (or less). When we are outrageous in what we ask for, the other person feels more powerful, and often inclined to be more generous. We ourselves feel entitled to get what we want. Think back to Chapter Five, where we described how favourably bosses respond to the stated ambitions of their (usually male) subordinates. At your next appraisal, when your boss asks for your personal development plan, do not be afraid to set your sights high. Big ideas draw people in far more effectively than small ones.

Strategy 2   *Live your life* as if

The key issue is to live your life *as if* you have power and you will be powerful. Hesitancy immediately undermines our credibility by casting doubt in the minds of others. Remember (again from Chapter Five): it is our self-belief that largely conditions how others respond to us. When we speak of our powers too – our intuition, our interpersonal and team-building skills, our concern for values and integrity – we must talk of them *as if* they have worth, *as if* they are the given of 21st century management competence.

Strategy 3   *Defy the rules*

By using the tactic of surprise we shake things up so that people are not sure what we'll do next. As in battle, so in business: the element of surprise is crucial. For example, if we can be magnanimous to our enemies we turn other people's expectations on their heads. We established earlier that rational approaches are not always effective in dealing with men, but if we use controlled emotion it can help us win. Rubin gives the example of tears.

Men, of course, would never cry in public, but at one point in a negotiation with her boss, when all else had failed, Rubin deliberately made herself cry. His response was to capitulate immediately: 'Well, if it means that much to you.'

Summary

Taking on new roles of authority and responsibility can be daunting whether you are a manager new to the role or already established on the career ladder. But whatever the circumstances certain rules hold good:

- Build your networks early. Learning from the experience of other women can be invaluable.
- Be aware of the corporate culture. Before joining any organization check that women-friendly policies and practices are in place.
- Turn gender games to your advantage by being charming, passionate about your work and unpredictable.
- Remain true to yourself and have the courage to challenge unacceptable behaviour.

In the next chapter we look at the specific skills needed to become a successful manager and how you can learn to develop them.

Visibility Action Plan

1 *Map the networks you need to participate in*

	Formal	Informal
Internal		
External		

How you will join these groups and do you need to be sponsored?
If so, who by, and how you will get their agreement?

2 *Key skills to acquire and develop*
  (This is explored more fully through the Career/Life
  Planning exercises in Chapter Nine.)
  Technical (e.g. IT); professional; communication;
  presentation; interpersonal
  Other . . .

  How will you acquire them?
  What are your priorities and timescales?
  What are the cost implications and how are you going to
  fund them?

3 *Ways to get involved in decision making*
  Project groups
  Committees
  Acting up
  Benchmarking teams

  Identify the methods you will choose.
  How will you get support from you manager?
  What are the time implications of your involvement?

4 *Voicing ideas/suggestions and demonstrating skills*
  Volunteering
  Working beyond your job specification
  Finding new/more cost-effective approaches
  Introducing new systems

  Where do the opportunities exist to add value in your job?

5 *Observing successful colleagues*
  Dress, speech and behaviour
  Vocabulary
  Attitudes to work
  Handling pressure
  Methods of work
  Managerial style
  Reflecting company values

  Identify the role models you will observe and could ask for
  coaching.

Notes

1 Interviewed by Michael Sheldon in the *Telegraph*, 27 May 2000.
2 With acknowledgements to Avivah Wittenberg Cox's research on MBA women.
3 Harriet Rubin, *The Princessa – Machiavelli for Women*, Bloomsbury, 1997. The name 'Princessa' comes from the Italian *principessa* – she who comes first.
4 See Susan Vinnicombe and Nina Colwill, *The Essence of Women in Management*, Ch. 6, Prentice-Hall, 1995.
5 With acknowledgements to Rebecca Tee, *Grow Newsletter 2000*, www.getupandgrow.co.uk
6 A. C. Poe, 'Volunteer for success', *Human Resources*, April 2000. Cited by Singh and Vinnicombe, 'Managing the promotion of high commitment/high performance through impression management', Cranfield School of Management, June 2000.
7 Elizabeth Mapstone, *War of Words*, Vintage, 1999.
8 Ibid.
9 Ibid.
10 Quoted in *Human Resources*, May 2000.
11 Speaking at the WIN Conference, September 2000.
12 Harriet Rubin, op. cit.
13 Quoted by Elizabeth Mapstone, *War of Words*, Vintage, 1999.
14 *The Valley of the Assassins*, 1934, cited in Carol Turkington, *The Quotable Woman*, McGraw-Hill, 2000.
15 Speaking at the WIN Conference, September 2000.
16 Quoted in *Human Resources*, May 2000.
17 Mapstone, op. cit., note 6.
18 Industrial Society research January 1998.
19 Mapstone, op. cit.
20 Ibid.
21 Ibid.
22 Ibid.
23 Cited in *Human Resources*, December 1999.

8
Becoming a better manager

Introduction

How many of us recognize that we work in a rather disorganized way and rationalize this to ourselves by calling it a 'creative' or 'organic' approach? We manage our daily tasks haphazardly, skipping from one thing to another. We fail to reassess our workload, commitments and deadlines regularly, and as a consequence are sometimes overtaken by the unexpected. We accept impossible deadlines because we are afraid to assert ourselves, and pass out vague requests to others for things to be done 'ASAP' because we are unable to be specific. We arrive at meetings overloaded with papers and then can't find those vital documents we need to refer to. Our desks are overrun with paperwork we don't want to deal with, and starting each day is a nightmare because we can't locate what we need. (I have often referred to my own desk as an excavation site – paperwork and files accrue on top of each other like the layers of civilization in an archaeological dig.)

We saw in Chapter Six that in order to move up the ranks of management we must prepare ourselves for challenging projects through better use of our time and more effective delegation. Also, we heard that women who get to the top consistently exceed expectations of their performance. This takes planning as well as effort and ability, and in this chapter we show you how to acquire some essential skills and techniques to increase your management potential.

Manage your time

To make the most of your time you have to be organized. And if you ever end the day with important work unfinished and wondering where the time went, then your first task is to discover what you really do with it. Keeping a diary or time sheet to log your daily activities for a week can be very revealing. There are two rules for this:

1 You must account for every minute of the day.
2 No cheating – put down everything from tea and loo breaks to chatting with colleagues.

After a week, analyse the results to find out your chief 'time robbers' – the activities that principally distract you from your work. For most people these include:

- Interruptions (from the telephone or people stopping by unannounced).
- Requests and invitations (to attend meetings; to take on additional tasks, etc.).
- Paperwork (often urgent and important to someone else) you have postponed until the last minute.
- Being disorganized (messy desk and unsystematic approach to work).

Interruptions: telephone

Set aside time each day for priority work when you don't take calls. Put your voicemail on telling people when you will be available and call them back at a more convenient time. You will feel much more in control and work more effectively.

Interruptions: people

If, like me, you love to communicate and cannot resist listening to people's problems and giving advice, you need a strategy for how to deal pleasantly but firmly with unwanted visitors when you are under pressure. The trick is not to make eye contact: glance up briefly and explain you are very busy and then look down again. This may require practice – and considerable self-discipline – but you will save time and accomplish much more.

Requests and invitations

Here you need to be very selective, and your criteria for deciding which to accept and which to decline must be:

- Do I really need to attend or could I send someone else?
- What benefit would I get from being there?

We have talked at length of the importance of networking, so if opportunities arise to mix with the right people then you should seize them. But if you are tempted to go along to some 'talking shop' out of politeness or a sense of duty, then think again. You surely have other tasks that should take priority.

Paperwork

Many of us postpone paperwork and other onerous but important jobs to focus on more enjoyable work, often of a lower priority. Deadlines may loom for your monthly sales figures or budget estimates, but reading that business magazine or dealing with your e-mail is more interesting. Time management experts would refer you to the Spanish proverb: 'Begin the day by eating a live frog.' The idea is to begin each day by doing the disagreeable job first – since by postponing it you will probably waste your time on trivia all day. The sense of achievement and virtue you get from following this advice is considerable – the rest of the day will seem wonderful.

Being disorganized: messy desk

If, as my old maths teacher used to tell me, 'An untidy desk reflects an untidy mind', then the inside my head must be a labyrinth of junk. The first step in clearing the debris is to try to handle correspondence only once. Read it through carefully and then make a decision: act on it, file it or bin it? And no, filing everything is not an option. Next, get rid of the junk on your desk and make it a habit to 'weed' your filing system on a regular basis. Ask yourself what would happen if you never saw that piece of paper again and throw as much paper as possible into the recycling bin. This may seem a daunting job when you first tackle it. But allocate an hour or two a day until you get it under control. It becomes easier if you file on a daily basis – keeping only those papers that are essential. Again, this will help you work more efficiently and feel more in control. Your desk will be tidy, uncluttered by depressing mess, and everything will be to hand.

Being disorganized: unsystematic approach

If you tend to flit from one task to another in a rather haphazard fashion you may find that, though things get done eventually, you end up doing them at the last minute and feeling stressed. Also, it is unlikely you will turn out your best work this way. (Remember the importance of exceeding performance expectations?) In order to focus your activities you need to set goals on a weekly, monthly and annual basis.

KEY RESEARCH FINDING
The 3 per cent of the population that sets career–life goals performs better and earns more than the rest of us.

These goals need to be written down, together with a plan of how you are going to achieve them, and you must review and update them regularly. (It worked for Nikki Beckett.) The career–life plan in the next chapter will be helpful in getting you started. The important thing to remember is that your goals must be SMART:

- **S**pecific
- **M**easurable
- **A**chievable
- **R**ealistic
- **T**ime-related.

Start small by writing down this evening your 'to do' list for tomorrow, preferably in order of priority. It will take only about five minutes, but you will be more focused, better able to concentrate on individual tasks, and you will have that lovely smug feeling at the end of the day when you have crossed off every item on the list. Keep a day-to-day book and note down calls to be returned and items to be 'brought forward', ticking off each one when completed.

As you start to work more systematically, take time out to reassess how things are going. Monitor your workload, commitments and deadlines and make any necessary adjustments to your schedule. Avoid accepting impossible deadlines: these would set you up for failure and this will reflect badly on you. Be careful of what you promise, but once having done so, stick to your word.

Set aside time for administration, perhaps late on Friday, so you can start afresh on Monday morning. And always allow space in your schedule to deal with the unexpected. Crises small and large are bound to arise and can be very time consuming if you have not planned for such contingencies.

When attending meetings try to arrive five minutes early and don't overload yourself with papers. Think carefully about what you will need and don't carry superfluous files as a 'security blanket'.

Establishing confidence and credibility in meetings

Lonely? Bored? Hate making decisions? Call a meeting. Get to know lots of people, feel important and offload those irksome responsibilities.

(Cartoon that went the rounds of our office.
Unattributed)

In Chapter Five we looked at confidence and credibility issues from the perspective of appearance and body language. Here we look at how we can behave confidently and credibly in day-to-day work situations that we may find challenging, specifically in meetings. We have seen earlier that meetings present a regular opportunity for you to show what you are worth to colleagues and senior managers. And whether you are a participant or chairing the meeting, how you perform is critical to your career advancement.

In meetings you reveal a lot about yourself and your potential. Specifically, it will be apparent whether you have skills in terms of leadership, communication, presentation and at an inter-personal level. People will also draw conclusions about your job competence, your trustworthiness and your reliability.

ACTION POINT

Thinking about the regular meetings you attend, who among your colleagues is always effective? What approach do they take? What can you learn from them? How could you make changes to your own style?

Let us consider the behaviours you should adopt at group meetings, whether at your regular team meeting when you want to achieve certain outcomes, or at board level where you may want to make your mark.

Attending as a participant

- When invited to attend, make sure you find out the objectives of the chairman to help you prepare.
- Never expect to 'wing it' in a meeting. Do your homework and be prepared to make a contribution. Try to be actively involved by stating your views succinctly. And avoid prefacing your remarks with hesitancy or self-deprecation ('I know I'm not really qualified to speak on this issue, but . . .').
- At group discussions no single individual has sole responsibility to sort things out – this responsibility is shared. You are there to contribute your expertise and, with others, to reach a collective decision or solution. Do not feel that all the responsibility rests with you.
- Avoid playing to win or score points as this causes resentment and may eventually lead to your exclusion. Once you are no longer at the centre of policy making your position becomes vulnerable.

Which meetings cause you the most anxiety? Write down what specifically worries you. What strategies could you adopt to reduce your anxiety level? (Being better prepared; getting to know the other participants socially; networking before the meeting to sound people out, etc.)

Leading a team meeting

This is an important opportunity to get to know your team better and to establish good working relationships between members.

■ Provide an agenda ahead of time or communicate the purpose of the meeting so that people can prepare. Give adequate notice so that people can arrange cover or reschedule their priorities.

■ Adopt a supportive and encouraging manner. You should aim to create a non-threatening forum for ideas and discussion.

■ Resist the temptation to finish people's sentences. Help the inarticulate or long-winded contributors by summarizing their contribution to check understanding.

■ Don't allow criticism of anyone at a personal level. The leader particularly should avoid shooting anyone down: this will silence the rest, causing resentment and negativity.

■ Appoint someone to take the minutes and note down action points, making sure these can be distributed within 24 hours.

■ Establish appropriate timetables and schedules for action planning and implementation, so everyone knows what is expected of them.

■ At the end of the meeting thank people for attending and say how much you appreciated their contribution.

How effective are your current team meetings? If they are less productive than you would like, what actions can be taken to improve them? (Give more advance warning; brief people on meetings skills; give feedback on past meetings; demonstrate that meetings have resulted in tangible outcomes; show how you value their contribution, etc.)

Team meetings with colleagues

When working with your peer group you should aim to be seen as collegial, but also be looking to earn authority and credibility as a leader.

▪ Prior to the meeting, if you have an agenda item, lobby key people to win their support. Be seen to be open to discuss the potential weaknesses of your proposals and appear open-minded and objective in your answers.

▪ Never show emotion about other people's objections. This weakness will be exploited by your opponents. Rather, persist in summarizing the benefits of your proposal, showing how they meet the objectives set.

▪ If the meeting is chaired by a senior colleague offer to take the minutes and submit them to him or her on behalf of the group.

POINT TO REFLECT ON

Write down how you think you are perceived by you peers. How would you like to be seen by them? What actions could you take to improve their perceptions? (By being more knowledgeable; by networking more actively; by being more supportive; by getting to know them better, etc.)

Meetings with senior managers

At these meetings you should take the opportunity to shine and showcase your talents. Aim to be seen as resourceful and collaborative on the objectives of the meeting and strike a careful balance between being a 'yes' person and a prophet of doom. The one gains no reputation as worthy of more responsibility, while the other is seen as making tiresome objections and no positive contribution.

■ Make your reservations known, but avoid getting a reputation as someone who always shoots down ideas. Leaders are positive people.

■ Avoid adopting the role of evaluator too often. Do not just weigh the pros and cons, have a decisive view sometimes.

■ Get involved in the meeting as this will bring greater visibility and responsibility. Do not just blend into the background – you have been invited to attend because you are assumed to have a contribution.

Some people seem to adopt the role of disrupter in meetings – they are often late, they dash in and out for messages and phone calls, and multitask when others are speaking. This self-important behaviour is rude and impresses no one, so do not be intimidated by it if it happens when you are presenting to the meeting. Politely ask the chairman to call the offender to order.

ACTION POINT

Ask for feedback from someone you trust (your mentor for example) about your performance in meetings. Draw up a strategy for how you can improve.

Where to sit

If seating has not been assigned, then think about what you want to achieve in the meeting. If you want recognition, sit where you can make good eye contact with key people. If you are making a presentation, get there early – 'Time spent in reconnaissance is rarely wasted.' Check out the room for the best place from which to speak. If you expect objections to your proposals, sit near to, rather than opposite, your potential adversaries – it is more difficult to attack people side on. If you are a new member, introduce yourself to the chairman and ask him or /her where you should sit.

Taking the chair

Being an effective chairman requires good preparation and good communication and management skills. People will be happy to attend your meetings if the agenda is tightly focused and you keep it within a reasonable timescale. Ensuring that everyone knows beforehand what is expected allows participants to prepare. If you are leading a working party or committee, do not be afraid to have a quiet word with those who persistently fail to pull their weight by turning up unprepared – or not turning up at all.

- To avoid passengers from joining (some groups are seen as bandwagons and people will want to jump on for the kudos) ask everyone who wants to attend to submit in writing their thoughts on the agenda and what they could contribute.
- Choose participants from people you know to be problem-solvers.
- Ensure the agenda is clear, thoughtful and comprehensive with items ranked in importance and an approximate timeslot allocated to each.
- Make sure the objectives and desired outcomes are apparent to everyone attending.
- Assign presentations ahead of time and ask key people (experts) to lead the discussion.
- Meet in the morning if possible, when people are fresh.
- Choose a meeting room that is large enough, well ventilated and adequately lit.
- Start on time and indicate clearly the finish time you are aiming for.
- Do not use a meeting primarily to schedule another. (It will be seen as a waste of time.)
- Ask for feedback on how useful the meeting was.

It is a myth that meetings generate good ideas. Research shows that brainstorming meetings are less effective than individuals working on their own and then coming together to discuss what they have formulated. Individuals don't like putting forward radical ideas if it means going out on a limb – keeping quiet is safer. Also, it is difficult to think when other people are talking – creativity needs peace and quiet. So be clear about what meetings can achieve. If you are looking for ideas, ask managers to poll their teams and present to you on a one-to-one basis.

POINT TO REFLECT ON

Do you feel confident that you are an effective chairman? In which areas would you like to improve your effectiveness? How will you achieve this?

Speaking and acting with authority

We have seen in Chapter Six that managerial effectiveness is closely linked to status in the organization – that power derives from the office held rather than from the office holder as an individual. And we have also established that there are pervasive gender stereotypes that assign higher status to men than to women, even where they are in the same occupation and at the same level. Aside from gender role expectations we can identify certain behaviours that either confer or undermine our status and authority. In particular we need to adopt a verbal style that is high status, but this is difficult for women because the way we address people tends to reflect our concern for the feelings and needs of others. We try to negotiate tactfully and to use our social skills, but in doing so we may, according to research, be perceived as less intelligent and knowledgeable than those who are more direct.

■ Too often we use the polite form to make requests: 'Would you please send out a copy of this report to Mr White?' This sounds more like a question than an instruction. A more authoritative form would be: 'I'd like this report sent to Mr White this evening, please.'

■ Using 'tag' questions can imply hesitancy and uncertainty: 'I did ask you send out that report to Mr White. Didn't I?' And using a questioning voice can weaken your apparent conviction about what you are saying. In this way it looks as though we need the approval of others and our status and authority are automatically lowered.

■ Using qualifiers like: 'Perhaps', 'I wonder if . . .', 'Well, I think . . .' also weakens the power of what we say. When you know that what you're saying is correct or your viewpoint is valid don't use qualifiers or disclaimers: 'I know this may sound odd but . . .' to weaken your position.

QUESTION TO CONSIDER

How would you describe your own verbal style and how could it be improved?

In addition to our verbal style we must consider the paraverbal – how we say what we say. Remember Harriet Rubin's advice: to speak more slowly and to lower your tone in order to gain attention? Much of men's power as speakers derives from the fact that they have deeper, more resonant (louder) voices. In addition they talk more, use more words and employ more summarizing statements. They also interrupt more – and the people they usually interrupt are women. Women, by contrast, allow themselves to be interrupted and often play a monitoring, peacekeeping and head-nodding role in mixed gender groups.

KEY RESEARCH FINDING

The most effective men and women are those that adopt some features of the communication style of the opposite sex.

To develop a more impactful verbal and paraverbal style women must learn to:

- Use more slang (particularly words relevant to your business).
- Use third person references ('In the *Economist* this week . . .').
- Use longer and more complex sentences (this is not the same as being verbose).
- Refuse to be interrupted (observe how politicians do this).
- Speak to the group as a whole rather than to individuals.

QUESTION TO CONSIDER

How will you incorporate these features into your communication style?

Finally, a few words about body language or non-verbal communication. Women tend to sit and stand in lady-like poses that occupy limited space. Men command more authority through more powerful poses and by occupying their space. Touching can also be a way to assert authority and establish empathy. Men touch women (non-sexually) more than women touch men because we live in a society where we 'touch down'. A brief touch on the forearm of whoever you are speaking to, or guiding them lightly by the arm conveys confidence and authority. Learning to maintain steady eye contact (as men do) is also critical to establishing your authority.

QUESTIONS TO CONSIDER

What gestures are you aware of using? Do they convey positive or negative messages? Overall, what changes could you make to improve the effectiveness of your communication style?

Enhancing your personal power

There are three principal types of power in the workplace: personal power, interpersonal power and organizational power.

We have already discussed the concept of 'locus of control' (whether individuals feel they determine their own fate or feel they are the victims of circumstance), and personal power is about feeling in control, feeling good about yourself and believing that you are powerful. Importantly, our self-belief strongly influences the way in which others respond to us. (Again, the concepts of self-belief and positive self-talk were introduced earlier in the book.) Our personal power can also be enhanced by the way we communicate:

- By using stronger and more assertive language (e.g. 'In my view . . .' rather than 'Well, I think . . .').
- By being more impactful in mixed sex gatherings (e.g. dressing for success; through confident posture; by speaking up and putting yourself at the centre of the discussion).
- By using your space effectively (e.g. do not be a shrinking violet; use positive body language signals; do not sit in cramped, defensive poses).

As women we can also draw on our interpersonal strengths to reinforce our personal power, by using our influencing and negotiating skills to get people to do things they would not other-wise have wanted to do. For even though our male colleagues have traditionally dominated organizational power – through the resources they command and their line authority – research shows that women are gaining the edge at work because they are increasingly perceived as more intelligent, more likeable and more successful than many of their male colleagues. And as more and more work projects depend for their success on informal communication and cooperation, rather than on formal chains of command, so women will have the advantage. The ability to mobilize resources in the knowledge economy will increasingly depend on our capacity to influence others. In this area women excel and so their power will inevitably grow. Get ready to seize it.

ACTION PLAN

Thinking about the changes you would like to make to your style, what particular challenges do you anticipate (e.g. how others will respond; feeling embarrassed or self-conscious initially; sustaining new behaviours)? How will you overcome these challenges? Set some goals and map out a plan of action with a timescale for implementation. Look at it regularly and monitor your progress, rewarding yourself for each achievement.

Managing the team

Start with good people, lay out the rules, communicate with your employees, motivate them and reward them. If you do all those things effectively you can't miss.

Lee Iacocca

In Chapter Six and elsewhere we stressed the importance of delegation as a means to free you to participate in activities that raise your profile and enhance your promotability. The purpose of building an effective team is to improve their problem-solving skills and to raise their effectiveness and efficiency. This enables them to work more autonomously with less supervision. Also, when your team works cohesively as a group then there is additional spin off in terms of higher morale and productivity, and well as lower stress levels, absenteeism and staff turnover. All of this will enhance your reputation as a manager, and over time you may find that some of the best people in the organization will gravitate to your team because they want to be part of what you are doing. Well-managed teams are winning teams and that experience is very exhilarating for team members.

Leading the team

Leaders must be seen to be up-front, up to date, up to their job and up early in the morning.

Lord Sieff

We have seen in Chapter Three that in some organizations women have not traditionally been accepted as leaders. Therefore they may have difficulty being taken seriously, and, for want of female role models, may lack confidence in their ability to lead. Many of the leadership challenges faced by women result from their early socialization that emphasizes relationships, conflict and risk avoidance and the importance of approval and popularity. Men's socialization has traditionally given them the edge in business: competitiveness, goal orientation, risk taking, following rules, taking responsibility and persevering. But the art of management is changing as more co-operative, consensual and collegial approaches to leadership gain widespread legitimacy.

It may be useful at this point to consider the difference between a leader and a manager. The Industrial Society has been spearheading a Campaign for Leadership and defines the difference as follows:[1]

- Managers plan, control, allocate resources and administer.
- Leaders innovate, communicate and motivate.

From comprehensive research they have compiled a Liberating Leadership Profile describing the skills, beliefs and behaviours exhibited by a leader:

- Liberate by freeing those closest to the job to take their own decisions.
- Encourage their staff and support them when necessary.
- Achieve the purpose for which their organization exists.

■ Develop people and teams and set an example by their own behaviour, building relationships on trust.

As competition intensifies and more emphasis is placed on customer service, and as patterns of employment shift to more flexible alternatives, so these qualities of leadership will come increasingly to the fore. If you want to enhance your own leadership skills, one of the ways you can do so is to consult the works of the great motivational speakers including Anthony Robbins[2] and John C. Maxwell.[3] I was once taught that 'Leaders are readers', and have since found this advice to be immensely helpful.

'When the best leaders' work is done, the people say: 'We did it ourselves'.

Lao-Tzu

(You can find out more about the Campaign for Leadership and about leadership profiling by contacting the Industrial Society on their website.)

Mobilizing the team

Working together to get results and benefiting from success is part of the ethos of a team, so the key is to create a goal or common purpose behind which they can mobilize. Assuming you have an existing team it may be apparent that conflicts and tensions exist. If they are to work together effectively, these must be resolved. Difficulties often arise as a consequence of misunderstandings and the failure of team members to appreciate each other's skills. One approach is to use the Belbin[4] framework for analysing individuals' team roles and to debrief this with your group, explaining that team members need to possess different strengths in order to create synergy.

ACTION POINT

Look at your personal job objectives and formulate some goals for your team. How will you communicate those goals and ensure that they are achieved? (Give clear instructions; put new or complex tasks in writing; make accountability clear; ensure that everyone has appropriate information and authority.)

Team activities

In order to break down barriers and develop team spirit you will need to organize a programme of formal and informal team activities. Some may have specific objectives – such as a training day to develop problem-solving skills or to enhance product knowledge. Others may be informal gatherings at lunchtime or after work to get to know each other socially. It is important that, as the leader, you attend all of these activities and see them as opportunities both to get to know your team better and to let them get to know other aspects of your personality.

In addition you will need to hold regular briefings where you consult the team for their suggestions about performance improvements. Set up groups within your team to brainstorm new ideas or to focus on particular tasks and report back to the team as a whole. Listening to the team is vital if you are to build rapport, capitalize on good ideas and anticipate problems. Regular information sharing should be a two-way communication process.

ACTION POINT

What conflicts exist within your team? How will you resolve them (counselling individuals; reallocating workload; transferring someone)?

Developing the team

Before you can delegate you must ensure your team has the necessary skills. Identify the experts within your team and ask them to mentor learners. Find out who would like to take on more responsibility and decide how this could be achieved – for example through job rotation or job shadowing. It is important also to lead from the front, to be a role model for exceeding high expectations and to teach by your own example. Your team must also have access to you at clearly defined times, so post 'office hours' indicating when you are available. Be scrupulously fair at all times, allocating work according to people's abilities and commitments.

ACTION POINT

How can you develop the talents of individuals in your team? What are the best ways to share expertise and transfer skills? Encourage contributions and initiative but also ask about implementation and the support they will need.

Decision making

We have seen that women's consultative style of decision making may sometimes be seen as indecisiveness or reluctance to accept responsibility. But it is crucial to involve your team in decisions that concern them, since they are much more likely to accept the outcome if they have been consulted. The key is to approach the task confidently by mapping out the problem or issue, your solution and asking for feedback. Listen closely to suggestions, acknowledging their validity and taking them on board where possible. Keep the team informed on progress.

Motivating your team

In order to motivate people you need to learn what makes them tick. So, take time to understand how your people see their jobs. Do they know what they want out of their work? Get them to talk about their career hopes and aspirations and encourage them to discuss their problems and challenges. To get the best out of people you need to focus on helping them to achieve success. The process must be to get your team involved, to monitor progress against targets and to give praise where it is due. And while it is important to deal appropriately with underperformers, if you are always giving negative feedback this will achieve very little. Try to present a praise sandwich – ensuring, whenever possible, that criticism is wedged between two slices of positive reinforcement. Being hypercritical damages people's self-esteem, and that provokes a downward spiral of performance. High self-worth means people work more effectively, so be liberal with praise and encouragement.

Learning to let go can be scary at first, but you must learn to trust your team and not to oversupervise them. Too much control will stifle initiative, cause resentment and create undue dependence on you as the leader.

ACTION POINT

Assess the capabilities of your team members and delegate work that matches their experience. Show how the tasks contribute to the team and organizational goals to foster a sense of common purpose.

Reward

Reward is an important adjunct to motivation, but not all individuals respond in the same way to the same rewards. We have already seen the marked gender differences that result in men and women deriving fulfilment from different aspects of their work. So it is with individual team members: for some pay rises, bonuses and status will be key drivers; for others recognition, praise or more challenging work will be more important.

Finding appropriate rewards for your staff is about reflecting their varying needs and offering something with recognizable value to the individual. The ground rules are not to give everyone the same, to be selective with rewards (lest they lose their effect) and to link reward to achievement by reference to goals and objectives.

ACTION POINT

List all the possible rewards you have the authority to offer. Think carefully about what motivates individual members of your team and then draw up a schedule of the rewards you will give as individuals achieve their objectives. Be fair and realistic – reward should reflect performance.

CASE STUDY

'Our first concern is that people should always know where the company is going', was how Martha Lane Fox described their approach to communication at lastminute.com, a company undergoing rapid change and whose culture is still emerging. The emphasis is strongly on open communication with both joint MDs accessible to staff on any issue. Early on they introduced the Jedi Council as a fun way to keep people in touch – they strongly believe that keeping people informed about what needs to happen encourages them to work better. The atmosphere is informal – staff can take a break to play table football and bounce ideas around. Food and fresh fruit are regularly ordered in to fuel those who wouldn't otherwise stop for a meal.

Managing change

If you do things well, do them better. Be daring, be first, be different, be just.

Anita Roddick, MD Body Shop

Communicate your vision

The need to demonstrate leadership is never greater than when managing change, and, in order to take her team with her, a leader must be able to inspire them through her energy and enthusiasm. You need to create and communicate a compelling vision of what the future state will look like, so that people can understand the goals they are being asked to achieve. Your role is to translate the vision from the strategic concept – for example 'To deliver customer service excellence' – into something more tangible and personal that you can share with your team: 'Imagine how it will feel when our customer satisfaction ratings are the highest in the company and people are saying how much they love dealing with us.' You will recall that many of the successful women we interviewed spoke of the importance of getting people to feel they work for *you*, and of having a strong personal vision of what you want to achieve, something about which you feel passionately. It is your conviction and commitment that will inspire the team and overcome obstacles and objections. Remember always that people connect with us at an emotional rather than an intellectual level.

Ways to share your vision include:

- Describing it in visual and practical terms. Nikki Beckett when training sales people encourages them to think about how it would *feel* to get the sale they had been working for.
- Explain the likely outcomes in a simple way ('When we introduce the new call management system we will have more time to deal with our backlog of customer enquiries.')
- Show the team how they can affect the outcome and let them get involved.
- Show your personal commitment to the change, but listen carefully to feedback from the team.
- Ask for their commitment, say why you need their support and ask what help they need to make the change happen.

ACTION POINT

Think about changes you need to implement in relation to what motivates your individual team members. How might you:

- Tap into the ambitions of those who want to move up
- Challenge those who like to stretch themselves
- Reassure those who distrust change or lack confidence
- Engage the interest or curiosity of those who like novelty?

A useful way of analysing the factors that facilitate or block change is the drivers and restrainers framework (sometimes referred to as force field analysis). A worked example is given below:

Drivers ⟶	**⟵ Restrainers**
Need to improve performance	Poor morale
Company declared values	Reality of existing culture
Need to raise customer satisfaction	Lack of ownership of problem
Staff satisfaction survey	Time pressures
Winning new contract	Conflict between team members

The idea is that in any situation there are identifiable factors (drivers) that you may be able to use to bring about change. But that, equally, there will be countervailing forces (restrainers) that you must overcome. Your strategy for managing change should focus on how you will deal with these issues.

Some pitfalls to avoid

It is most important that you feel personally inspired by the vision you want to communicate. If not, you will not be convincing and you will not be able to sell the benefits of the change, nor to deal with the concerns of others honestly and openly. When you give out mixed signals people will pick them up. And remember, you are the leader: if you are lucky they may do about 40 per cent of what you do right, but they will do 100 per cent of what you do wrong. Bear in mind the potentially negative effects of change – it does not always benefit everyone. The drivers and restrainers framework will help you identify risks early so you can plan to minimize negative effects. Also beware of trying to implement changes that are doomed to failure. Be realistic:

- Is the business ready for the change and how will it be bedded in?
- Beware of change overload. Have previous initiatives been properly absorbed yet?
- Have sufficient resources been allocated? Calculate realistically the initial investment required to bring about the change.
- Will there be enough support for people through training and development?

Finally, you will need to set some targets with your team and give them feedback on progress. Let them know the success criteria, but limit them to a manageable number and make sure they are consistent.

ACTION POINT

Before discussing a new proposal with your team, can you sum up in one memorable sentence what the change is about?

Delegation

*And the trouble is, if you don't risk anything, you risk even
more.*

Erica Jong

Relinquishing control

If you are to move up the career ladder you need, as we have seen,
to shift your focus away from detailed and repetitive tasks and to
concentrate on networking and increasing your visibility through
high-profile work. Initially you may need to overcome the pull
both of your perfectionism and of wanting to do what you enjoy.
Also, the idea of relinquishing control and trusting others to do
as good job as we ourselves would do can feel quite scary. But if
you are going to take a more strategic view of the business you
need to develop your team and to entrust the lower priority
tasks to them, leaving you to concentrate on what you do best.
However, it is important not to delegate only the grunt work.
Remember that your role as leader is to develop your team too,
so pass on interesting and challenging assignments as well the
routine stuff.

Your guiding principle should be: what do I personally need to
attend to in order to reach my goals and objectives? Anything else
can be delegated.

Who to delegate to

When choosing someone for a task, ensure that the person is
competent and that his or her schedule is not already overloaded.
Understanding your team's capabilities is essential if you are to
delegate confidently.

Give clear instructions

Take time to explain the task, stating clearly what you want. For
example if you want a database set up, explain how you want to

use it. Resist the temptation to overmanage – let people do things in their own way so that they feel a sense of ownership and learn to work with initiative.

Monitor progress

Make sure you are available to answer questions. Queries can arise as the work progresses and your team may need help. Set a clear deadline for completion with milestones along the way to check how things are going. If you are approachable and open then nothing dramatic can go wrong. Small mistakes are not a problem – that's how people learn.

Celebrate success

It is important that people feel their contribution has been recognized, so be generous with praise and offer some informal reward or treat in proportion to the achievement. This maintains morale and wins loyalty.

ACTION POINT

Audit your workload to identify the tasks you should delegate. Draw up a matrix mapping your team's capabilities and allocate tasks according to their aptitudes.

The art of successful negotiation

Always bear in mind that your own resolution to succeed is more important than any other one thing.

Abraham Lincoln

Knowing your value

When we think of negotiation it is often in the context of a formal bargaining situation where a contractual relationship is being formed. However, successful managers learn to negotiate in less formal ways in order to achieve a range of objectives including salary increases, access to greater resources, involvement in new projects or rescheduling priorities. Remember that this is not a fair world – you will not be given the salary increases, perks and promotions you want just because you work for them. You need to know your value and to lay claim to what you want.

Uncovering agendas

We saw earlier in the book how gender stereotypes can act as barriers to our progress. Therefore, at an early stage in any negotiation we need to uncover any hidden agendas and assumptions that we may be expected to acquiesce to. For example, it may be assumed that, because we are women, we will make concessions to try to keep the peace. If we buy into these assumptions, we are dead in the water. That is not to say that we cannot turn being a woman to our own advantage. No harm in disarming your opponent by appearing warm, friendly and cooperative. Listening closely to the other person makes them feel we understand their viewpoint and that we are taking their feelings into consideration.

Make your value visible

If someone is prepared to negotiate with you it is because they believe you have some value to contribute. This value must be made explicit and become the focus of the negotiation to strengthen your position. To build this value you will need to have used your impression management skills to raise perceptions of your performance.

Seek a solution

Your opening position in the negotiation should be to present your problem and to ask for support: 'Although I've achieved/exceeded all my targets this year I don't seem to be in the running for promotion. And I'd really appreciate your help with this.' At this stage you don't want to antagonize your boss (if that is who you are negotiating with). You need to listen to his or her response and to stay cool and rational, agreeing with whatever points you can.

Seek an ally

Your primary objective at the next stage is to get the other person to accept responsibility for your problem and its resolution. Communicate clearly what you would like to happen without recourse to references about your 'rights'. Talk calmly and with conviction about how the other person could help bring it about. Remember not to be afraid of asking for everything (Harriet Rubin) – it can make the other person feel both more powerful and more inclined to be generous if you set your sights high and believe in your power to win.

Seek a win/win

It is important that the other party in the negotiation should not feel that he or she has made too many concessions and lost face. Be a gracious winner and show your appreciation for what the other person has agreed to. Make clear the advantages and benefits to the other person from the agreement you have reached.

You may be disappointed if you fail, but you are doomed if you don't try.

Beverly Sills, opera singer

Become irresistible

Our lives – not only at work, but also in most interpersonal situations – are a constant negotiation. In order to succeed you have to be really good at getting people to accept your agendas and proposals – it is a competitive world. The skill involved is mainly verbal communication, and Philippa Davies,[5] a psychologist and communications expert, has put forward the concept of *irresistibility* to describe some techniques we can adopt to win people over. She has identified a number of 'laws of irresistibility' that govern human interactions and, once aware of these, we can use them to our advantage to sell ourselves and influence others. They are:

■ **Reciprocity**   The idea that if you do someone a favour they feel obliged to return it. This is because most of us feel uncomfortable when obligated to others and so we seek to discharge the obligation by repaying it. This technique is particularly useful when networking or when selling your services as a consultant or freelancer. Offer advice or ideas, provide information or pass on the details of a useful contact and the favour will come back to you.

■ **Comparison**   We are always measured against what has gone before, so we must always be conscious of differentiating ourselves from our colleagues (if we are seeking promotion) or from other competitors in business. Think carefully about how you describe yourself and your capabilities. Seek to build a career portfolio with an unusual combination of skills (e.g. marketing with finance or IT experience) that singles you out.

■ **Consistency**   Determine early on the personal image and reputation you want to establish for yourself (e.g. creative innovator; powerful networker; subject expert; flexible team player). Ensure this is congruent with the culture of your chosen profession and act consistently with it. Also, when interacting with clients, be aware of their culture and value systems and ensure your negotiations take this into account (e.g. fair play; expert knowledge; analytical approach to problem solving).

■ **Scarcity**   The perceived value of any commodity rises when it is seen as rare and desirable. Cultivate what Philippa calls an air of 'busy-itis' so that you seem constantly in demand – those plum projects you want will become more accessible as a result. In job negotiations with a new company, do not reveal your current salary on your application. Rather, indicate you would be prepared to discuss this face to face, and then imply that the potential employer may not be able to afford you.

■ **Liking**   Use your warmth and charm to get people to like you (people buy people). Be sensitive to what is important to others (dress code; good manners; punctuality; formality/informality) in order to overcome any barriers to communication.

■ **Authority**   As business communication is increasingly characterized by informality, so it becomes more difficult to signal authority. But it is important to do so because people are strongly influenced by those who have it. If you must 'dress down' to fit into your work environment, then you will need to find other means of establishing your status. Being efficient, businesslike and appearing always in control (though not unfriendly) are the marks of authority, particularly if supported by an effective verbal and paraverbal style (see above).

Other aspects of your communication style to focus on, according to Philippa, include giving an 'auditory cuddle' to your audience. Breath control, voice projection and good articulation are important whether presenting to a group or in one-to-one discussions, but using a confiding style of delivery can really win people over. Philippa suggests we act as though what we are saying or offering is exclusively for that person: when handing over any object – a brochure or your CV, for example – relate to it as though it were precious. Hold it almost reverently and say something to emphasize its value before passing it over.

The most flattering way of communicating is by giving the person your full attention and appearing not to want anything from them. (Think of the all too rare occasions when this has happened to you and how it made you feel.) But while eye contact is important, you should avoid dominating others with your gaze, as this can be intimidating. Break the contact by looking from one eye to the other and then down at the person's mouth.

Dealing with failure and rejection

Philippa Davies has some very helpful advice to offer on this subject. First, don't feel worthless just because you didn't get that

new job or promotion: perhaps it wasn't meant to be, and maybe
you should find another route to your goals. She recommends
'reframing' your memories of what happened – seeing others as
prats and yourself as heroine, and using humour to distance
yourself from the experience. Do something pleasant to distract
you from the memory and resist the temptation to be obsessive
about it:

> *If you're not failing from time to time, you're not moving
> on.*

Humour at work

Traditionally humour has been kept out of the workplace – the
business of making money being considered too serious to
trivialize with fun. But this is changing: delayering has resulted in
smaller teams having to work together more closely, and there is
an increasing acceptance of new management styles that take
people's feelings and needs into account. Good relationships are
now at a premium, so fitting in, being likeable and having a
sense of humour are important criteria for selection. Humour is
important in enabling us to maintain a positive attitude. It helps
us to keep a sense of proportion in times of difficulty and can
defuse potentially explosive situations. It is not, therefore, about
telling jokes, but rather about the ability to laugh at ourselves and
recognize our imperfections.

By encouraging your team to have fun together outside
working hours you will foster an environment of openness and
trust, particularly if you also hold regular team meetings to
discuss how things are going, rather than convening them only
when things go wrong.

Humour is a great stress buster, and stress has been shown to
build when people don't enjoy their work and feel isolated. As a
consequence they may then become less productive, resentful
and difficult to handle. The physiological effects of laughter are
well documented – it lowers blood pressure and relieves tension.
But the psychological benefits are less well known: it engages
the creative side of the brain and so may stimulate creative
thinking.

ACTION POINTS

In what situations might you use humour to manage your team more effectively? Think about:

■ **Communication** how can you break down barriers by sharing humour to put others at ease and create rapport? In particular, how can you encourage your team to overcome shyness and contribute ideas?

■ **Negotiation** can you get someone to laugh with you when things become confrontational? This lowers defences and opens up the position.

■ **Problem solving** when progress is mired in detail or conflict, can you loosen the tension and bring in a new perspective with humour?

■ **Giving feedback** criticism can be less threatening if softened with humour. Think about how you would deal with someone who regularly misses a deadline using humour. Note: it is important to focus on what the person is doing wrong rather than on them personally.

While using humour can be highly productive, it has its limitations and we must beware of sending out mixed messages. Experience and judgement will teach you when humour is or is not appropriate. In particular you should consider how the other person might interpret your humour: will they take you less seriously or think you frivolous? Never make jokes at other people's expense. You will alienate them and make them your enemy.

Total absence of humour renders life impossible.

Colette

Your professional development

Preparing for leadership

We have talked extensively of the need to build your portfolio of skills and qualifications, and emphasized that in the knowledge economy your competences must be constantly broadened and updated. To maintain and further develop your effectiveness as a manager and to prepare for promotion you must make your professional development a priority. But what form should it take? Naturally, you will want to keep abreast of developments within your profession, and your professional association or institute will provide a programme of regular updates in which you should participate. But how will you acquire new management and leadership skills?

The MBA route

It is now well established that women's development needs differ from men's and that traditional management development programmes alone do not adequately meet women's requirements. Vinnicómbe and Singh argue that the MBA, for example, was originally designed by men, based on male experience and targeted at an almost exclusively male group of managers.[6] Women-only development programmes are therefore needed alongside conventional management training to enable women to explore issues relevant to their lives and experience. Currently only about 25 per cent of MBAs are women and this, according to Mary Mattis of Catalyst perpetuates inequalities in the workplace and constitutes a barrier to women's progress.

> ... it is time to acknowledge that women's development is different from that of men. This needs to be reflected in the design of management development programmes specifically for women, so that their progress in the new century can better reflect their talents and potential contribution to management practice.[7]

There are many reasons why so few women enrol on MBA programmes, not least because at the age when most people do the programme – late 20s to mid 30s – women may be coping with the most demanding phase of family responsibilities. The MBA, too, has a reputation for its highly analytical approach and for being formulated around an essentially male model of managerial identity and experience. The thinking and learning styles are male-oriented and women prefer to think and learn in different ways. The researcher A. Sinclair, cited by Vinnicombe and Singh, has identified four sources of tension for women MBAs:

- The centralization of authority and power in the classroom.
- Reluctance among participants to admit uncertainty and ignorance.
- Learning by benchmarking and best practice rather than experientially.
- Knowing through mastering analytical techniques rather than through emotional or intuitive connections.

This whole approach produces a narrow set of values that are far removed from the experience of many women (and indeed of some men). As an MBA graduate myself, I recall a feeling of having endured and survived the programme rather than of having enjoyed it. There was a strong sense of achievement that I had measured myself against my (predominantly male) peers and not let myself down. But this was tempered by a great deal of frustration that what we had learned discounted much of my experience and many of my perspectives. I did, however, find the 'Women in Management Module' (led in fact by Susan Vinnicombe and her then team) immensely helpful in allowing me to reflect on and reinterpret my experience with other women. We were able to discuss in a safe environment issues such as organizational politics, our working styles, patterns of career development and how to achieve balance in our lives.

It is important to acknowledge the issues specific to women and to learn how to deal with them effectively. Our problems in handling organizational politics and using impression management techniques demonstrably hold us back in our careers, and we often experience competitive and aggressive business cultures as stressful, not least because we set out to please everyone, take on too much and risk physical and emotional exhaustion. We accept unrealistic and excessive burdens by trying to combine home and work demands, and we need a forum where we can share our problems and learn from one another's experience.

It may not be possible or appropriate to lobby within your own organization for women-only programmes (though there are many companies, including BT, that have run them successfully for many years). An alternative might be to approach your professional organization, or one of the many women's networks, to find out whether they provide relevant management training for women. A list of women's organizations can be found in 'Useful Contacts' at the end of the book.

Playing the numbers game

Although far from being a financial wizard myself, I have found it immensely helpful to understand something about key financial ratios. They provide insight into your own company's performance and help you understand more about your competitors. It is particularly important to familiarize yourself with them if your work is outside the financial sphere and the principal benefits you will derive from this are:

- **More professional image**   top management live and breathe these ratios. Being able to understand their thinking will enable you to gain visibility by asking informed questions about business performance.
- **Better business decisions**   many of these ratios are referred to as the 'levers of profitability' – you will be more informed about the links between performance and financial results, so that you manage your resources better in relation to profitability.
- **Better insight**   being able to track your company's performance will give you clues about what the future may hold for you.
- **More powerful presentations**   by being able to demonstrate how your proposals impact the key ratios, your reports and presentations will have greater effect.
- **Improved management skills**   you will be better able to understand and communicate budgetary decisions and generally feel more confident about financial issues.

Financial ratios

Financial ratios fall into five groups: profitability ratios, efficiency ratios, leverage ratios, liquidity ratios, and market value ratios.

They can all appear ambiguous and misleading if used incorrectly, so buddy up with a financial 'expert' (trade some of your skills in return) to check out your results until you are more experienced.

The purpose of the ratios is as follows:

▓ Profitability ratios measure how efficiently a company is using its assets.

▓ Efficiency ratios are often used as measures of the internal performance of the business. *These are the ratios you are most likely to use to monitor your business plans.*

▓ Leverage or gearing ratios tell you about the relationship between debt and capital and between interest and earnings. Usually the debt referred to is long term, but it is sometimes defined to include all liabilities other than equity.

▓ Liquidity ratios tell you about the company's relationship with cash. They measure the firm's ability to access cash to meet payments and continue operating. Beware: they are volatile and can change quickly.

▓ Market value ratios are not day-to-day controls, but are useful in that they combine both accounting and (where appropriate) stock market data.

How to work out these ratios

Profitability ratios

$$\text{Pre-tax profit margin} = \frac{\text{Profit before interest and tax (PBIT)}}{\text{Revenue}}$$

$$\text{Return on capital employed (ROCE)} = \frac{\text{Profit before tax and interest}}{\text{Capital employed}}$$

$$\text{Return of shareholder funds} = \frac{\text{Profit before tax and interest}}{\text{Reserves plus share capital}}$$

Efficiency ratios

$$\text{Profit per employee} = \frac{\text{Profit before interest and tax}}{\text{Total number of employees}}$$

$$\text{Sales per employee} = \frac{\text{Revenue}}{\text{Number of employees}}$$

$$\text{Profit per } \pounds \text{ of pay} = \frac{\text{Profit before interest and tax}}{\text{Total salary bill}}$$

Leverage ratios

$$\text{Debt ratio} = \frac{\text{Long-term debt}}{\text{Capital employed}}$$

This is the usual measure of financial leverage and shows the ratio of long-term debt to total long-term capital.

$$\text{Debt equity ratio} = \frac{\text{Long-term debt}}{\text{Share capital plus reserves}}$$

This shows a company's long-term debt over its equity.

$$\text{Times interest earned} = \frac{\text{Interest}}{\text{Profit before interest and tax}}$$

This is a measure of a company's ability to repay interest. It shows the extent to which interest is covered by profits, before payment of interest and taxes plus depreciation.

Liquidity ratios

$$\text{Current ratio} = \frac{\text{Current assets}}{\text{Current liabilities}}$$

Also known as the liquidity ratio, the current ratio is a straight comparison of current assets in relation to current liabilities. It gives a broad measure of the company's ability to meet short-term obligations. The final figure should approximate $1:1$ – every £1 of liability should be covered by at least £1 of assets.

Market value ratios

$$\text{Quick ratio (or 'acid test')} = \frac{\text{Current assets} - \text{stock}}{\text{Current liabilities}}$$

This is commonly used by banks to assess risk by scrutinizing those assets that can quickly be converted to cash (primarily: cash at bank, marketable securities and receivables). It shows the 'quick' (liquid) assets in relation to the current liabilities.

$$\text{Stock turnover} = \frac{\text{Revenue}}{\text{Total stock (as indicated on the balance sheet)}}$$

This shows how often a company turns over its stock and measures the cost of goods over the average stock held. The quicker you turn your stock the better.

Finally, it is most important to be able to read financial statements: the profit and loss accounts and the balance sheet are central to a company's annual report. You will not fully understand what is going on in your own company, what your competitors are doing or how successful your customers' operations are without this valuable information. If you have not already done so, enrol on an introduction to finance course as soon as possible – make it a personal development priority, today.

Business communication skills

The first and most important aspect is being a good listener. We have already seen how being an attentive listener wins people over and helps build rapport. Let us consider the practical measures we can take to ensure we listen effectively.

We can identify three levels of listening:

- **Active**   where we pay full attention and attempt to understand the subtext of what is being said.
- **Superficial**   where we are emotionally detached from what is happening and do not really participate.
- **Tuning in and out**   where we fake attention, listen passively and chip in a contribution occasionally.

When we listen only superficially or tune in and out we may think we are faking attention but our body language often gives us away. Gestures of impatience, negativity or even hostility may signal to others that we are not really interested in what they have to say.

The reasons why we don't listen effectively may be emotional (we bring preconceptions to the discussion and don't listen objectively); or they may be due to distraction (we may be attempting to multitask while listening halfheartedly.) So, the keys to effective listening are to:

- Give the other person your full attention and not to use their speaking time as your thinking time.
- Avoid interrupting or finishing other people's sentences.
- Maintain eye contact in a non-threatening way.
- Listen actively by nodding and reflecting back what the other person has said.
- Summarize the discussion periodically and check understanding.
- Pause before replying to show you have taken on board what they have said and are not responding with a predetermined answer.

ACTION POINT

Be aware of how you listen to others. What triggers you to switch off and lose concentration? (e.g. dealing with people you don't like or find boring.) What techniques could you use to maintain focus?

Summary

Becoming a better manager means taking some simple steps to improve your effectiveness:

- Get organized and manage your time better.
- Improve your meetings skills and impress others with your professionalism.
- Speak and act powerfully.
- Build a strong, autonomous team around you and learn to delegate.
- Free up your time for challenging, high profile projects.

■ Focus on your interpersonal and negotiating skills to reach win/win outcomes.

■ Become a leader through lifetime learning and self development.

■ Take personal responsibility for changing the way things are for women at work.

All the successful women we interviewed attributed their success in part to the fact that they set themselves goals and made plans for how to achieve them. The next chapter provides a framework for developing your personal career/life plan, an essential step in taking charge of your own destiny.

Notes

1 www.indsoc.co.uk/cforl/liberating_leadershp_profile.htm

2 *Awaken the Giant Within*, 1992.

3 *Developing the Leader Within You*, 1994; *Developing the Leaders Around You*, 1996.

4 R. Meredith Belbin, *Management Teams – Why They Succeed or Fail*, Butterworth Heinemann, 1998.

5 Philippa Davies, *Irresistibility – Secrets of Selling Yourself*, Hodder & Stoughton, 2000.

6 Susan Vinnicombe and Val Singh, *Taking Stock: The Making of Women Managers*, Centre for Developing Women Business Leaders, Cranfield School of Management.

7 Vinnicombe and Singh, op. cit.

9

Career–life planning

Introduction

This book was written to support women already working as, or aspiring to become, managers. In Chapter Six we explored some of the major challenges confronting working women and saw that, aside from gender stereotyping and structural barriers to progress within organizations, many of these challenges centred on the issue of work–life balance. We considered some of the choices open to us as women: directing our energies primarily into our careers and opting to be childless; combining work with family life and making some compromises; taking a career break to concentrate on motherhood and possibly having to retrain or remarket our skills. If you are still undecided as to which option suits you best, or if you are wrestling with some deep-seated dissatisfaction in relation to your life choices, then undertaking career–life planning could help resolve your dilemma.

We rarely acknowledge how little conscious planning we put into managing our lives – save on a day-to-day basis. So concerned are we to get through the coming days, weeks and months (usually until our next holiday when we can get off the treadmill for a while) that we fail to take control of our lives by thinking deeply about what we want and deciding how to go about achieving it. So we muddle on, juggling our work and domestic responsibilities, sometimes in unfulfilling jobs, occasionally shaken out of the *status quo* by one of life's crises – illness, relationship break-up or possibly redundancy. And so enmeshed are our working and non-working lives that it is often difficult to see the wood for the trees when we try to pin down the cause of any dissatisfaction we feel. Is it the long hours at work or the lack of domestic support from our partner that is causing us stress (often experienced by women as anger)? Are we unhappy at work because we are not progressing quickly enough, or because we are fundamentally bored and frustrated in our chosen career? (So many people choose a 'safe' career to please their parents, rather than something more exciting and consequently risky.) If, for any reason, you feel unsure about the next move in your life, then take time to set some goals and work out a career–life plan. Remember that the 3 per cent of people that do so are more effective and more successful than the rest of the population. Why not take some simple steps to enable you to join them?

Pause for reflection

Looking back

The first task we suggest is to gain some more personal insights, building on earlier exercises in Chapter Five. One way to do this is to look at your past life to see what has shaped you and brought you to where you are today. Think back over your 'history' and write down the main events and experiences that have been important to you so far. This may take some time, since you may not be able to recall everything at one sitting. Keep a notepad with you to jot down ideas and memories as they come back to you. Now, read through your notes to see whether you can identify any themes or patterns.

■ Are there recurring thoughts, behaviours, feelings or events that crop up frequently or from time to time?
■ Are there any constants in your life that have always been there?
■ What do you count as your major achievements so far? (Whether in connection with career, relationships or personal development.)

You may find it helpful to review the list with a trusted friend or partner and to talk over how you think and feel about what you have written.

Assessing the present

The next task is to think about issues in your life at the moment. Are any themes from the past spilling into the present in the form of unresolved questions? What do you feel are the current priorities you need to deal with? Do you anticipate having to make any important decisions soon? Write everything down. Again, review your notes with a partner if possible, to see whether you can trace any patterns and themes. What are your feelings about what you find?

Looking into the future

List the goals you would like to achieve. These may relate to personal relationships, to work, to your personal development and to material wealth or anything else you can think of. Imagine yourself as the person you would like to become. What would that person be like? Visualize some ideal future state in your life. What does it look like? Who is in the picture with you? What are you doing? How does it feel?

Setting priorities

The next stage in the process is to determine some priorities from all the data you have collected. Five would be a good number with which to begin, depending on how major and how complex each of your chosen priorities turns out to be. For each priority, briefly state the issue to be addressed, how it is affecting you and how you would like things to be. Then consider some alternative strategies you could pursue – there is usually more than one way to resolve any issue:

■ **Take action** Could you do something positive to address the issue or change the situation you find difficult?
■ **Reframe the situation** Can you change the way you see and relate to it, or learn to live with it?
■ **Look at yourself** Could you modify your attitudes or some aspect of your behaviour to improve things?

▥ **Find an exit route**   Can you find some constructive way
to move on?

Choose the best approach for you, having weighed the pros and
cons of each option, and then decide what action you will take to
follow it through. Be realistic: what do you need to do to make
things happen, and when and how will you take the action(s) you
have decided on? You may like to use the drivers and restrainers
framework introduced in the previous chapter.

Example
▥ Issue: personal fitness
▥ How I am: tired and stressed, slightly overweight
▥ How I want to be: more energetic, slimmer
▥ Strategies: visit a gym; go jogging; use fitness video at home;
  eat more healthily
▥ Best option(s): visit gym and eat more healthily
▥ Action(s): join gym at weekend – plan fitness regime with
  trainer; cut out junk food; shop for and eat more fresh fruit
  and vegetables; reduce alcohol intake.

Writing an action plan

1 Having selected the five or so priorities you are to begin with,
  write them down (see below). Start with the easiest to tackle
  – something that will show results fairly quickly – in order to
  build your morale and strengthen your determination to stick
  with it.
2 Review the list on a weekly basis to check your progress and
  complete the right-hand columns as appropriate.
3 As you achieve your goals, reward yourself for the progress
  you have made.
4 Keep adding new priorities as you complete earlier tasks, so
  that the plan constantly rolls forward.

You will be more successful if you focus your energies and do not
try to do too many things at once. Tackle things in ascending
order of difficulty so that you build on your experience.

Priorities	Date started	Milestones achieved	Date completed
1			
2			
3			
4			
5			

Managerial development

The exercise overleaf (p. 280) is designed to help you determine which managerial skill sets you need to develop. It enables you to measure your current level of ability regarding your present job, as well as in relation to your career aspirations. This will help you to prioritize the development areas you need to focus on.

ACTION POINT

Having completed the managerial skills exercise, you may find it useful to talk through with your mentor or manager how your development priorities could be addressed. First, formulate your own solutions (training courses; open learning; job shadowing; a job swap; involvement in specific projects; etc.) and put together a realistic programme with some timescales and cost estimates to use as a basis for discussion.

Creating work–life balance

If you are seriously dissatisfied with the course of your present career, it may be helpful to work through (with your partner if you have one) a matrix of goals and priorities for your future.

1 Give some careful thought to what is important to you now and for the future (refer back to the first exercise above) and set some parameters for each goal or area of priority. For example, how important is your income? Are you hoping to downshift in terms of the demands of your job (and perhaps to settle for less money), or are you looking to move up a gear in terms of your earning potential?

2 Set the income range you need or would like to achieve and decide similar parameters for the other priorities and goals you have identified. In our worked example below these include job satisfaction, working hours, geographical location and the business or industry sectors in which you would like to work. You will need to assign a weighting to each of the factors, since they may not all be of equal importance.

3 Decide what options are available to you and rank them on a scale of 1 to 10 in relation to each of your goal criteria. Work out the score for each option by multiplying the ranking by the weighting. The method is illustrated in a worked example on p. 282, after the managerial development exercise.

Building your power and reputation

In this exercise we are going to develop a plan for managing the impression you make and building your reputation at work. We saw throughout Chapter Five (and elsewhere in the book) how critical these issues are for career success and now is the time to begin a concerted personal PR campaign to get you noticed and advance your career.

The first step is to identify the 'stakeholders' you need to impress. Whose view of you is most influential in your career? List them in order of priority. They may include:

- Senior managers/partners in your company or firm
- Colleagues (with whom you work directly or indirectly)
- Members of your team
- Clients
- Suppliers, co-suppliers and subcontractors (anyone with whom you negotiate or work in collaboration)
- External members of your industry sector or profession.

Managerial activity	A Your ability[1]	B Importance in your job[2]	C Difference A–B[3] (+/−)	D Importance for future career[4]	E Difference A–D[5] (+/−)
Time management: planning and prioritization					
Personal development: continuing professional and personal development					
Team building: development, motivation and empowerment					
Team working: within and across functions, 'virtual' teamwork					
Managing power: impression management, influencing and negotiation					

Interpersonal skills: networking, relationship building and communication				
Decision making: working under pressure, risk taking and effectiveness				
Work–Life balance: prioritizing, planning; managing your support network				
Financial management: budgeting, cashflow, financial statements				

[1] Rank 1–5, where 1 = V. poor; 2 = Poor; 3 = Fair; 4 = Good; 5 = V. good

[2] Rank 1–5 where 1 = Unimportant; 2 = Little importance; 3 = Some importance; 4 = Important; 5 = V. important.

[3] In column C calculate the difference between A and B, indicating whether this is a + or a −.

[4] In column D rank the importance 1–5, where 1 = Unimportant and 5 = Very important.

[5] Calculate the difference between A and D and enter with a + or a − in column E.

Minus scores (especially high ones) indicate development priorities. High plus scores may imply that your talents are not fully employed by what you are currently doing.

Goals and Priorities	Weighting 1–5	Option A Ranking	Score	Option B Ranking	Score	Option C Ranking	Score
Min. income £40k	4	7	28				
Job satisfaction	5	3	15				
Flexible hours	3	8	24				
Location	3	4	12				
Business sector	2	6	12				
Total			91				

Note: Option A might, for example, be working for a charitable organization where job satisfaction is high and the hours flexible, but which requires you to move to a city location that is not your first preference.

Stakeholders

1

2

3

4

5

6

Expectations

Identify the top three stakeholders you want to influence. Now, from your experience and observations, list the behaviours that these people expect from you when you interact with them. Then, try to evaluate how far you are seen to meet those expectations and whether your reputation is high, medium or low with each stakeholder group:

Stakeholder expectations	Reputation score
(a)	
(b)	
(c)	
(d)	
(e)	
(f)	

Purpose and goals

Next, you must decide how you want to be perceived by these individuals or groups and to do this you will need to think about the reputation you would like to build for yourself. In the light of what you know of stakeholder expectations, which are the main areas you will need to focus on improving?

	Reputation I aspire to	**Improvement opportunities**
1		
2		
3		
4		
5		
6		

Impression management plan

Finally we need a strategy and plan for how we will bring about change by modifying our attitudes and behaviours.

First, think about the key messages you would like to be able to communicate to your stakeholders? For example, I am ready for more responsibility; I am committed to my job and to the organization; I have successfully completed some important projects/brought in significant revenue/made valuable innovations for the company; I would like to be considered for the fast track.

Next, how will you need to behave in order to communicate these messages? For example, will you need to speak up more in meetings; network more actively; volunteer; develop your presentation skills; draw attention to your achievements? Lastly, what actions will you need to take and when?

Key messages	New behaviours	Action plan and timing
————	————	————
————	————	————
————	————	————
————	————	————
————	————	————
————	————	————

Summary

Career success for most of us will hinge on demonstrating personal effectiveness through focusing on our own and our organization's goals. Therefore:

■ Identify your main problems, prioritize and tackle them early.
■ Identify and address your development priorities for professional and managerial skills.
■ Evaluate your career–life choices and match them to your goals.
■ Remember to 'influence up' through impression management techniques.

I wish you every success, wherever your career–life plan takes you, and I sincerely hope that it brings you great fulfilment and satisfaction.

In the final chapter we consider how the world of work is changing, the opportunities that are developing for women, and how we can best take advantage of them.

10

Workscape of the future

Introduction

A major driver for change will be the growing power of women. Despite the low starting point, these changes are likely to have significant impacts – with women taking dominant positions in some sectors. As a result, the 21st century may eventually come to be known as 'the women's century'.[1]

Although some attempts have been made by government to legislate for change in women's working lives, social, economic and technological changes must also coalesce to produce an environment in which our contribution is valued and our skills are in demand. This final chapter now attempts to project forward to show how the world of work will evolve over the next 10 to 20 years, highlighting the opportunities that will be created for women and how we might capitalize on the workscape of the future.

Increasingly organizations will need to tap into people's creativity. Brain is replacing brawn and people skills are becoming more highly valued. Women's skills, therefore, are especially useful – and with the increasing demands of knowledge organizations, women will become a key asset.

Fiona Reynolds,
former Director of the Women's Unit,
The Cabinet Office

The labour economy of the future

The news headlines

As we saw earlier, the labour market today remains broadly traditional – flexible working, home working, teleworking and other innovative work forms have yet to make any serious impact on the UK economy. Looking forward 10 to 20 years, however, the picture will be very different.

KEY RESEARCH FINDINGS[2]
Employment in 2020:
- 20–25 per cent of the workforce will be temporary workers and many will be working flexibly
- 25 per cent of people will no longer work in an office
- 20–25 per cent of the workforce will be self-employed.

With these developments will emerge new types of workers (some of the new typologies are considered later). And with the continued rise of double income households there will be a parallel growth in domestic and other services to support materially affluent, but time-poor couples. A key driver of change will be technology. Not only will the desktop PC grow ever more powerful, but technology is expected to revolutionize both the office environment and the commuting methods by which we reach our work.

Increasingly in the future, people will work anywhere they can be connected to a computer, while the office itself will be dramatically transformed both in terms of its role and its layout. Companies expect to see significant organizational change, some of which will be massive. Meanwhile entrepreneurship will flourish and the feminization of the workplace will continue. Higher levels of skills will be even more in demand, with technology expected to up-skill rather than 'dumb-down' the workforce. The Web will transform education and training, providing access to skills and qualifications not only for the educated, but also for those who missed out at school.

Real incomes are expected to double over the lifetime, with male and female pay converging further. Staff retention problems will continue, and firms will introduce new forms of remuneration packages to try to resolve the problem.

So what are the implications for women of these radical changes and how can women prepare to take advantage of the emerging opportunities?

Working hours

We have already observed the growing demand for flexible work patterns from all quarters of the workforce – whether for annualized hours, term-time working, job-sharing or shortening the working week by a day or half day. At this point, even though two-thirds of employers say they believe flexible working is viable, only 20 per cent of employees currently have flexible work arrangements.

KEY RESEARCH FINDINGS[3]

Flexible hours:
- ■ Only 25 per cent of people want to work 9 to 5
- ■ 49 per cent want flexible hours
- ■ 29 per cent want the option to work any time of the day or night.

Predictions made a decade ago about the advent of a leisure society with a two- or three-hour day are unlikely to come true. The reality though, according to the Kelly research, is that by 2020 we should have reduced our working time to six hours a day, with the flexibility to drop off and pick up our children from school.

The 24-hour society – particularly in cities and urban centres – is already here and further moves in this direction will considerably relieve the time pressures felt by many employees. The option of late night shopping will be closely followed by later access to other services previously only available 9 to 5: hairdressers, dentists and doctors are all expected to offer more flexible hours of business.

The impact of 24-hour working will benefit transportation, by greatly reducing traffic congestion at peak hours as commuter travel becomes more evenly spread throughout the day.

The current cost of office accommodation averages £6000 a year per employee (rising to £8000 and more in London). The obvious attractions of 'hot desking' (whereby workers timeshare a desk) in reducing costs will spur employers to adopt the practice more widely and at the same time to stagger shifts over 24 hours. The key driver will be the need to provide late night services in the retail, restaurant and entertainment sectors, as well as on-line services and telephone banking.

Again, we have already established the importance to all employees – and especially to women – of achieving a degree of work–life balance. And it is this, together with the need for companies to provide their customers with 24-hour global services, which will drive the adoption of flexible working.

Working from home

At present only about 2 per cent of people in the UK work from home. Despite optimistic forecasts of a shift to home working, this has been held back by a combination of factors: people (especially women) like the social contact work affords; some feel isolated by the prospect of working from home, whilst others don't have the facilities do so. But this is set to change.

KEY RESEARCH FINDING
Growth of virtual companies:
By 2020, 10 per cent or more FTSE 100 companies will not have a traditional physical headquarters.

Not unexpectedly, the driver will again be technology, which will alter significantly the cost : benefit trade-off for home working. Video conferencing and the paperless office will facilitate home working: the one will replace less important face-to-face meetings, while the other will mean less space is required for the home office. This means, too, that for many the nightmare of rush hour commuting will be at an end, with the opportunity to reclaim two to three hours a day of previously dead travelling time. This will simultaneously make travelling less congested for those who remain office-based – and this will be around 75 per cent of us, due to the need for employee contact and team working.

TECHNOLOGY NEWS
UPDATE FOR 2020

- Fifth generation mobile phones provide global digital video contact
- Mobile personal networks allow development of in-car infotech systems
- Voice recognition systems enable us to create and manipulate vast amounts of information while on the move
- Global positioning systems (GPS) automatically navigate and redirect traffic
- High-speed levitation trains shuttle between cities at 350 mph
- Global commuters speed to the USA or Far East in space shuttles.

Skills shortages and the need to retain staff will transform the workplace into a community with lifestyle and fitness facilities as today's 'concierge' services expand to meet the needs of tomorrow's employees. On-site corporate crèches and nanny services will finally have become a reality, and regarded as an essential, not a luxury. The cyber café of today will also evolve – into a 'work contact centre', functioning as a meeting and communication point to support telecommuters and the self-employed.

Technology will undoubtedly change our work patterns. Skills shortages combined with technological innovation will force a paradigm shift, and workers will experience much greater flexibility, freedom and control in their working lives.
Julia Penny, Deputy President, Institute of
Chartered Accountants, Thames Valley branch

What skills will be in demand?

While some specialist skills (IT again) will undoubtedly be important, in the future the critical ability will be the rapid acquisition of new knowledge and skills. It is even now apparent that one set of skills will not last a working lifetime. The concept of lifetime learning is already current and the practice of continuing professional development is spreading. Employers of the future will be desperate to recruit employees with leading edge skills, and keeping this edge will mean constant retraining as knowledge becomes obsolete quicker than ever. Later in this chapter we look at the skills profile of the manager of the future. But for the moment let us remember the critical importance of maintaining the habit of learning whatever our employment situation, and think about the kinds of personal development and refresher training we need to undertake to keep up with – or even ahead of – our peers.

Create value. Be flexible. Acquire some key skills that are
portable and layer on these breadth and depth of experience.
Early on, focus on building a foundation of any discipline to get
you into the arena where things happen.

Leigh Woods, CEO, ntl UK

Key occupations of the future

We noted in Chapter Two that some women may be disadvantaged in the 'new economy' for lack of IT and technical skills. Fortunately, however, not all the best jobs are expected to be in the IT sector, as innovation will not be confined to technology alone. And as the flexibility of the workforce increases, so traditional contracts of employment will shift to non-standard forms to accommodate this.

New ways of working and emerging business and consumer needs will create new types of workers, the characteristics of which are described in the Kelly Services research.[4]

KEY RESEARCH FINDINGS

Workers of the future:
'Insiders and Outsiders': Companies will retain a core of highly skilled workers, while less skilled workers will perform various tasks on a subcontracted basis.

■ **Gurus** Highly paid individuals with skills in strong demand.
■ **Past masters** Post-retirement working becomes the norm.

■ **Past pros**   Automation of non-manual work results in job insecurity.

■ **Servicers**   New army of mainly domestic workers created to service time poor dual career couples.

■ **Superkids**   Bright teenagers employed to work from home on skilled IT-related tasks.

Becoming an Insider

In order to become an Insider, enjoying a high level of remuneration and a degree of job security, core managers and professionals will need to develop two key sets of competences:

■ High levels of education and/or
■ Entrepreneurial skills.

Because their skills are highly marketable and widely sought by other companies, these Insiders will have the negotiating power to demand family-friendly or indeed person-friendly working conditions. Higher level management qualifications – including the MBA – are expected to command a much higher remuneration premium in the future than is currently the case.

> *The new economy is very female-friendly: technology provides greater flexibility and the scope to do things differently. This is what women are good at.*
> Colette Graham, Head of Internal Communications,
> Centrica plc

Choosing to be an Outsider

In the economy of the future, Outsiders will represent another dimension of outsourcing, primarily of administrative and back-office tasks. And this form of short- or long-term contract work may prove attractive to some women seeking to downshift at times when non-work commitments need to take priority. However, the key here will be for Outsiders to maintain their skills at a sufficient level to ensure they are not forced to market themselves solely on price.

People management training is invaluable. You need to know what motivates people and makes them happy. Learn to look at things from other people's perspectives. Your concerns are not necessarily theirs.

Joy Kingsley, Managing Partner,
Pannone & Partners, Solicitors

Gurus of tomorrow

A higher form of Outsider, Gurus will be freelance consultants and portfolio workers very highly paid for their exceptional skills and experience. The key to being an effective Guru will be the ability to bundle skills and experience into high added value services, for which individuals will be able to command high daily fee rates to compensate for the uncertainty of self-employment and the downtime required for business development.

Again, this may be an option in the future for many women seeking greater flexibility and control in their working lives by operating their own businesses, working freelance or in a loose network of consultants. Self-employment has many attractions for women – though there are downsides in terms of risk. Women often acquire a broad portfolio of experience and competences, and these, coupled with their communication, coaching and other interpersonal skills, form the perfect foundation for the Guru role.

In the future we will see more high growth businesses run by women as they discover it can be done. The Internet has already begun to change how women see the possibilities – the big stories about Internet start-ups have all been about women.

Louise Campbell, MD, Venture Partnership

KEY RESEARCH FINDING

Self employment:
By 2020 an estimated 20–25 per cent of people will be self employed – 40 per cent of these will be women.

Self-employment is at present an option taken up by only 12 per cent of the workforce. The Kelly Services research showed that almost half the workers in the UK would like to be their own boss, including 44 per cent of women surveyed (compared with 53 per cent of men). The time of the small niche business is dawning, driven by new technology and the Internet that will dramatically reduce business start-up and promotion costs.

There is a revolution going on in the world and it's coming from the grass roots. It's the revolution of sustainable entrepreneurs – mainly women – and it's about personal growth as well as an economic tool for being financially empowered.

Lynne Franks, Founder of SEED[5]

And if women have any doubts about their entrepreneurial skills, those should be dispelled by a study showing that, though women may have different management strategies than male business owners, they achieve comparable financial results.[6]

Women tend to build businesses based on passions, and they are very focused on long-term profits and delivering value for their companies, employees and investors. Men often look at short-term scenarios, and many men-led businesses are exit strategy-focused from the outset.

Diana Reid,
Forum for Women Entrepreneurs[7]

Past Masters work on

Given that their projected earnings over the lifetime are much lower than those of men, women are particularly vulnerable to relative poverty later in life. Those who have made insufficient pension and savings provision will be forced to work past retirement age either full or part time. Some people may, however, welcome the prospect of remaining in work and relish the opportunity to foster the expected flowering of entrepreneurship by drawing on their experience to help others or to start their own businesses. (Those concerned about financial planning might like to refer to the list of addresses in 'Useful Contacts' that include financial advisers specializing in helping women.)

> *The future of work for women is a mixed picture. Women will stay in the workforce longer – especially those over 50. But women have advantages later in their careers: they are generally healthier and more adaptable to change.*
> Rabbi Julia Neuberger, CEO, The King's Fund

The fate of the Past Pro

To those who prefer the security of an Insider role, a word of warning: many of today's secure occupations will experience high levels of uncertainty tomorrow. Those in non-manual occupations, where little value is added by their activity, are particularly vulnerable to the automation of their jobs. Solicitors, for example, may in future be under attack from on-line conveyancing. In order to avoid becoming a Past Pro, the key will be to up-skill and retrain before redundancy strikes.

> *Women have a great future fuelled by their own empowerment. As older men leave business, women have huge vistas.*
> Fiona Price, CEO, Fiona Price & Partners

Servicers

The need for support on the home front for dual income couples will cause a steep rise in the demand for domestic services. Not all these will be low skilled, however, since the penetration of high-tech gadgetry into the home will require an army of skilled people to help manage and maintain it. We will even see domestic consultants employed to advise us on how to choose and use new devices to make our lives easier. Catering for the working couple, office support services for the self-employed, as well as traditional domestic help will all create opportunities for many women to open businesses. For though many of these 'Servicers' will be self-employed, many will want to work through agencies, and this is a business sector where women have traditionally been well represented.

Career management in the future

The imperative will be 'up-skilling' in the workplace of the future and this will create demand for training and education as never before. The American management guru, Peter Drucker, believes that education service provision both to businesses and to consumers could become the greatest economic growth area of the future. The key driver will be the Internet. But already in place are distributed and distance learning systems provided both by companies to their employees and, more widely, by colleges and universities operating in an increasingly global marketplace. Opportunities will be created both for training providers and for a parallel industry of support services to help people find their way around the confusing mass of courses and materials that 'webucation' – education on the Web – will offer.

A second strand of service provision will also be required for those freelance or portfolio workers we earlier termed 'Outsiders' and 'Gurus'. The projected growth in temporary work will produce a cadre of people needing advice and support on training and employment. New forms of recruitment agencies will develop to fill this gap, and, again, opportunities for women will grow as the self-employed increasingly look for life coaches and personal trainers to help them manage their careers.

Skills shortages

KEY RESEARCH FINDINGS

26 per cent of manufacturing companies say skills shortage is their biggest single problem.

In June 1999 the venture capitalist group 3i reported that more than half of British businesses were suffering from a shortage of skilled employees. While some employers were attempting to resolve the issue by increasing training and by raising pay levels to retain staff, there were pockets of serious shortage that required more drastic action. In the financial services sector, for instance, there will be severe challenges over the next 10 years, brought about by the failure of education and training systems to deliver the workforce employers need for the future.

KEY RESEARCH FINDINGS

By 2003 Western Europe may lose out on over £230 billion of trade if it fails to make good the shortfall of nearly 2 million IT professionals.[8]

The problems of skills shortages within UK businesses are allegedly compounded by ineffective management. A government report in December 1999 showed that British industry was suffering from a shortage of good managers, lacked innovation and had a workforce whose literacy and numeracy skills were inadequate. Despite the long hours culture in the UK, it achieves relatively low productivity rates, even though employees work harder and longer than their counterparts in Germany, France, Italy, Canada and the USA.[9]

British managers now face two challenges:

■ How to help employees work smarter rather than harder
■ How to promote innovation.

It is clear that management performance needs to improve. The UK's poor investment record is due in large measure to deficiencies in management skills and attitudes.

3i plc

So, if these are the deficiencies that Britain desperately needs to address, what is the ideal profile of the manager of the future? And to what degree do women's skills and characteristics fit the parameters of that profile?

The 21st century manager

We are becoming the men we wanted to marry.

Gloria Steinem[10]

Successful managers in the 21st century will need to develop a completely different set of skills and techniques from those of their counterparts in the last century. *Business Week* highlights the following essential qualities:[11]

- ■ Charm
- ■ Flexibility
- ■ Quickness
- ■ Foreign languages
- ■ Understanding of technology.

Change will be the only constant in tomorrow's business world and, to meet this challenge, managers will need to be far more entrepreneurial. Following established procedures and waiting for direction is not the name of the game. The race will not only be to the swift, but to those able to lead change and to empower teams, encouraging them to use their skills and ideas to the benefit of the organization.

> *The core qualities of intelligence, passion and an ability to motivate will, of course, remain fundamental for future leaders. But managers in the new millennium will also need humour, spontaneity, a team orientation and genuine concern for the intangible needs of employees. The ability to acquire knowledge will be less important than the ability to obtain, distribute and act on that knowledge quickly. The new executives have not only to make fast decisions in a tough environment, they must also motivate and empower their staff to follow suit.*
>
> Diane Brady[12]

Do you see your male colleagues in these descriptions? Probably not – subverting established procedures and worrying about their teams' emotional needs are not archetypal male behaviours. They are, however, second nature to many of the successful women we interviewed.

Concern for others was mentioned frequently:

> *Women are better at appreciating what others might think ... at understanding what others might feel. Consequently people*

say things to women that they wouldn't say to a man. Because women are open and nurturing, people are able to ask questions and give suggestions and feedback.

Julia Penny

Seeing the big picture is a skill many women possess:

Women are better at getting information from people because they show more interest. They are good at seeing the big picture as well as the small one. They don't use silly jargon and are not afraid to admit what they do not know.

Fiona Price

Women find ways around barriers to change:

There is a new way of working that women are not afraid of. Issues and behaviours that block change are often unspoken but women can usually understand what these might be. They are sensitive to personal agendas and have the skills that organizations need.

Sue Slipman, Director, External Relations
and Compliance, Camelot

We like to lead change collaboratively through others:

I'm less bothered about hierarchy – I like to make things happen and am driven by affecting the world and getting it right. I'm passionate about people getting things through ... and very much against sloppy thinking.

Kate Barker,
Chief Economist, CBI

A recurring theme among the women in our research was an impatience to get things done and an intolerance of unnecessary delays and bureaucracy.

I brought a different mind set to traditional legal problems because I did not come up through the conventional route and therefore my thinking was not hampered by the way things had always been done. I always just ploughed through the middle of everything (red tape) and somehow I got away with it. But I'm fiercely competitive – once I'm in the race, I've got to win.

Hilary Meredith, Managing Partner, Donns Solicitors, and former athlete

Education and training for the manager of the future

While marketing and finance will remain key business disciplines, there will be a return to the preference for a liberal arts background, rather than early specialization in a first degree. The ability to think laterally will be key and here, again, women score highly. Their ability to use different modes of thought – commonly referred to as 'intuition' – will increasingly need to be recognized and legitimized. The growing requirement for managers to make decisions quickly, based on piecemeal information perfectly fits the decision-making style of many women. For what is intuition but the ability to process information rapidly at a subconscious level and, based on experience, to see connections not always apparent to highly rational analytical thinkers?

Furthermore, recent scientific research has highlighted women's superior ability to observe and interpret body language, and that gives them a significant advantage in business, where reading gesture and facial expression accurately is critical in many contexts.

A small group of thoughtful people could change the world. Indeed, it's the only thing that ever has.

Margaret Mead

Business Week also refers to the rising value of an eclectic background. This too fits the profile of women, many of whom can boast a portfolio of five careers or more by their 40s. Unlike most of their male counterparts, who generally remain within the same specialism for most of their careers.

CASE STUDY

'While I was living in the USA and looking back at the UK I realized that I could be influential with the portfolio of experience

I had acquired.' Julia Neuberger, who studied archaeology, then attended Rabbinical college and became a congregational Rabbi, before getting involved in healthcare and being awarded a scholarship to Harvard to study medical ethics. She is now CEO of The King's Fund, a leading healthcare charity.

Winners will accept constant change, making themselves adaptable to whatever comes their way.[13]

Speed of change and the need for adaptability are the watchwords for tomorrow. I recently met a Russian woman – whom I came to admire – at a women's conference in Milan, and as she told me her extraordinary story I realized just how resilient and resourceful women can be:

CASE STUDY

'Before *perestroika* I was a musician and teacher. Then I lost my job and because my husband earned only a small salary I desperately needed to get work. One day, in the hallway of the block of flats where I lived, I met a neighbour. She was very smartly dressed and carrying a briefcase. I recognized her as a woman who had been a housewife only months before. I asked her what she was doing now and she replied that she worked at the Stock Exchange. I asked her how she got the job and she said she had some commercial qualification and that this work was not for people like me. But anyway, I went to the Stock Exchange building to enquire about qualifications and, of course, they laughed when I said I was a musician. But a few weeks later the course prospectus arrived and I enrolled. After I qualified I was very successful. I now educate my children abroad and I am paying to do an MBA through the University of Barcelona. Now I am very interested in working in a big international corporation and getting to the top – just to see if I can do it.'

Valentina, Russian stockbroker

Does anyone doubt for a moment that Valentina will achieve her goal? I recently heard a wonderful saying: 'Women are like tea bags – you never know how strong they are until they get into hot water.' And, if the pundits are right, there will be plenty of hot water around as this century unfolds.

Interpersonal and
influencing skills come to the fore

Another area where women's special interpersonal and collaborative skills will be needed is in helping to manage the complex
web of relationships between organizations and their suppliers,
co-suppliers and customers and in creating workable partnerships and alliances. Women are quite comfortable with the looser
spans of control required to produce more responsive organizations. For they are generally happy to empower their teams,
allowing their innate resourcefulness to surface. This practice of
empowerment has also been shown to create a more satisfying
workplace because people feel their ideas and contributions are
valued. This will be critical in motivating and retaining the key
workers of the future.

*Women are different in positive ways and businesses would be
stronger if they were better able to deploy women's skills in
team working and juggling multiple priorities.*

Leigh Woods

And there is compelling evidence that young workers especially
will not tolerate being ordered about – they want guidance,
respect and an opportunity to show their worth. Who better to
manage these people than women, with their highly developed
nurturing skills?

*Whereas women particularly used to have to fight for
everything and were grateful to be given opportunities, trainees
today don't accept that. They complain about what they don't
like and don't want to do. They want everything on a plate.
But as a Training Principal myself, I'm inclined to be very
protective of my trainees.*

Hilary Meredith

So the main story for the next ten years is the accelerating pace
of change and the need for businesses to recruit the best talent
to steer them through the turbulence. If *Business Week* is correct
and '. . . listening skills and a passion for helping people could
well become the hallmarks of a successful manager',[14] then

women's time has truly come. Above all, future managers will need a sense of humour and the ability to keep a sense of perspective.

I get a bit of a buzz from the publicity, but it's transitory and makes me a bit embarrassed. I know what I haven't achieved in comparison with my peers.

Joy Kingsley

And this is our abiding memory of the interviews with the women who have so generously contributed to this book: not only their wisdom but also their ability to laugh (often ironically) at setbacks and always to remain grounded by their own values.

It would be very easy to believe all the publicity telling you that you are important. You crash and burn if you do. Remember always that this is just a moment in time.

Dianne Thompson,
CEO, Camelot

Life in the new economy

KEY RESEARCH FINDINGS
Business to business (B2B) e-commerce could increase GDP by 5 per cent over 20 years.
GDP of the EU could rise by 1.5 per cent by 2002 from productivity gains created by IT.[15]

During the Main Event 2000 (organized by womenfuture.com) it emerged that a number of factors make e-commerce an attractive prospect for women, not least its flexibility and collaborative ethos. Women are now the fastest growing group of Internet users, accounting for around 40 per cent of the Internet community. What is more, the proliferation of sites dedicated to women is almost matched by the growth in Internet companies founded by women – around 30 per cent and rising. (This is predicted to reach 50 per cent by 2002, a level it has already achieved in the USA.) Importantly, too, because the Web is growing so quickly, it is still wide open for start-ups.

*There's no glass ceiling because the offices haven't been built
yet. Either you have the skills or you don't.*

Eva Pascoe,
MD zoom.co.uk

Internet successes are largely dependent on the effective formation and management of alliances and partnerships, and
women's management style is perfectly adapted to these requirements. Interpersonal, negotiating and nurturing skills are all
brought into play and dot.coms welcome creativity and entrepreneurship. New ways of thinking and the ability to be flexible
are also an advantage. As we saw earlier in the chapter, women
relish the opportunity to find new ways of doing things and to
overcome barriers and blockages to change, and the ability to rise
to new challenges is key to succeeding in a dot.com.

*There is no history to tell us what will and will not work. We
operate on instinct and courage. The Internet economy allows
women to get fair play. There are tremendous differences from
traditional businesses in terms of what surrounds success.
Intuition can be the defining talent. Hierarchy and politics are
superseded by value creation.*

Adriana Kampfner, President StarMedia
Network Inc., Mexico[16]

But there are dynamic tensions within the e-commerce sector.
On the one hand dot.coms are undoubtedly rewriting the
rulebook for starting up and operating a business. They are not
hidebound by traditional hierarchies, protocols and cultural
norms which is helpful for women:

*I don't want glass ceilings, walls, boxes and labels telling
me who I am. Performance is what matters here. What I
deliver in value is what I am valued for and that makes me
happy.*

Adriana Kampfner[17]

Yet at the same time, many are driven by a work ethic of total
dedication and very long hours reflected in the myths of people
sleeping under their desks:

I've probably only had three Sundays off since Christmas.
Emmanuelle Drouet, founder of Iglu.com[18]

*Work is always at breakneck speed until 10, 11, 12 at night,
seven days a week.*
Martha Lane Fox, joint founder and MD,
lastminute.com[18]

This isn't a J-O-B, it's a lifestyle.
Serena Doshi, founder Liv4Now.com
(commenting on needing to work a
16-hour day, six days a week)[18]

The paradigm shift from a traditional to an Internet business can be summarized as follows:[19]

Traditional business	Internet business
Charted waters	New territory
Established goals	Unstructured
Salary package	Reward linked to success
Security	Risk
Job description	Self-management

However, at the moment, one problem of virtual trading is the virtual money that goes with it. Few Internet entrepreneurs have so far become wealthy in real terms – many have paper fortunes estimated in the millions, but very little net worth. They recognize they would be better off working for someone else, but few would trade this for the freedom of being their own boss in such a dynamic environment.

It was evident from a report in the *Sunday Telegraph* (18 March 2000) that many women involved in the Internet are truly evangelical, not only in relation to the opportunities it can offer, but also in terms of its potential to bring about fundamental change on a global scale. In 1998 Julie Meyer, fresh from INSEAD, drew together her dinner party skills, an interest in people and her network of contacts to set up First Tuesday, a club where venture capitalists can meet entrepreneurs. From a membership of 50 the club became a website – firsttuesday.com – with 30 000 registered users and an estimated flotation value of

£50 million. Meetings are now held in over 60 cities in the UK and the rest of Europe.

Individuals change society, not governments. Entrepreneurs are heroes. They need to be supported ... given the chance to change the world, why would anyone walk away?

Julie Meyer[20]

Women's knack of combining business and IT experience with issues close to their hearts is a feature of many Internet companies founded by women. Women, it appears, see the Internet as a means to pursue personal fulfilment on several levels: the satisfaction of creating a business, achieving financial success and independence, and, importantly, doing something worthwhile to boot.

From a joint background of television, computer sales and Internet access provision Emma Crowe and Carol Dukes set up ThinkNatural.com, a website selling natural health and beauty products which successfully raised over £2 million in venture capital. Meanwhile Emanuelle Drouet, a keen skier with a background in evaluating real estate in the French Alps, decided that people needed to see the chalets they were being asked to book and Iglu.com was born. She put together a business plan and in three months raised £3 million venture capital. However, in order to do so she had to move from France, where the Internet industry is less advanced, to the UK. The downside, however, is that she now no longer has time to pursue her passion for skiing. Indeed, so addictive is the excitement of working on the Internet that she says anything else would be 'very dull'.

Eos Ventures, created by Dafna Ciechanover, came about because, as international director of marketing at Excite, she was besieged with entrepreneurs looking for advice. Eos now provides support to novice entrepreneurs in e-commerce businesses. She is a great advocate of the Internet as a career for women and sees the nurturing of enterprise as an essentially female role.

Her passion for women's issues eventually led Jayne Buxton to found Flametree.co.uk, a website where women can access information to change their lives. It focuses on the real concerns of women: how job shares really work; how to be an effective parent. She says the turning point in her life, after a highflying career in management consultancy, was 'letting go of other people's definitions of success and their timetables in which you should achieve it.' Her dedication to finding work–life balance, not only for herself but also for other women in terms of a new work paradigm, led her to write *Ending the Mother War*[21] where she tried to define a new world of work better adapted to women's needs. She found this for herself when she created Flametree:

> *We were in control, with no one telling us when to start or when to leave. But we were the only dotcom start-up not working its people to death.*

Another proponent of changing the work paradigm for women (and men) is Susan Willett Bird. A lawyer by training, she is now the president and founder of womenfuture.com, a website out of which sprang the Main Event[22] – a global tele- and webcast debate – involving audiences in several hundred sites around the globe simultaneously – about how women see themselves creating the future.

She differentiates the new work paradigm from the old in the following way:

Old	**New**
Think big	Think big
Start big	Start small
Don't screw up	Make lots of mistakes
	Correct as you go
	Scale up quickly

We'll let her tell her own unique story:

CASE STUDY

'I began as a litigator and I liked to argue and win. It was fun to be at war and win at a man's game. Eventually, though, it got harder to get up each morning. I made some changes and became a "serial entrepreneur". Working as a business mediator I learned how disputes could be settled by creating alliances and new solutions. And this special skill is common to many women – the ability to say: "This isn't working. Let's get people together and solve it in a new way." So we created the Main Event by gathering together 40 world business leaders and held conversations on seven topics that were then telecast to live audiences across the world in an interactive event. It was international because today you can't *not* be international. And we used the Internet because this has finally made legitimate the way women have always led: non-hierarchical; inclusive; through networks. We had a BHAG – a big hairy audacious goal – to set an agenda and have a global conversation. We predict that people will look back at the 21st century as the last time we resolved conflict by fighting. Women are the key to change because they know how to have a conversation and form alliances to create the right solution. Assuming there is a right answer and only one way is very "old economy".

Susan Willett Bird,
presenting at the WIN Conference in Milan,
September 2000

The Main Event organizers recognized that they were missing a trick by not including men. For if they are ever to understand how the process works, men need to be able to observe it. For future events, on a similar principle to 'Take your daughter to work', they propose: 'Take your guy to women.future.'

Is e-commerce for you?

With one or two notable exceptions, the new generation of e-commerce women are all in their late 20s and early 30s and all report that current work demands exclude almost completely the social and family aspects of their lives. Any business start-up is demanding and the terrifying pace of technology means that dot.com start-ups are all-consuming. The pressures to get to scale fast, establish a compelling market offering and make a return to investors are unbelievable. So, particularly in the early stages of development, this is not an environment either for the faint hearted or for those seeking flexible work patterns. At lastminute.com when the airline relations manager had a baby she was able to negotiate a four-day week, comprising three days in the office and one day working from home. But, in an environment where most people need to give 150 per cent, such accommodations are not easy.

Martha Lane Fox, MD of lastminute.com, dismisses the idea that the new economy is easier for women, because of the fast pace and long hours – particularly in start-ups. What is more, technology forces people to work harder and longer because they are always accessible wherever they are by phone, or e-mail. It also takes its toll personally as reality bites:

CASE STUDY

'In the early days when the Internet was flying in the USA it looked cool – full of bright people and interesting ways of doing business. At lastminute.com we wanted to create a great service for the customers and bring people to the vision. I loved the idea and wanted to see it work. But the changing demands of the job require you to adapt to meet new challenges. You have to grow up when the spotlight of the media is turned on you.'

Martha Lane Fox

Whilst Martha is proud to have brought the Internet to people's attention and to have shown how young people can do things differently, she admits the high profile role of co-founder can be isolating. Typecast by the media as the 'dotty blonde one', her Oxford pedigree and management consulting credentials are often overlooked. Even to the extent that when she originally fronted the business it was assumed to be a cynical ploy to generate publicity. She hopes that lastminute.com will be an example to women entrepreneurs, but warns that there is a trade-off to be made: you need enormous strength and resilience to withstand not only the rigours of the job but also the pressures of being constantly in the public eye.

So, it appears that dot.com start-ups, though incompatible with work–life balance, are a great opportunity for young women to make their mark:

My message to very young women is to be hugely ambitious.
Go as fast and as far as you can as early as you can . . . I hear
a lot of women saying: 'I'll drop out and start a company', or
'I'll become a consultant'. But it takes preparation: you can't do

*it when you're pregnant. Before you go off the pill, take a look
at your CV.*

Avivah Wittenberg Cox[23]

Avivah herself holds a remarkable portfolio of skills and
experience: computer consultant, corporate communications
consultant and dot.com entrepreneur. She also has two children.
But her experience in 1999 as partner and director of MBA-
Exchange.com, a website for alumni of top European business
schools, taught her that women cannot have it all. She worked at
a frenetic pace to the neglect of her family ties and subsequently
decided to opt out. She now works as a career counsellor at
INSEAD, chairs the Paris Professional Women's Network and is
writing a book about MBA women. Her observations about
working on the Internet make interesting reading:

> *The web has tremendous potential for women who need
> networking but don't have the time to do it. This Internet site
> (MBA-Exchange.com) used everything I had ever done. And it
> was so much fun ... I discovered that I too had limits. In a
> corporation you know what your objectives are and what is
> expected of you. But in a dotcom the only measure of success is
> your own ...You set your own goals and they tend to be a lot
> harder to achieve than anybody else's. Nobody ever says: 'Stop!
> Great job!' Except for your kids who say: 'Stop! Lousy job over
> here!'*

Avivah Wittenberg Cox[24]

By contrast, when dot.com businesses are being prepared for
flotation, and in the later consolidation phase, recruiters see
opportunities for those with greater experience to play a role.
Broad teams representing cultural diversity will become the
norm. The VenturePartnership.com sees a positive future for
women in the global economy, where recruiting to the traditional
WASP profile is no longer relevant. The IT companies are
actively seeking more women and there is a determination within
dotcoms, headed by young entrepreneurs, not to discriminate
against women and minorities.

What is more, women managers may very well prove the ideal
bridge within dotcoms between youth and experience. With their

nurturing skills and less confrontational style, women may be seen as less of a challenge to young entrepreneurs when management teams and boards of directors are being recruited. Their greater sensitivity to the feelings of others will enable experienced women to offer direction without appearing directive and to lead change without provoking resistance. In conclusion, there are undoubted opportunities for women within the new economy. For those with unbounded energy, entrepreneurial flair and no other commitments dot.com start-ups could be an option. Meanwhile, for those women with a track record in pre- and post-flotation management, there will be ample scope for a safe pair of hands to steer later dot.com development. In either context women can expect to experience an immense feeling of liberation in a culture free from traditional corporate constraints, which for many will more than compensate for the long hours and frantic work schedules.

Desperately seeking diversity

KEY RESEARCH FINDINGS

A *Sunday Times* survey of the Top 100 companies showed that the most successful companies are those with the most diverse boards and personnel drawn from a wide range of backgrounds.

Undoubtedly 'diversity' is one of the buzzwords of the 21st century, but isn't it simply a new spin on equal opportunities? And if there is any substance to the new style, what are employers doing about it and how will it affect women?

Managing diversity is a comprehensive managerial process for developing an environment that works for all employees.
R. Roosevelt Thomas[25]

The Domino Consultancy, UK specialists in diversity and equal opportunities,[26] would say that, though there is still a tendency for people to refer to specific groups – women, ethnic minorities and the disabled – diversity is everyone's business, and good business at that. One problem with the concept of equal opportunities is that it is exclusive – people assume that if they don't fall into one of the groups above, it has nothing to do with them. By contrast, the focus of diversity is the concept of difference. And because we are all different, diversity becomes everyone's responsibility. The key differences are summed up as follows:[27]

Equal opportunities	Diversity
Driven by legislation	Driven by business need
Piecemeal initiatives	Holistic strategy
Assimilation	Inclusion in open culture
Removing barriers	Nurturing potential
Improving numbers	Improving the workplace
Assumptions about certain groups	No assumptions/judgements

Domino stresses that diversity awareness and training is less about getting people to change their attitudes, than about challenging them to move out of their comfort zones and to see that, if they have a problem with someone, it is probably more to do with themselves than the other person.

The primary requirements for diversity within an organization are that:

- Everyone has a right to their own value system.
- No one has a right to impose their value system on others.
- Organizations must make clear the value systems they hold, championing behaviours that support those systems and defining as 'unacceptable' behaviours that do not.

The business case for diversity is immediately apparent within consumer products companies: their marketplace becomes increasingly diverse as internationalization intensifies. There is a pressing need for the profile of employees to reflect that of customers for a number of sound business reasons:

- Customers want to see their values and norms represented in the companies they buy from.
- The changing needs of diverse groups of customers will only be met if the teams developing products and services can respond to that diversity.

And women's purchasing power continues to rise as more women enter the workforce and as they take control of an increasing proportion of the family budget. Modern businesses need to reinvent themselves because the world is increasingly defined by women's changing needs. This challenges companies in every sphere – in recruiting the best employees, in forming business partnerships and, of course, in attracting and retaining customers. Marissa Brambilla,[28] Vice President of Avon Products Inc., identifies four key areas where corporations must change if they are to capitalize on women's greater independence and economic freedom: their values; their focus on women; modernization; and globalization.

> *Life is change. Try to adapt; don't resist – it may be better as well as different.*
>
> Marissa Brambilla

■ **Values**   corporations need to develop more 'human' values, relevant to women's lives, so they are able to work in an environment of trust where openness and teamwork are valued. Women (and men) need to be free to express themselves and their differences. There must be recognition that the organization may not always be right and that it doesn't always have the answers. Change and responsiveness are the future imperatives and yesterday's way of doing things may not work tomorrow.

> *If you always do what you've always done, you'll always get what you've always got.*
>
> Anon.

■ **Focus on women's needs**   to succeed in future, companies must understand women's aspirations and relate to women, both as people and as professionals. Through their products and services and through the work environments they create they must strive to make women's lives easier and more enjoyable. (Avon has a corporate goal that 50 per cent of managers in the company will be women by 2005.)

■ **Modernization**   products and services need to reflect women's changing lifestyles and product innovation must be more about pursuing an enduring vision of what the

customer wants than about gimmicks to stimulate sales in
the short term.

■ **Globalization**   and as companies reinvent their products,
so they must reinvent their culture. In a world that is
growing smaller and more accessible, the emphasis is on
delivering the best value.

So far embedded is the diversity concept within Avon's business
strategy that they do not see it as an issue to be 'managed'.
Rather, it is a reflection of all the different viewpoints and
experiences of the individuals that make up the Avon workforce.
Small wonder that in September 1998 Avon topped the Working
Woman magazine poll for best company for women executives.

An example of a company changing 'beyond recognition to
meet (these) challenges' is the white goods manufacturer,
Whirlpool. Corry Wille, Vice President HR, describes what
diversity in action means within Whirlpool:

CASE STUDY

'Diversity initiatives at Whirlpool are directly linked to innovation
initiatives. Our brand was virtually unknown 10 years ago – it's
now number one in Europe in volume terms. Positioning the
brand was about recognizing diversity as fundamental to our
success, as a means of leveraging the talents of our people to
bring about innovation. Teamwork, respect and integrity are key
values and ours is a truly international company. The flow of
people between our European operations allows a free exchange
of talent and has been central to securing competitive advantage.
We were chosen by Ikea as a partner because of our ability to
deliver a common standard in our product and our way of doing
business across Europe.'[29]

And diversity within Whirlpool is not only about the international
dimension, but also about increasing the number of women at
managerial level and above, through targeted recruitment and
development to key leadership positions. But it goes further than
just women's issues, to recognize the need to include both ends
of the spectrum in all human experience: male and female; work
and home; youth and maturity; north and south; experience and
inexperience.

Embracing diversity has meant a complete paradigm shift, to a corporate mindset where differences are actually seen to create value. The Talent Pool Committee – a 'think tank' for new product development – is an example of this new paradigm in action. In a mature market, such as that for white goods, innovation is the accelerator that stimulates demand, and the Talent Pool comprises people drawn from all levels and backgrounds within the company to lead the innovation strategy. Whirlpool has seen how diversity can stimulate a new culture, provoking discussion and challenging old ways of doing things. Faster, more dynamic communication processes have been created that break down traditional hierarchies and facilitate the non-linear changes from which competitive advantage is developed. Everyone becomes a leader in this new way of working, with junior level employees making convincing presentations about their projects and achievements. Indeed, so far has the democratization process advanced that Whirlpool has even introduced 'reverse mentoring', whereby junior employees work with their bosses to raise the bosses' awareness and understanding of business issues.

The business case for diversity

While it is difficult directly to correlate the implementation of diversity programmes with bottom line improvement, increasingly there is perceived to be a link between the two. An article in *Human Resources* magazine[30] described how the Dominion Mutual Fund of New York has introduced a diversity ranking for company funds, measuring against seven criteria including hiring and promotion policy and board level representation of women and minorities. The link between successful diversity policies and stock market performance has been researched by Professor David Thomas of Harvard University:

The effective management of a diverse workforce translates into bottom line results.[31]

'Effective' implies that the policy has led to diversity in the leadership of the organization, whereby a wide pool of talent has been drawn up through the ranks benefiting the company in terms of different ideas and viewpoints. Unless and until talented women and minorities move to the top of organizations, we cannot call a diversity policy successful, say the experts.

There are several reasons why diversity and business success should correlate, according to Amy Hillman, a professor at Ivey School of Business. Diverse businesses may attract superior talent; they are likely to encourage creativity and innovation; companies can access and better understand new markets; and morale is probably higher. Further, diverse companies appear less risky for investors because they make better business partners and merge more smoothly with other organizations. Given that a clash of cultures often undermines mergers and acquisition activity, diverse companies have a significant advantage in being more ready to accept and accommodate differences.

Ultimately, however, perhaps firms should worry less about the bottom line and more about doing the right thing:

> *There are perhaps times when the bottom line is not being completely and aggressively served by diversity ... Diversity in the workplace may be simply the right thing to do.*
> Johnetta Cole, Professor of Anthropology,
> Emory University[32]

The hallmarks of organizational diversity

Since the adoption of diversity policies can significantly enhance the working environment for women, by encouraging greater openness and acceptance of differences, what should women in future be looking for in the organizations seeking to recruit them?

AdvancingWomen, a website for working women,[33] suggests that, whatever its written policy, you check that the company 'walks the talk':

> *Companies which already have diversity in their ranks, generally support more diversity of all types: ethnic, gender and*

orientation. Companies with women as owners or directors, with substantive numbers in management have gone on record in a meaningful way as being in support of women in the workplace. When you elect to work for one of them you are stacking the deck in your favour.

AdvancingWomen

In describing its vision of the 'Ideal Workplace' Advancing Women refers to the following hallmarks:

▪ In its approaches to both staffing and development it will have processes that support the values of diversity.
Managers will:
- Provide opportunities for visibility
- Explain and interpret organizational politics
- Map out clear development goals and
- Support you in achieving them.

Of course, there is bound to be some disparity between the ideal and the present reality. But AdvancingWomen points out that these criteria can both serve as goals for companies to work towards and as benchmarks against which women can measure potential employers. Some specific questions to ask include:

▪ How many women currently serve as board or executive directors? ('If you see a vacuum, run the other way' advises AdvancingWomen).
▪ What does the company pay women? (As we saw in Chapter Two, this can be significantly less than men even at senior levels.)

It is a widespread, societal practice to promote fewer women and pay them less.

AdvancingWomen

However, having short listed companies that are women-friendly and diversity oriented, women will find that the values form a 'cluster': respect for differences and the desire to deal with people fairly are broadly concomitant with the provision of equal pay and equal career opportunities.

In the ideal company, formal systems of mentoring will be underpinned by informal support processes. Through these, people in authority will ensure that key people are not excluded from the informal networks that are crucial to career advancement. Equally, there will be ways to ensure that women gain line management experience to build their career capital and so qualify for the next round of promotion.

> *... if you are in an ideal workplace, or one which has values aligned with your interests and is working on putting them into practice, you are on the right path for career success.*

AdvancingWomen

Finally, as AdvancingWomen stresses, it is important to have career goals and to align these with the opportunities you find within your company.

CASE STUDY

We have already cited BT as a best practice example in relation to flexible working. Its diversity policy is but one facet of a comprehensive strategy of championing women in what has traditionally been a man's world. In recent years BT has attempted to change its corporate culture through the creation of a top-level equal opportunities steering group; the appointment of a 'gender champion', the introduction of an equal pay review and monitoring system and the investment of resources into line manager training. BT believes strongly in diversity and, especially, that a gender mix in the workforce is vital in representing its customer base and thus to improving its competitiveness. By amending job titles and broadening job descriptions (as well as holding a 'Daughters to Work Day') BT has introduced initiatives to encourage the recruitment of more women graduates. To ensure the advancement of existing women employees it also offers four training programmes comprising the Women's Development Portfolio, as well as two work-life projects – Freedom to Work and Lifestyle Working – to address women's concerns about balancing home and work.[34]

Summary

Technology is driving dramatic changes in the workplace. To survive and prosper firms must take radical new approaches both in the way they serve their customers and how they manage their employees. In this context demand for women's managerial skills will grow markedly. To take advantage of the new opportunities women should:

▨ Acquire and maintain a portfolio of expertise, retraining and up-skilling regularly.

▨ Consider entrepreneurship more confidently, taking encouragement from the lead given by women's success in dotcom start-ups.

▨ Set the agenda for equality and diversity by checking the credentials of companies before taking up employment.

Women need no longer feel things are stacked against them, for as Tom Peters proclaimed,[35] we now hold the entire deck of fifty-two playing cards. All we now need to do is learn to play them to our advantage. Take heart – the future is bright, the future is woman.

Notes

1 'The New Power of Women', Centre for Strategy and Policy, Open University Millennium Project.

2 'Tomorrow's Work – a report into the future of the way we work', Commissioned by Kelly Services (UK) Ltd. Author: Graeme Leach, Chief Economist, Institute of Directors.

3 Ibid.

4 Ibid.

5 Quoted on the www.womenfuture.com website: 'Welcome To Your Revolution'.

6 Research Institute for Small and Emerging Businesses, July 2000.

7 Quoted in *Business Week* online. Copyright © 2000, The McGraw-Hill Companies Inc.

8 Reported in the *Guardian*, 23 March 2000.

9 'The UK Competitor Indicators Report 1999', DTI.

10 Cited in Carol Turkington, *The Quotable Woman*, McGraw-Hill, 2000.

11 'The 21st Century Corporation – The New Leadership', *Business Week*, 28 August 2000.

12 Ibid.

13 Kelly Services (UK), op. cit.

14 Diane Brady, *Business Week*, 28 August 2000.
15 Datamonitor, IDC & Goldman Sachs research reported in the *Guardian*, 23 March 2000.
16 Quoted on www.womenfuture.com 'Internet time: why now is the time for women to soar'.
17 *Business Week*, op. cit., note 12.
18 All quoted in the *Sunday Telegraph*, 'The rise of she-commerce', 18 March 2000.
19 With acknowledgements to Marie Francey del Bono, co-founder Bizywoman.com
20 *Sunday Telegraph*, op. cit.
21 Jayne Buxton, *Ending the Mother War*, Macmillan, 1998.
22 Now to be held annually in April.
23 Speaking at the WIN. Conference, September 2000 and quoted in the *Financial Times*, 10 July 2000.
24 Op. cit.
25 *Beyond Race and Gender*, McGraw-Hill, 1997.
26 www.dominoconsultancy.co.uk
27 With acknowledgements to the Domino Consultancy.
28 Speaking at the WIN. Conference, September 2000.
29 Speaking at the WIN. Conference, September 2000.
30 *Human Resources*, Society for HR Management, vol. 44, no. 13, 1999.
31 Ibid.
32 Ibid.
33 www.advancingwomen.com.
34 'BT: championing women in a man's world', *Women in Management Review*, no. 84, p. 14, March/April 1999, Ref: 28AL723.
35 Women Future telecast April 2000. See www.womenfuture.com

Useful contacts

Some of the organizations mentioned in the text may be useful for future reference and their contact details are given below:

AdvancingWomen Workplace Strategies A free women's engine from AdvancingWomen.com. Resource to access advancement strategies, advice on starting up a business plus lots of helpful news items, articles and links to women's networks and other business and career-related organizations. www.advancingwomen.com

Catalyst The leading US-based non-profit organization working with business to advance women. Contact them for news about events, discussions, research and information centre, books and reports. Works in the UK with Opportunity Now. www.catalystwomen.org

Domino Consultancy Development and consultancy organization with expertise in helping companies establish a strategic approach to diversity, as well as supporting the implementation of equal opportunities and women's development initiatives. www.dominoconsultancy.co.uk

Equal Opportunities Commission Invaluable resource publishing reports relating to equal pay and work opportunities. Advises on a range of legal employment issues. Acts as advisory body to government on policy making. www.eoc.org.uk

Fiona Price & Partners Financial services company set up to meet the specific needs of women. Tel: 0207 611 4700

Flametree UK website aimed at helping women balance their lives. Wealth of practical information on business, entrepreneurship, careers, childcare, employment rights. Helpful and interesting articles and discussions on all aspects of women's life and work. www.flametree.co.uk

Future Foundation   An independent think tank advising companies on how to plan for the future. Publishes related news digest and research reports on future trends impacting consumer markets. www.futurefoundation.net

Globaltmc   Training organization specialising in intercultural training, expatriate issues and women in management, as well as general management and business skills development. www.globaltmc.com

Grow   An organization for personal and professional development; offers you a newsletter, a website, an information service and entertaining workshops, as well as information about books, products and networking for self-development. www.getupandgrow.co.uk

Industrial Society   'The Industrial Society are the UK's leading thinkers and advisers on the world of work. Everything we do – from consultancy to research, from training to advocacy, from education to advisory services, is driven by our commitment to improve working life.' The Industrial Society can be found at: www.indsoc.co.uk

iVillage Career   website for the working woman with message boards, advice on jobs, news items and job listings. www.ivillage.com/career/

Online Women's Business Centre   If you run your own business or would like to do so, then access this site for information about finance, management, market research, training and technology. www.onlinewbc.org

Praxis   A training, coaching and mentoring organization set up to support women's development. Contact nkazerounian @gitmail.com to discuss personal image, impression management and managerial skills training.

The Federation of Image Consultants (TFIC)   Contact them if you want professional help with your personal image. Tel: 07010 701 018. info@tfic.org.uk / www.tfic.org.uk

United Women's Voice   Launched as the UK's first interactive newspaper for women, this website aims to inform, entertain and amuse – but importantly also to enable women to speak up on important issues. Useful Salary Checker can be accessed to find out whether you are being paid what you're worth. www.unitedwomensvoice.com

Woman Abroad 'The world's first international magazine devoted to helping women away from their home country to develop their careers, improve their skills, cope with third culture family problems and enjoy a new world of networking with like-minded women.' Monthly magazine, subscriber service and network membership are available at www. womanabroad.com

Woman Lawyer Forum Conference held annually focusing on issues relating to women in the legal profession. www. womanlawyerforum.co.uk

Women Future Focused around their annual Main Event – a global tele- and webcast 'conversation' that brings together 'thought leaders' to share their vision of the future. Join the conversation at www.womenfuture.com

Women in Management Now a special interest group of the Institute of Management (IM). Information can be accessed via the main IM website at www.inst-mgt.org.uk or e-mail wim@imgt.org.uk

Women's International Networking Conference (WIN) Held annually in September in Milan, this three-day conference includes lectures, panel discussions, workshops, training groups and networking sessions (as well as some superb socializing!). An unmissable event for women looking for personal and professional development, and seeking to extend their network internationally. For more information and to register contact: www.winconference.com

Working Women Business resource centre for women with features on work issues, free business listings and job classifieds. www.wwork.com

Index